Welcome!

Three years ago, my husband Chris and I
Glimpses of New Zealand, inspired by our
The book featured a series of 35 quilts, each of them representing a peep through a half-open door into the landscape, fauna and flora, language and history of the Land of the Long White Cloud. The series took me two years to stitch, and one day, just as I was just finishing the final quilt, I mentioned to Chris that I wasn't sure what to work on next. 'That's easy,' he replied: 'Glimpses of Britain.'

What an intriguing idea! My mind started working nineteen to the dozen: what does Britain mean to us, its people? What do people abroad think of when they picture the British Isles? When visitors come to our shores, what do they most want to see? I realised very early on that this series of quilts was going to be a big challenge. In Britain we have so many layers of history, plus the specific characters of the individual countries, countless different cultural influences and so on. I knew that each quilt would have to combine several layers of meaning and inspiration.

So, I began thinking and designing. We decided to do 24 main quilts, then include a project alongside each one – something inspired in some way by the theme of the original quilt. All the projects include complete instructions and step-by-step diagrams, and most of the templates are full size. If you're completely new to quilting, we've slipped in a techniques section at the back of the book which will give you some useful extra tips.

We've also included lots of our favourite photographs of the British Isles, most of them taken by us and some by friends. And at the end of the text on each subject, we've included an *Inside Information* section packed with interesting websites and other info. All together these make up our ***Glimpses of Britain***. Whether you live in (or come from) England, Ireland, Scotland or Wales, or whether you're a visitor or an armchair traveller to these islands, we hope that you'll enjoy this celebration of our beautiful and complex land.

CONTENTS

Four Countries

The emblems of England, Ireland, Scotland and Wales celebrate our different cultures and histories.

When we decided to launch this book in 2012, we really hadn't registered how many significant events and anniversaries were taking place. We knew Britain would be hosting the Olympics, of course, but we'd almost forgotten that it would also be the Queen's Diamond Jubilee. Then came the 200th anniversary of Dickens' birth – as well as that of Edward Lear (supreme nonsense poet), and Augustus Pugin (master of the Victorian Gothic revival). And so it went on. 2012 marks 100 years since the sinking of the Titanic (see p29), and since Scott's Terra Nova expedition set out. 50 years ago the Beatles (see p46) launched their first single (***Love Me Do/PS I Love You***), and the ***Sunday Times*** published their first colour magazine. It's 10 years since Spike Milligan died, 30 years since the Falklands War, 35 years since ***Abigail's Party***, and the 80th birthday of Frank Dickens, who draws the delightful Bristow cartoons. What's now known as the Chelsea Flower Show began life as the Great Spring Show in 1862 – 150 years ago. The theme of the opening ceremony for the London Olympics, taken from Caliban's speech in ***The Tempest,*** is *Isles of Wonder*; that would be a good subtitle for this book, there's so much going on in this part of the world!

Before we go any further, let's unpack the confusing topic of what actually constitutes Britain. The various territories that make up the British Isles have had uneasy relationships down through the centuries, often related to whether Ireland, Scotland or Wales were going to be considered extensions of England/Britain, or as countries in their own right (read more below). As these political boundaries and alliances have been re-drawn down the centuries, what might be meant by 'Britain' in one century can be completely different a couple of hundred years later. So, assuming that Scottish Independence isn't going to happen between me writing this and the book being published, let's have a look at where we are at the moment!

• The British Isles

The group of islands including mainland Britain, the whole of Ireland (north and south), and six thousand-odd smaller islands around our coasts.

• Britain

This strictly refers to the United Kingdom (England, Scotland, Wales and Northern Ireland), but is often used as shorthand for Great Britain.

• Great Britain

This is the name of the big island that comprises England, Wales and Scotland; it's often used though to mean Britain, which includes Northern Ireland (still with me? I'm confused, and I live here!)

Materials

The quilt is a mixture of silk, cotton and synthetic fabrics. I used gold metallic thread for the machine satin stitch, and gold fusible bias binding for the stained glass patchwork. For the lettering I used a particularly sparkly fabric paint.

Techniques

The flower and plant designs were built up using reverse appliqué, which I also used to apply the border patches and the banner shapes. The lettering was painted, using a very fine brush to keep the serifs sharp; while the paint was still damp, I sprinkled very fine fabric glitters across the shapes. I quilted the background of each panel with a geometric design in machine satin stitch, then outlined the patches of fabric with stained glass patchwork.

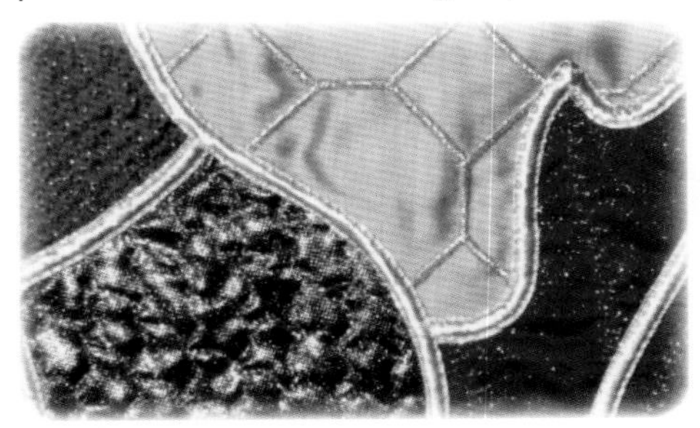

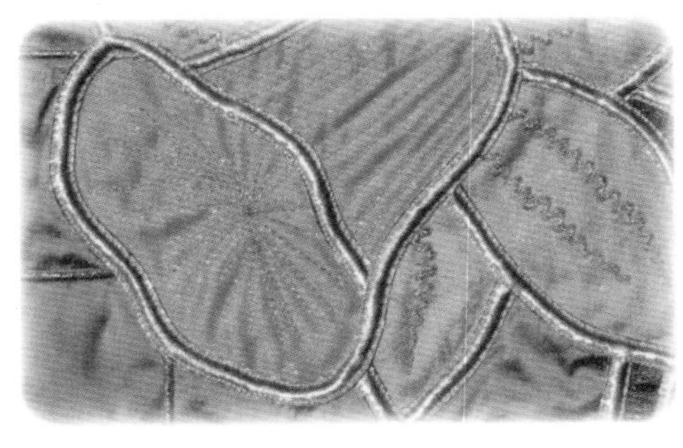

Backing and binding

For the backing I found a gold-coloured satiny fabric that complemented the bias binding, and bound the outside edges of the quilt in gold ribbon.

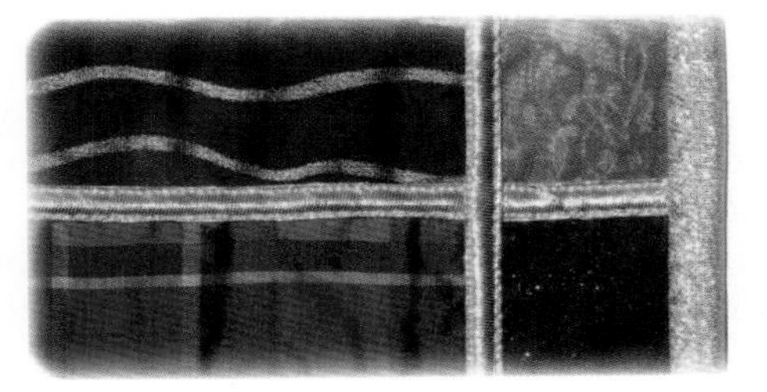

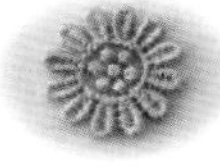

• United Kingdom

The UK is legally one sovereign state, comprising England, Scotland, Wales and Northern Ireland. (I know, I know ...)

• Ireland

This can either refer to the whole of the large island off the coast of Wales – which includes both Northern Ireland and the Republic of Ireland (Éire) – or it can simply mean the Republic of Ireland.

OK – got that?! For the sake of unity, we have decided to cut across all political, religious, historic and nationalistic lines and make our ***Glimpses of Britain*** a celebration of **all** the countries in the British Isles. Scotland, Wales and Ireland each have their own quilts, and we'll have a look in a minute at the characters and histories of those different countries, but first of all let's take a peep at the British people. Many authors have written wonderful observational books on us as a race, and it's fascinating (and also sometimes embarrassing ...) to see ourselves through other people's eyes. Because English is the main language across the British Isles, the term 'English' is often conflated with 'British,' so many of the books about the English are actually about all of us.

Recently both Chris and I read the novel ***Mr Rosenblum's List***, subtitled *'or friendly guidance for the aspiring Englishman,'* by Natasha Solomons. It's based on the real-life experiences of Jews coming to Britain to escape the Nazis; each refugee was given a leaflet to help them 'adjust' to life here, providing a great insight into British society at the time. Particularly, it was all about respectability: there was plenty of advice about not making yourself conspicuous by speaking loudly, or by manner or dress. Hungarian George (György) Mikes, who came to Britain in 1938, has similar advice: 'the Englishman, even when he is alone, forms an orderly queue of one,' and 'on the continent people have good food; in England the people have good table manners.' Kate Fox's ***Watching the English*** is subtitled *'the hidden rules of English behaviour'*; fascinating too is Bill Bryson's ***Notes from a Small Island***.

Stoney Middleton's 2011 well-dressing, designed by Joy Devereaux

The English language has given us all kinds of wonderful words; like our surnames (see p34, 68, 108 and 125), our language is a melting-pot of influences from different countries and eras. Some of my personal favourites include gallimaufry, palimpsest, serendipity, flippertigibbet. If you'd like explore some of the other unusual words in our rich language, have a look at www.worldwidewords.org/, hosted by Michael Quinion. In addition to our general words, each part of the country has its own particular vocabulary – as well as, occasionally, their own distinct languages or dialects.

Like our language, our land itself is astonishingly varied, and it provides a wealth of inspiration for artists. Marie Angel was a calligrapher who painted exquisite wild animals and birds alongside her letterforms. As I child I became captivated by Arthur Rackham's eerie depictions of woods and forests. Stanley Spencer's poignant painting set transcendent events in his home town of Cookham. Some modern landscape painters we've discovered include David Inshaw, Colin Smithson, Terry Rosser and Andrew Waddington. Recently we bought two prints by Takumasa Ono, a Japanese artist who paints our landscape with an enchanting Oriental touch.

Partly because of all the varied habitats, the British Isles supports a phenomenal number of different native trees, birds, insects, butterflies and wild animals. If you'd like to know more, explore any of the following sites:

www.ukbutterflies.co.uk/
www.britishbugs.org.uk/
www.rspb.org.uk/wildlife/birdidentifier/
www.wildaboutbritain.co.uk/
www.british-trees.com/

There are also many organisations devoted to protecting different aspects of our islands' heritage. On the pages devoted to each quilt we've included some websites and other information that you might find useful, but there are a couple of general organisations that we need to mention.

The National Trust (www.nationaltrust.org.uk/) maintains many historic houses, gardens and other significant sites in England, Wales and Northern Ireland; equivalent organisations in the other countries are the National Trust for Scotland (www.nts.org.uk/), and The National Trust for Ireland/An Taisce (www.antaisce.org/).

English heritage (www.english-heritage.org.uk/) preserves many historically important sites. North of the border is Historic Scotland (www.historic-scotland.gov.uk/), and the whole of the Emerald Isle is covered by Historic Ireland (www.historic-ireland.com/). In Wales, Cadw, the Welsh Assembly Government (cadw.wales.gov.uk/), oversees the historic sites. For inside information on all that Britain has to offer, go to www.visitbritain.com/.

So, we've explored Britain (and the Britons) in general: what about the individual countries that make up our islands? Let's look at them one by one.

England

Up until the 9th century, Anglo-Saxon England consisted of seven independent kingdoms: Wessex, Kent, Sussex, Essex, Mercia, East Anglia and Northumbria. As some of these monarchs (notably the kings of Wessex) conquered others, we ended up with various kings of almost-all-of-England: one of the first was Alfred the Great. In the 920s, Athelstan hoovered up the final patch (Northumbria), and adopted the title *Rex Anglorum*. The unification was partly a reaction to the threat from Scandinavian forces; the Vikings already had a large foothold in the north of the country (see p125), and were also making themselves a nuisance further south. After a few years of these raids, the English began to lose their famous sense of humour, and thought that perhaps the forces would go away if we gave them some gold – a ransom known as the Danegeld. Perhaps predictably, though, the Danes simply kept coming back for more: if the English would hand over gold without even fighting, so much the better!

Despite being a small country geographically, we have always had ambitions that belie our size (see p50!). Our Age of Discovery (see p39) began the English/British conquest of regions that eventually became the British Empire. This geographical spread explains the worldwide influence of our language, religion, place names and culture. The English political and legal systems have been the models for those of numerous other countries, and the Royal Society, founded in 1660, developed the principles of modern scientific experimentation. The Industrial Revolution began in England in the 18th century, and the National Geographic Society, founded in 1888, has always been in the forefront of exploration and conservation.

TOP LEFT: George and the dragon sign in Ashbourne; ABOVE: The Angel of the North by Antony Gormley; BELOW LEFT: oast house in Kent; BELOW RIGHT: the beautiful Lake District

The geography of England is highly varied, and includes the rocky coasts of Cornwall, west country moorland, flat East Anglian Fens, the chalky North and South Downs, the magnificent slopes of the Lake and Peak Districts, and the sandy beaches of Northumberland. Until 1066 (spot the date – see p34), the capital of England was Winchester; it's now London, which is also the capital of the United Kingdom, and our largest city. England's population is just over 50 million, which is roughly 85% of the UK's total population.

For inside information, explore www.visitengland.com/; for lovely photographs of the British countryside generally, try www.fineartphotographs.co.uk.

Ireland

I was apparently conceived across the Irish sea, although I can't say I remember a great deal about the event ... in recent years, though, Chris and I have been fortunate enough to visit Ireland several times, and those trips have proved highly memorable. Ireland is a dramatic and beautiful land, and the many loughs (lakes and sea inlets – the equivalent of the Scottish lochs) are highly photogenic; Lough Neagh is the largest lake in the British Isles. We stayed once at the foot of the spectacular Mountains of Mourne; these granite giants even have their own song. Irish peat bogs (see p61) are some of the most extensive left in Europe, and support their own distinctive fauna and flora.

The Emerald Isle has had quite a turbulent political history. During the 12th and 13th centuries, Norman influences dominated just as they did in England; during the 14th and 15th centuries, the balance swung back in favour of homegrown Irish culture and law. In 1542 Henry VIII recreated the title of King of Ireland, and the country came under the English thumb again. Over the next couple of centuries the resulting wars and conflicts established and entrenched the sectarian divides that have flared up many times since.

For many centuries Ireland was the poor relation in the British Isles, with hundreds of thousands of people living very close to the breadline. When blight hit the staple crop, potatoes, between 1845 and 1852, there were no resources to fall back on; during the Potato Famine, roughly one million Irish people died, and another million emigrated to seek a better life on other shores. On the shores of Clew Bay a poignant sculpture, called the Coffin Ship (see p59), is a memorial to all the lives lost during what's known in Irish as *an Gorta Mór* (the Great Hunger), or *an Drochshaol* (the Bad Times).

During the 19th and 20th centuries, Irish Nationalism became a force to be reckoned with. After much unrest, the Anglo-Irish Treaty was signed in 1921; this devolved a great deal of power to the newly-christened Irish Free State. In 1949 the southern part of the country officially became the Republic of Ireland, or Éire; the Republic is home to about 4½ million people. Six counties in the north form Northern Ireland, which is part of the United Kingdom and has a population of just under 2 million.

Well-known sons and daughters of Ireland include George Bernard Shaw, Bono, Bob Geldof, Roddy Doyle, Dana, James Galway, Kenneth Branagh, C S Lewis, Edna O' Brien, Oscar Wilde, Terry Wogan, George Best, Liam Neeson, the Cusack dynasty of actors, and the Day-Lewis dynasty of actors and poets; various others are mentioned on page 58.

For inside information on visiting Ireland, try these websites: www.discoverireland.ie/, and www.tourismireland.com/. You can learn more about Irish history at www.museum.ie/, and see gorgeous images of the land at www.beautifulirishphotos.com/.

Top left: rainbow against a stormy Irish sky; Below: the Giant's Causeway; Bottom: heading towards the hills of Achill

Scotland

When I was a teenager I lived in Scotland for a year; it was the first time I'd ever visited the country, and along with many other visitors I fell in love with its wild landscape and ever-changing light. Since I married Chris we've listened to Scotland's siren call and visited as often as possible; *Caledonia, you're calling me* as the traditional song says. As well as its main land mass, Scotland includes nearly 800 islands, stretching right up to Unst,

the northernmost island of Shetland. As I write this, we're planning a trip to Shetland in the summer, and I can't wait to see its wide vistas and bright seascapes. Scotland's three main cities have each played a significant part in the country's development for different reasons: Edinburgh (the capital) is one of the largest financial centres in Europe; Glasgow (Scotland's largest city) was for decades one of the world's great industrial centres; and Aberdeen is near the country's massive offshore oilfields.

Scotland is informally divided into the Highlands and the Lowlands. The Highlands are both further north and (on average) higher above sea level; its mountain ranges include the highest mountain in Britain, Ben Nevis. Nowadays this part of Scotland is sparsely populated; this is partly because the traditional Highland way of life was outlawed after the Jacobite uprisings, and partly because of the Highland Clearances of the 19th century, when many traditional crofting families were evicted. Many Highlanders died (the Potato Famine, see p6, also affected the Scots badly), and many more emigrated.

The Lowlands go from the southern Highlands down to the Border country. Although they're not anything like as mountainous as the Highlands, they do have their own ranges of hills, particularly in the confusingly-named Southern Uplands. The terrain of the Lowlands makes them more suited to agriculture and forestry, and there are also large areas of moorland. Scotland contains Britain's most northerly point. Because I love the name, I'd like to tell you that this is Muckle Flugga, just off the coast of Shetland – but in fact there is a small rock just slightly further out: Out Stack.

Famous Scots abound, and include John Logie Baird (the inventor of television) and Alexander Graham Bell (the inventor of the telephone). Just imagine how different our modern lives would be – for both better and worse – without those two people! Others include John Buchan, Evelyn Glennie, Robert Adam, Willie Carson, Joseph Lister, Sean Connery, Kenneth Grahame, Flora MacDonald and Charles Rennie Mackintosh – and others are mentioned on page 73.

Some of Scotland's official websites are www.scotland.org/ and www.visitscotland.com/; another gem is undiscoveredscotland.co.uk/.

Above left: Up Helly Aa boat burning (see p125) on Shetland; Above: Highland cattle; Below: the mysterious shore of Loch Lomond

Wales

Wales is on the western side of the British mainland; its proximity to Ireland makes it a useful jumping-off point for crossing the Irish Sea. Wales was inhabited by Celtic tribes during the Iron Age and until the time of the Roman occupation of England (see p109); between the years 48 and 78AD, the Romans gradually took charge of Wales too. They were particularly interested in Wales' mineral deposits – gold, copper, silver, zinc and lead. Like the Scots, the Welsh didn't take kindly to being occupied and tended to resist. The Romans, never slow to take up the opportunity for a bit of fortifying, responded by building over 40 forts and 'fortlets' to quash the uprisings.

After the Romans withdrew, in around the 5th century, Wales went back to minding its own Celtic business; for several centuries it was a loose alliance of tribes, each one ruled by a separate king. In 844 Rhodri the Great became king of a large amount of the country, but during the 1050s Gruffydd ap Llywelyn was recognised as the first king of all Wales. The death of the confusingly-similarly-named Llywelyn ap Gruffydd in 1282 was the final stage in Edward I of England's conquest of Wales. Edward too built numerous castles and defensive walls to keep the Welsh in their place, many of which can still be seen along the Wales/England border.

Between 1400 and 1415, Welsh hero Owain Glyndŵr briefly restored Welsh independence; once the rebellion had been reversed, the English parliament brought Wales under English law. During the 19th century there was a strong resurgence of Welsh nationalism and politics. The National Assembly for Wales was created in 1999, and has legal responsibility for various matters which affect the country.

A great deal of Wales is mountainous; its tallest peak is Snowdon (Yr Wyddfa). The country's dramatic landscape includes three National Parks and five Areas of Outstanding Natural Beauty. The Welsh language, jealously guarded by its native speakers, is all but impenetrable to outsiders. Although its pronunciations are perfectly logical, names such as Llanfairpwllgwyngyll and Maesycrugiau reduce the non-Welsh to gibbering inarticulacy. Famous sons and daughters of Wales include Dylan Thomas, Harry Secombe, Augustus and Gwen John, Ivor Novello, Griff Rhys Jones, Richard Burton, Tessie O'Shea, Ruth Jones, and Siân Phillips. Songbirds Shirley Bassey, Bryn Terfel and Robert Tear all hail from Wales.

For information on the good things that await you in Wales, have a look at www.visitwales.co.uk/; you will find lovely photos of the landscape on www. photographsofwales.co.uk/.

Top left: Tintern Abbey on the Welsh border; Above: Gail stitching the Welsh quilt (see p103) in Wales; Below: looking across Golden Valley

PROJECT

Fancy Flowerpots

The national flowers of England, Ireland, Scotland and Wales decorate these fabric vases. Of course (!?) the pots aren't waterproof, but you can use them for dried flowers, decorative twigs or pot-pourri. Or, as I've done here, use them as slip-covers over the plastic pots your plants sit in, to create prettier alternatives. The secret to creating a firm vase that keeps its shape is to use heavy fusible interfacing; I used the heavyweight version of Fast2Fuse™, which is fusible on both sides.

finished size: each pot is 5in (13cm) high and 6in (15cm) wide

For each pot you will need:

- one piece of heavyweight fusible interfacing, 26 x 6½in (66 x 16.5cm)
- two pieces of print background fabric, 26 x 6½in (66 x 16.5cm); if your fabric is strongly directional, you might need a bit more to ensure that you can cut all the pieces out in the correct orientation
- 4½in (12cm) square of double-sided bonding web
- large reel of toning or contrasting thread for the outer stitching, plus a reel of strong thread (eg button-hole thread) in the same colour
- pencil, paper scissors; if pencil won't show on your chosen background fabric, you will also need a chalk marker or coloured pencil in a colour that will show up
- A4 piece of template plastic
- small patches of fabric for your chosen motif:
  - for the daffodil, 4½in (12cm) square of yellow, and 2in (5cm) square of orange
  - for the shamrock, 4½in (12cm) square of emerald green
  - for the thistle, 4in (10cm) square of pale green for the leaves, 2in (5cm) square of mid green for the thistle base, 1½in square of mauve for the thistle-head
  - for the rose, 3½in (9cm) square of pink for the flower, 2 x 3in (5 x 8cm) piece of mid green for the leaves
- sewing threads to match the fabric patches

Instructions

1 Trace the templates for the pot (A and B) onto the template plastic, then cut them out along the marked lines (**a**).

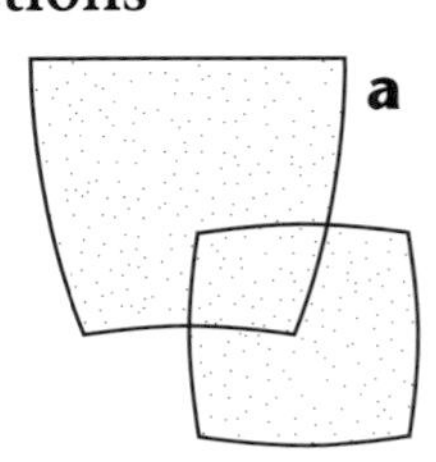

2 Use a hot iron to fuse the background fabric strips onto the strip of interfacing, then use pencil or other marker to trace round the side template A four times, and the base template B once, as shown (**b**). Cut these shapes out along the marked lines (**c**).

3 On the paper side of the bonding web, trace the shapes needed for your chosen motif, and cut these out roughly (**d**); if you are using one fabric for several patches, you can cut the shapes out as a group.

4 Fuse these tracings onto the wrong sides of the relevant fabrics, and cut the shapes out along the marked lines (**e**).

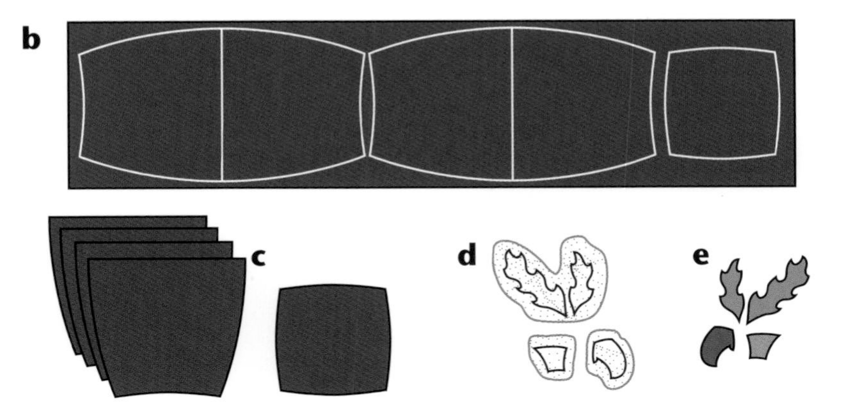

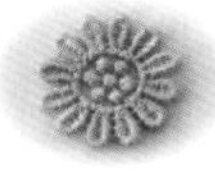

5 Choose which side panel you would like to be the front of your pot. Peel the papers off the bonding web shapes and position the patches on the pot front to create an attractive motif (**f**); once you're happy with the positioning, fuse the shapes into position. Use a small machine zigzag to go round each of these patches in matching thread (**g**).

f

g

6 Follow the tips on page 37 to set your sewing machine up for satin stitch; the stitch width should be about 4. Stitch all the way around each piece of the pot, including the base (**h**). On each side panel, begin and end the stitching line on one of the corners at the bottom of the piece; then any unevenness will be hidden when you join the sides to the base.

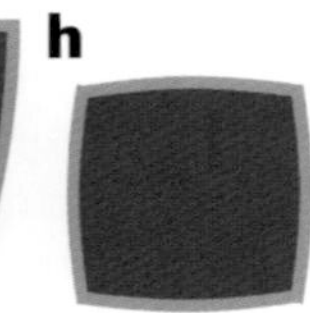

h

7 Set your sewing machine to zigzag stitch, about 2.5 width and about 1.5 length. Lay the base under the sewing machine foot with the vase front panel next to it, both right sides down; stitch the two together using the zigzag. When you get to the corner of the base, turn the work by 90° and continue stitching to join the next side in the same way. Carry on until you have added all the side panels (**i**).

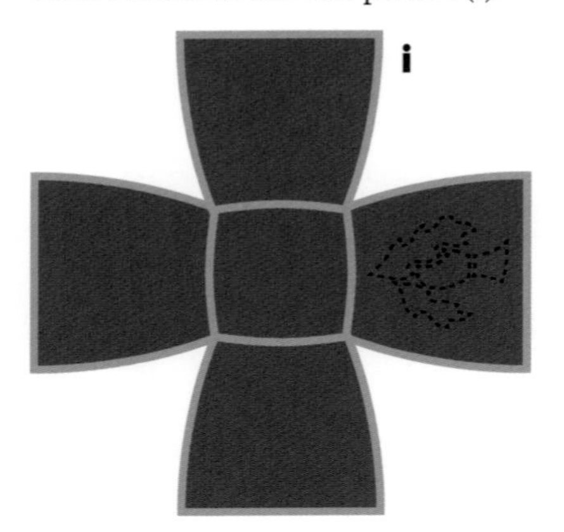

i

8 Thread a hand-stitching needle with the strong thread. Working from the top downwards, join two of the sides using ladder stitch (if you're new to ladder stitch: take a straight stitch, parallel with the join, into each side piece alternately).

TIP

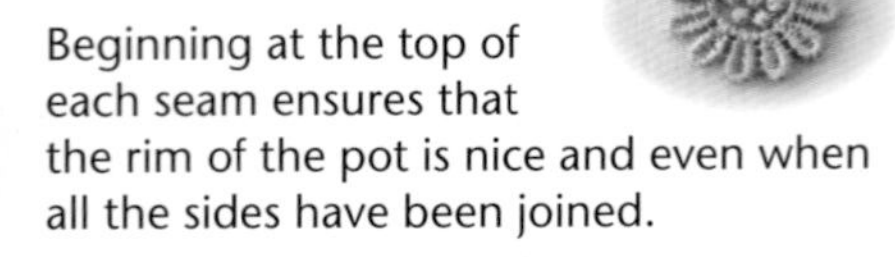

Beginning at the top of each seam ensures that the rim of the pot is nice and even when all the sides have been joined.

9 You will probably find that the pot has become a little distorted as you've handled it. To restore its firm shape, set your iron to steam; lay each side of the pot in turn on the ironing board and put the nose of the iron into the pot, pressing each side flat for a few seconds. As you press, hold the edges firmly at right angles where they join.

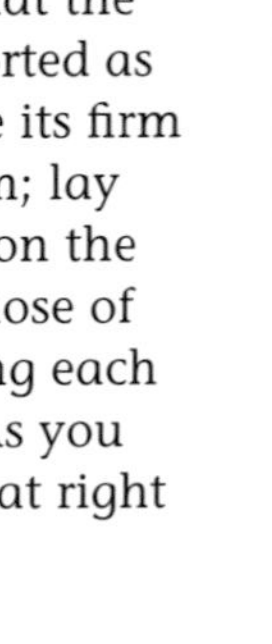

VARIATION

If you have a really attractive fabric, perhaps a bright batik or a very striking print, you can use this for your pots without adding any extra motifs. The art deco shape of the pots would lend itself very well to 30s-style print fabrics; or you could use floral prints for a more old-fashioned feel.

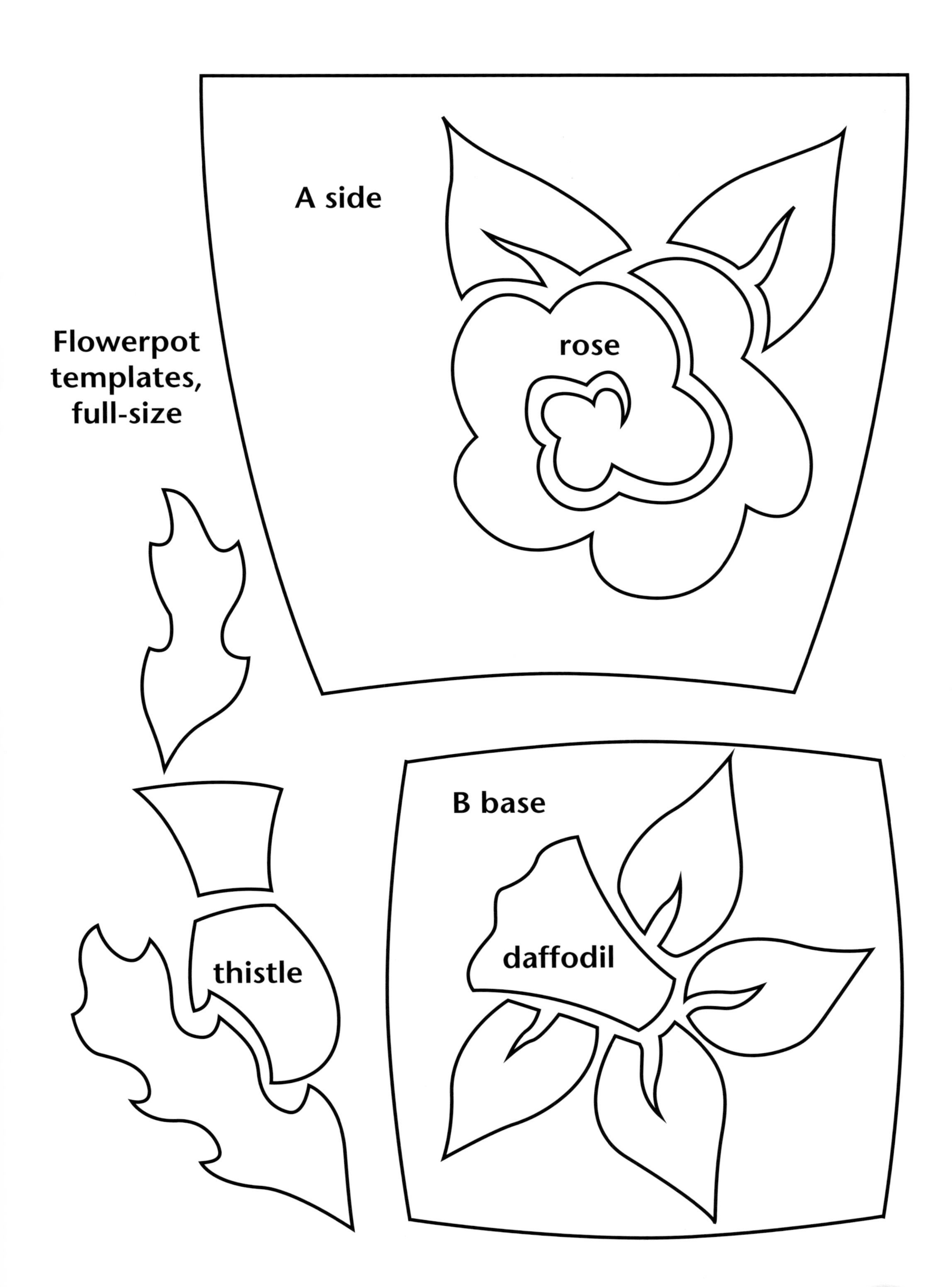
A side
rose
Flowerpot
templates,
full-size
B base
thistle
daffodil

Weather

Is there a subject that the British love to talk about more than the weather? I doubt it!

When I was first thinking about this book, I asked quite a few people what themes would have to appear in the quilts: one of the most common answers was The Weather. Many years ago, an American friend said to me 'I can see why the British talk about the weather all the time: you go into a store and it's summer, and when you come out it's winter!'

I think that there are two reasons my fellow countrymen (and women) love to talk about the weather. One is because it does change very frequently. I can remember one day when Chris and I were walking by the Adur river; it was only February, so there were still snowdrops out on the river banks, but it was unseasonably warm – so sunny that it had tempted dragonflies out from hibernation (or from being nymphs, or booking their holidays or whatever they spend the cold weather doing). Was that day part of winter, or spring, or summer? We can't really decide by the calendar any more.

Rainbows are always special, and particularly so for us. On an October day in 1977, Chris and I had just gone back to university and had been food shopping. On the way home we got soaked in a heavy storm, and a fabulous double rainbow arced all the way across the sky; we stood on the flat roof of the hall of residence and admired it for ages. Then later that day Chris asked me to marry him …

The weather in Scotland is notoriously rainy, but on our frequent visits there we've often had lovely sunny weather, even though the sky over the western isles changes every ten minutes. When we first visited the west coast of Ireland, we discovered

Rainbows arcing over Clew Bay, County Mayo, in the shadow of Croagh Patrick (see page 58)

that the weather changes even more frequently than in Scotland, and over the hundreds of islands in Clew Bay rainbows are commonplace visitors. (Incidentally, those little bits of rainbow that appear in other parts of the sky are called, rather unromantically, sun dogs.)

'Weather events' (as they've recently come to be called, for some reason) often play significant parts in our literature and films. They can be used to move the plot in a particular direction; there's nothing to beat a good shipwreck, flood, storm or baking-hot summer for creating new possibilities in a story. For instance in ***Sense and Sensibility*** impetuous Marianne gets caught in the rain and twists her ankle, and the dashing cad Willoughby comes to her rescue, beginning her infatuation with him. And the weather can be symbolic, too; for instance, the storm at the end of ***King Lear*** echoes the turmoil going on in the king's heart. And we mustn't forget the most famous lightning flash in the world, emblazoned on Harry Potter's forehead.

Inevitably, our islands have spawned numerous songs relating to weather; one of the first live gigs I ever went to involved crowding into a dark hall in Watford, listening to Lindisfarne sing (among other things) ***The Fog on the Tyne***. Here are just some of the others; you'll no doubt be able to come up with many more. ***Here Comes the Sun*** and ***Good Day Sunshine*** (the Beatles), ***Flowers in the Rain*** (the Move), ***Here Comes the Rain Again*** (Eurythmics), ***I Wish it Would Rain Down*** (Phil Collins), ***Let it Rain*** (Eric Clapton), ***Right as Rain*** (Adele).

Interesting, isn't it, how rain features so often?! Even our nursery rhymes aren't immune from downpours: think of ***It's Raining, It's Pouring***, and ***Doctor Foster went to Gloucester*** (*in a shower of rain*). And a 16th century poem/song begins '*Westron wynde* (western wind), *when wilt thou blow, the small raine down can raine.*' The city of Manchester has acquired the nickname The Rainy City, for obvious reasons. (Manchester was also site of the world's first railway station, and where scientists first split the atom – good thing that it went well, otherwise we could have had a very different apocalyptic weather icon for that part of the country.) Sea shanties, not surprisingly, often feature the elements behaving badly; lines that come randomly into my brain include '*And now the storm is raging, and we are far from the shore.*'

The restless weather throughout the islands has been immortalised by many artists: Constable was one of the first painters to make notes in his sketchbook on what the cloud formations etc were like, and the notes enabled him to reproduce the weather conditions faithfully in his finished oil paintings. I used to wonder why Constable always painted vegetation in particular grey/green tones, with greyish skies, until early one evening I visited the countryside that inspired him; the colours I saw then were just like a Constable painting come to life.

To represent the weather in my quilts, I was drawn to the idea of a map on which, like a real-life weather forecaster

from my youth, I could move the symbols around (these days they've taken all the fun out of it by doing it electronically). So I've created a series of weather icons which include all the usual suspects: sun, cloud, dark cloud, mixed sun and cloud, fog, rain, hail, snow, storm (with lightning flash). I've also included some extra icons based on favourite British sayings: on one panel it's raining cats and dogs, and there's also a red sunset (*red sky at night, shepherds' delight; red sky in the morning, shepherds take warning*). And you'll see a rainbow, too, with the ever-elusive pot of gold at the end.

There's a popular belief that our weather in Britain is becoming more extreme, so on my quilt I've added some extra weather icons to reflect this; there's a typhoon and a tsunami, and the volcano reflects the ash clouds that have disrupted so many flights recently. The earthquake represents the tremors around Blackpool, apparently caused in part by fracking operations. Every so often a space nerd spots an asteroid that they think spells certain destruction for our planet, so one of those is heading our way, but I don't think it's big enough to do any harm.

We're told that, with global warming, our summers will get hotter (bring it on, as far as I'm concerned). So I've added a desert icon, complete with lizard and blazing sun. We're also told that we'll soon see invasions of pests usually associated with hotter countries, so I've included assorted plagues of Egypt: locusts, flies, frogs and gnats. And every schoolchild knows that you don't get eskimos and penguins in the same place, as one is found in the Arctic and one in the Antarctic; but presumably if the icecaps continue melting, maybe icebergs will float from both ends of the planet and meet in the middle? And you can bet your bottom dollar that, if they do, they'll rendezvous in Britain, so I've predicted that meeting; now that ***would*** give us something new to talk about on the weather forecast.

Inside information

The Weather Channel (uk.weather.com/) will tell you everything you need to know about the weather forecast in your area, and also for any other region of the world you're curious about.

If you're interested in snowflakes, two websites you'll enjoy are www.cco.caltech.edu/~atomic/snowcrystals/, and snowflakes.barkleyus.com/. Still on an icy theme, check out www.londonicesculptingfestival.co.uk/ to see some of the amazing things that can be done with frozen water.

Materials

The background map, lettering and water are cotton fabrics; I used a rainbow-print fabric behind the word WEATHER. For the icons I used a mixture of cotton, synthetic and metallic fabrics, fused over firm interfacing and attached with velcro so that they can be moved around the map. The lettering and weather icons are embellished with beads, buttons and charms.

Techniques

I used simple machine appliqué for the map and the lettering, and machine-quilted the water in a pattern of stylised waves; the lettering is edged with machine satin stitch. On the weather icons the patches were fused in place on the interfacing, then quilted with a small machine zigzag around the fabric shapes; the ovals are edged with machine satin stitch.

Backing and binding

The wonderful fabric on the back of the quilt features a well-known symbol of the British countryside (as well as a great British invention): the Wellington boot! It's also a sideways reference to a much-loved British icon, Paddington bear. I cut the edge of the quilt to an uneven shape, to reflect the movement of the waves, then bound the edge with a very narrow double strip of bias binding, cut from the same fabric I'd used for the sea.

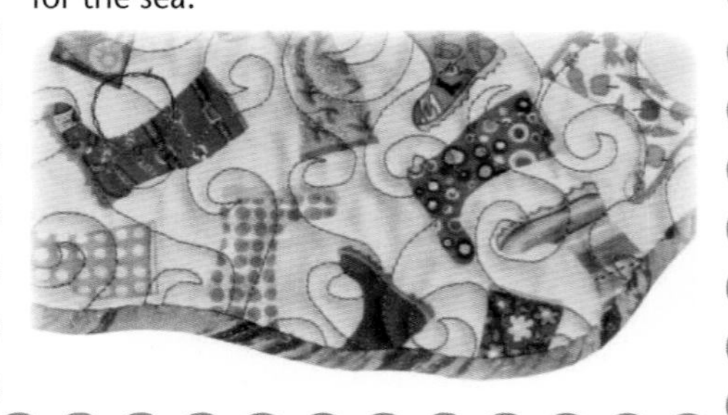

PROJECT

Today's Weather

Any small child would love this weather chart, complete with moveable symbols – just like the ones on the grown-up weather forecast! The symbols are stitched onto thick interfacing, so they're easy for little hands to hold, and if they get grubby they're even washable (I'm talking about the symbols, not the kids, but I guess the same holds true ...) I used a multicoloured dotted fabric for the background; find something that all the symbols show up clearly against. For the border I picked a mid-blue print that looks a bit like sky or water.

finished size: 24in (61cm) square

You will need:

- 22in (56cm) square of background fabric
- contrasting fabric for the border: two 22 x 3in (56 x 8cm) strips two 27½ x 3in (70 x 8cm) strips *(note: if the border fabric is strongly directional, bear this in mind when you cut the strips)*
- 24in (61cm) square of wadding
- 24in (61cm) square of backing fabric
- eight 5 x 6in (13 x 15cm) patches of cotton fabric for the sky, one patch for each symbol. I used:
  - four patches of ordinary sky/ cloud print
  - one patch of blue spotted with white for hail
  - one patch of snowflake print on blue for snow
  - one patch of blue with raindrops
  - one dark blue batik patch for the storm
- 12 x 6in (30 x 15cm) bright print cotton fabric for the lettering
- 22 x 12in (56 x 30cm) double-sided bonding web, or the equivalent in smaller bits
- eight 5 x 6in (13 x 15cm) patches of white cotton fabric for backing the symbols
- eight 5 x 6in (13 x 15cm) patches of firm fusible interfacing (eg heavyweight Fast2Fuse™)
- 5 x 6in (13 x 15cm) template plastic; pencil; paper scissors
- cotton fabrics for the symbols:
  - 10in (25cm) square of white (use a thickish fabric so that the background prints won't show through)
  - 8 x 4in (20 x 10cm) bright yellow for the suns' rays
  - 6 x 3in (15 x 8cm) yellow-orange for the suns' centres
  - 5 x 4in (13 x 10cm) dark grey for the dark cloud
- 6 x 5in (15 x 13cm) translucent fabric for the fog
- scrap of bonded silver fabric for the lightning flash
- 1yd (1m) stitch-and-stitch velcro
- large reel of navy thread for edging the symbols
- sewing threads to match the background fabric and border, plus yellow, orange, white, black and grey threads for stitching the symbols
- non-stick ironing sheet, or grease-proof paper
- extra strip of fabric for a casing, or fabric or ribbon strips for making hanging loops

Instructions

1 Trace templates A-J onto the paper side of the bonding web; you need to trace template A six times, to create all the different clouds, and the rest of the shapes once each. Cut the shapes out roughly; if you group the patches that will be cut from the same colour when you trace them, you can cut them out as a group (**a**). Fuse all the

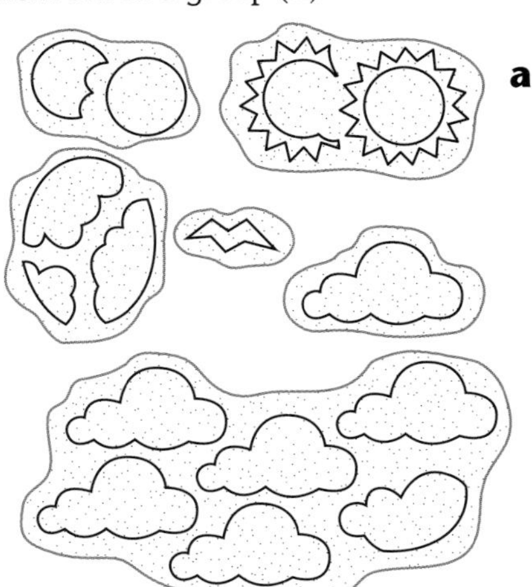

patches onto the wrong sides of the relevant fabrics (use the non-stick ironing sheet to protect the fog and lightning fabrics), and cut the shapes out along the marked lines (**b**).

2 Lay the eight backing fabric patches right side down on the ironing board. Cover these with the patches of interfacing, then with the different patches of sky fabric, right side up (**c**); fuse the fabrics into place with a hot iron.

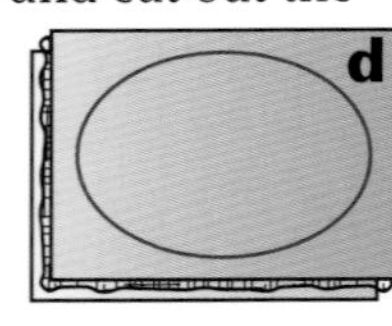

TIP

Turn the patches over and iron them on the back as well, to make sure that all the fabrics are firmly fused.

3 Trace the oval template (K) onto the template plastic and cut out the shape along the marked lines. Use this shape to draw an oval onto each sky patch (**d**).

d

4 Peel the papers off the coloured patches, and lay them in position, right sides up, on the correct sky pieces as shown (**e**). Once you're happy with the positions, fuse them into place; use the non-stick sheet or greaseproof paper to protect the translucent and silver fabrics as you iron.

5 Cut out each oval shape (**f**), then use a small zigzag in a matching colour to stitch round the edges of all the fused coloured patches. You don't need to stitch round the patches where they coincide with the edge of the oval; this will be done at the next stage.

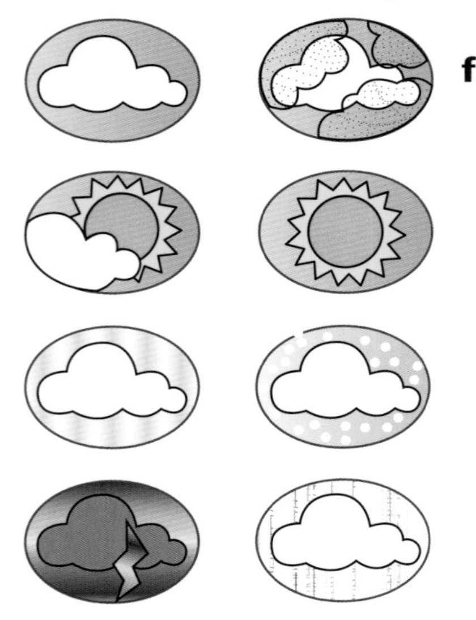

6 Using the navy thread, work a fairly wide satin stitch, about size 4, around the raw edge of each oval (**g**); see page 37 for hints on doing a good satin stitch.

7 Trace the letters onto the paper side of the bonding web; fuse them onto the back of the bright print fabric, then cut out the shapes (**h**).

today's weather h

Lay the background square on a flat surface, right side up. Peel the backing papers off the letters, and lay them in position, with the ovals in the layout shown (**i**); it doesn't matter which oval

is where – it's just the positioning that we're looking at. Make sure that all the design elements are at least 2in (5cm) in from the edges of the fabric square. When you're happy with the positions, push a pin through the centre of each of the ovals; where the pin hits the background fabric, make a small pencil cross. Now you can remove the ovals, and fuse the lettering in place.

8 Using ½in seams, add the shorter border strips to the top and bottom of the background square, then add the side borders (**j**). Lay the fabric right side down on a flat surface, and position the wadding on top so that there is an even border of fabric all the way around. Lay the backing fabric, right side up, on top, aligning it with the edges of the wadding; use your preferred method (see p136) to secure the quilt layers.

9 Cut the velcro into eight 4in (10cm) strips. Separate the two parts of each strip, and pin the hooked sections onto the background fabric, centring them over the pencil crosses. Use a machine zigzag to stitch these strips in place (**k**). Pin the looped sections onto the backs of the weather symbols, and stitch these on by hand (use hand-stitching so that it's not visible on the front).

10 Stitch round the edges of all the letters to quilt them, using a small zigzag. Fold the raw edges of the border to the back, and slipstitch them in place, then add any other quilting you wish; I did a line of wavy stitch just inside the edges of the background square, and another down the centre of the border.

11 Add a hidden casing on the back of the work, or stitch hanging loops of ribbon or fabric along the top. Check the weather outside, then you're ready to put the symbols in position (**l**)!

VARIATION

This idea of moveable symbols on velcro can be adapted to many other themes. How about a garden that the toddler can design himself or herself, with flower and tree motifs, a pond, a shed etc? An underwater scene, complete with fish and other sealife, a wreck, treasure chest and perhaps a submarine? Or Noah's Ark, with pairs of simple animal outlines?

Today's Weather lettering templates, full-size

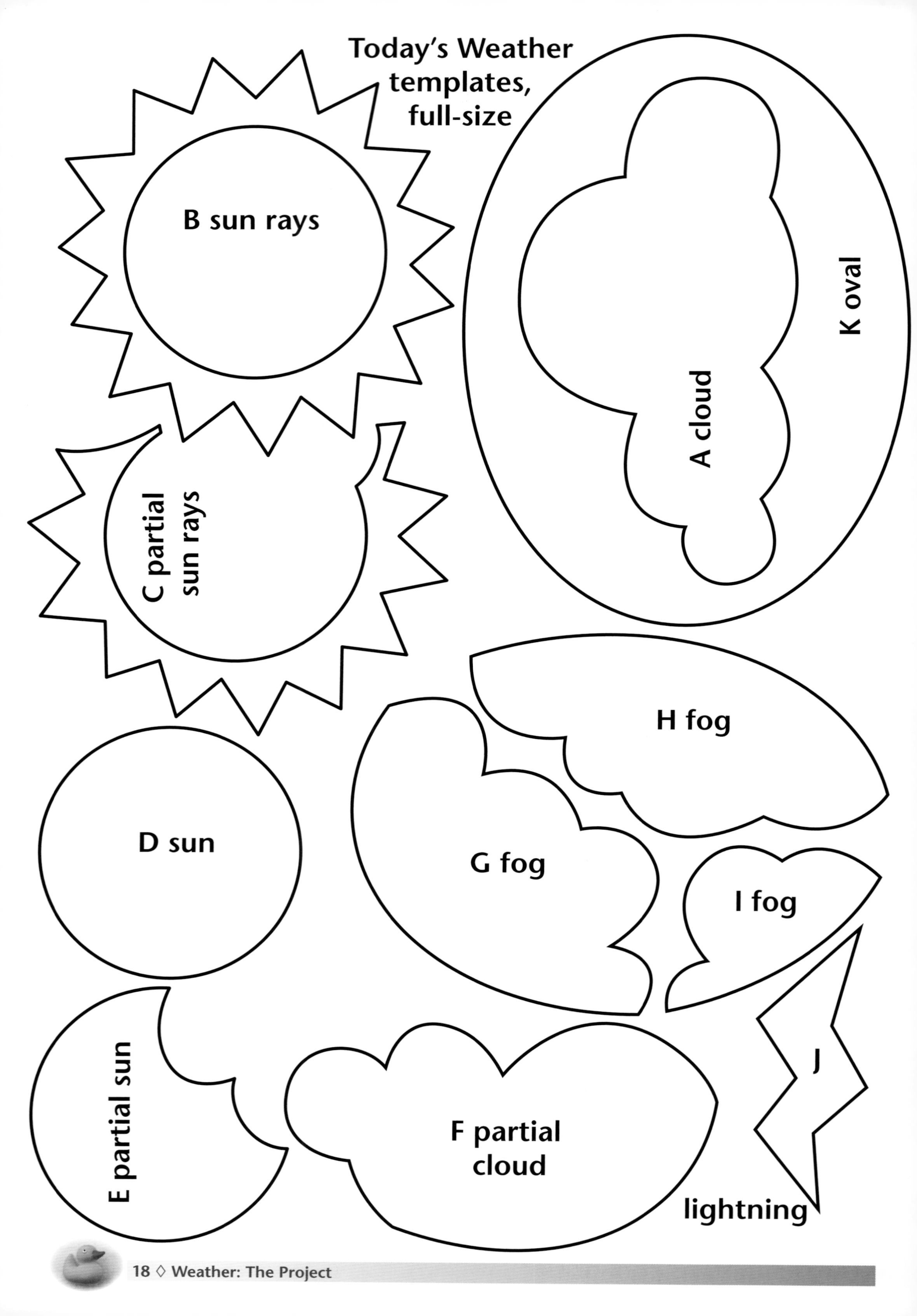
Today's Weather
templates,
full-size
B sun rays
K oval
A cloud
C partial
sun rays
H fog
D sun
G fog
I fog
J
E partial sun
F partial
cloud
lightning

Ancient Stones

The menhirs, dolmens and sarsens of our ancestors stand sentinel over more modern stone structures.

Our islands are covered with massive monuments built by our stone-age ancestors; stone has been an invaluable building material for millennia, for both functional and symbolic structures. One of the oldest is the passage tomb at Newgrange in Ireland; when the sun shines in during the winter solstice sunrise, it illuminates the oldest known carving of a triple spiral design (this event is so dramatic and so famous that tickets to witness it are allocated by lottery).

But there's no doubt that the most iconic of all these structures is Stonehenge, set at the edge of Salisbury plain, and dating back to at least 2000BC. This dramatic construction is famous throughout the world; because of the flatness of the surrounding land it's visible from many miles away. Stonehenge currently draws around a million visitors a year, and appears as the backdrop to many pieces of art and literature; John Constable did a watercolour of a double rainbow above the monument, and Thomas Hardy's Tess of the D'Urbervilles spent her final night of freedom sleeping on Stonehenge's altar stone.

Hundreds of stone circles can be found across our countries, too (as well as thousands of single standing stones); some of these are tiny, found in the middle of a dense forest or on top of a small mound, but some are massive. One of the most famous is Avebury, also in Wiltshire; the beautiful Castlerigg circle in the Lake District commands spectacular 360° views of the surrounding countryside, and the Ring of Brodgar and Stones o' Stenness on Orkney are elegant circles of tall slender stones.

So what on earth was the purpose of all these megaliths? That's a subject of endless debate. Some of them are obviously burial places, but others don't have any immediately obvious purpose. Some academics think that they're ceremonial, others that they are primitive calendars, and still others that they are boundary markers: perhaps they were all of the above, or something totally different that we know nothing about (giant games of skittles? results of drunken macho bets – 'I've got £10 that says you can't lift that stone up and shove it in the ground' etc?) Certainly it's hard not to stand in awe of the organisation and physical strength that led to their construction. Many years ago Chris and I visited Wayland's Smithy, near the Uffington White Horse (see p87), a Neolithic chamber tomb lined with massive stones, and we've never felt such a sense of our civilisation stretching back for millennia.

But what about more modern uses of stone? Because we have such a complex geological structure for such a tiny land mass (see p82), many different types of stone have played important parts in our heritage, from the softest sandstone to the hardest granite. As well as being used

for constructing buildings, stone is also used for wall, monuments, gravestones, milestones, and in art; one of my favourite Land Artists is Andy Goldsworthy, who uses all kinds of natural items, including stone, in his work. As I write, a modern coliseum known as Achill-Henge is causing a great stir in Ireland; it's been built in concrete on the spectacular Achill island, apparently by a local builder disillusioned with the local authorities.

Millstones were generally carved from a hard rock known as Millstone Grit, found in northern England and northeast Wales. I wanted to include a utilitarian use of stone alongside the ceremonial, and the attractive design of the traditional millstone was just right. This combination also gave me the chance to bring in references to two heroines of English literature, both of whom met rather unhappy ends: the strawberries relate to Tess, who shared the fruit with the evil Alec (hiss), and the millstone and reeds refer to Maggie Tulliver from George Eliot's ***The Mill on the Floss***, who met her death entwined with the reeds in the millstream.

I wanted the name of the quilt just to appear subtly in the sky, so I did it in a style that celebrates another group of people dedicated to preserving our heritage: the lexicographers who compile our dictionaries and encyclopaedias. The most famous of these is Samuel Johnson, (pictured left) who produced his ***A Dictionary of the English Language*** in 1755 after nine years of work. In honour of our lexicographers, I used the words Ancient Stones in their phonetic forms, based on dictionary pronunciation guides.

Inside information

You will find many websites devoted to our ancient stones; the official sites for Stonehenge and Avebury can be found at www.english-heritage.org.uk/daysout/properties/stonehenge/, and www.nationaltrust.org.uk/avebury/. The Megalith Map (www.megalith.ukf.net) gives the location of every known stone circle and stone row on the British Isles. The map is based on the exhaustive work of archaeologist Dr Aubrey Burl, and a good introductory book on the subject is his ***The Stone Circles of Britain, Ireland and Brittany.***

Materials

The henge stones are different grey cotton fabrics, marbled and batik; I added extra depth to them using fabric crayons. The dramatic sky is hand-painted cotton poplin, and the millstone is a patch of speckled grey that gives the impression of granite. The ground is green batik, and the reeds are plain green fabric which I added tone to by quilting them with variegated thread.

Techniques

The main design was assembled using invisible machine appliqué. I used what I call 'vermicelli with gaps' to quilt the stones on a layer of wadding, then cut the wadding back to the outline of the stones; this gave the henge shape extra depth and dimension when it was layered up. The sky is free machine-quilted, and the ground is stitched in a grassy pattern.

I cut the leaves from fabric fused onto thick interfacing; they are quilted and appliquéd in one go by stitching the leaf veins. Each strawberry was made by gathering red fabric over a padded card shape; small dits of fabric pen create the pips. The flowers began as little Suffolk Puffs, appliquéd using the yellow stitching in the centre, with added free-machined tendrils; the reeds are appliquéd using machine satin stitch.

Backing and binding

A simple marbled cotton provides the quilt backing, and I bound the edges with a slightly sparkly grey cotton fabric.

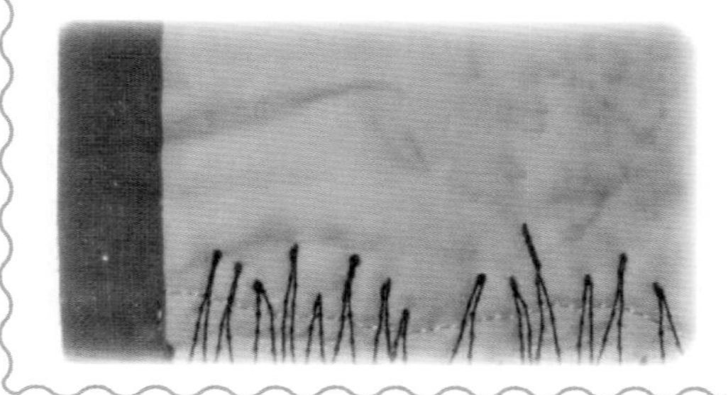

PROJECT

Stone Circle

The ancient stone circles of Britain have a timeless fascination – why are they there? Who put them in place? Centuries – or even millennia – later, they still stand majestically in the landscape, keeping their secrets. This project gives you the chance to create your own quilted stone circle in fabric; much easier than handling all those heavy rocks! The basic design is fused, and once all the pieces are in place you can use any simple machine-quilting method to quilt the panel. If you choose a dramatic fabric for the sky (I used a Mickey Lawler sky-dye piece), you can make the finished wall-hanging look even more atmospheric.

finished size: 21 x 30in (54 x 75cm)

You will need:

- sky fabric 8 x 30in (20 x 75cm)
- ground fabric 14 x 30in (35 x 75cm)
- flat wadding 21 x 30in (54 x 75cm)
- backing fabric 21 x 30in (54 x 75cm)
- large scraps of different grey or stone-coloured fabrics in a variety of tones; marbled or batik fabrics look particularly good. You will need a piece roughly 6 x 3in (15 x 8cm) for each stone. You could use 14 different fabrics, one for each stone, or use some of the fabrics for several stones.
- 18 x 13in (45 x 35cm) bonding web
- 18 x 13in (45 x 35cm) dark brown or black tulle net to create shadows for the stones (optional)
- 3yd (3m) toning or contrasting fabric strip for the binding: I used a bias strip of marbled brown, 1½in wide. If you prefer a straight binding rather than the wiggly one I've given my quilt, you can use a straight-grain strip of fabric rather than bias.
- sewing threads for joining the sky and ground, and to match the binding
- your choice of machine quilting threads. I used a clear thread to quilt across the whole design in random wavy lines; if you want to stitch around the edge of each stone shape, you can do this in matching or contrasting threads
- pencil; tracing paper or template plastic; paper scissors
- non-stick ironing sheet, or grease-proof paper
- extra fabric strip for making a casing, or ribbon/tape for creating hanging loops

Instructions

1 Using a ¼in seam, join the bottom of the sky piece to the top of the ground piece; press the seam open (**a**).

a

2 Trace the five stone templates (A-E) onto paper or template plastic and cut them out. Use these as templates to draw 14 shapes on the paper side of the bonding web, reversing some of the shapes so that you have a good variety. Cut the shapes out roughly, outside the drawn lines (**b**).

b

3 Fuse each bonding web shape onto one of the 'stone' fabric patches, making sure that you put the rough side of the web onto the wrong side of the fabric. Cut the shapes out roughly, using the marked lines as a general guide but wiggling the scissors as you cut to roughen up the edges a bit (**c**).

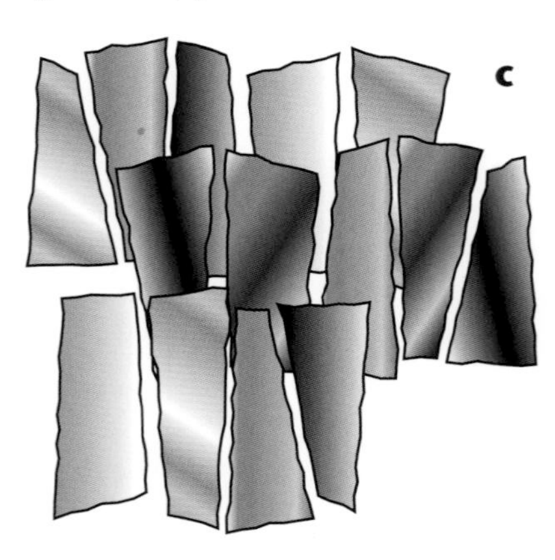

4 If you're using net to create shadows for the stones, cut a piece of net out to match each stone shape (**d**); pin them together in pairs so that you don't forget which shadow goes with which stone.

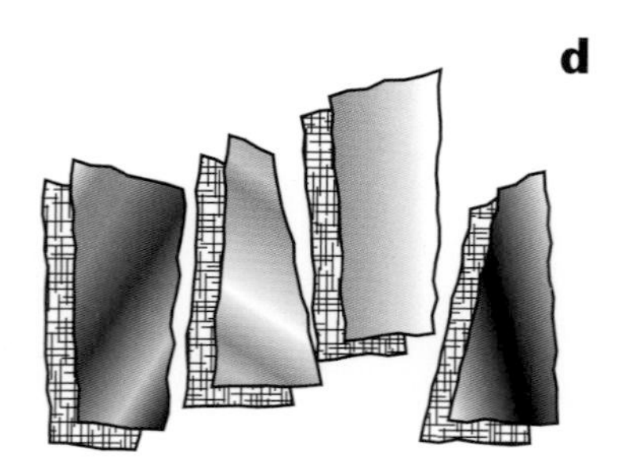

5 Decide whether you'd like the light stones at the back of the circle and the dark ones in front, or the other way around (this will probably depend on what the tones are in the sky and ground fabrics); take this into account when you decide which side of the stones to put the shadows. Lay the stones (and their shadows) out to create the circle, moving them around until you're happy with the arrangement. Once you are, peel the paper off each stone patch and pin it on the background, trapping the net shadow so that it emerges about ½in below and to one side of each stone (**e**).

6 Using the non-stick ironing sheet or greaseproof paper to ensure that you don't melt the net, fuse the shapes in place on the background, removing the pins as you work.

TIP

Try the temperature of the iron out on a scrap piece of net and fabric (laid under the ironing sheet or greaseproof paper), just to ensure that it isn't too hot.

7 Lay the backing fabric on a flat surface, right side down, and position the wadding on top; lay the fused design, right side up, on top, and use your favourite method to secure the layers (see p136).

8 Use your chosen method to machine-quilt the design (**f**); you can either stitch around each stone, using a small zigzag or a decorative stitch, or you can do as I've done and stitch random lines (or patterns) across the whole quilt.

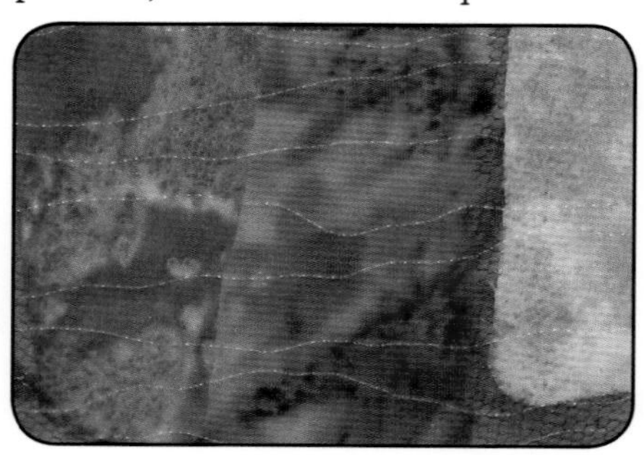

9 Trim the edges of the quilt, either straight or wiggly, and follow the instructions on page 136 to attach the binding. Add a hidden casing on the back of the quilt, or stitch hanging tabs of ribbon or tape to the top edge.

VARIATION

You could depict your stone circle on a sunny day, with a blue sky (perhaps with some dramatic clouds) and a grassy green print or batik instead of the brown batik ground I've used. Or you could create your circle against a starry or moonlit midnight sky.

Left: dovecote (doocot) in Linlithgow; Above: figure on the front of Wells cathedral; Right: gravestone from a churchyard on the Welsh borders.

Stone Circle templates, full-size

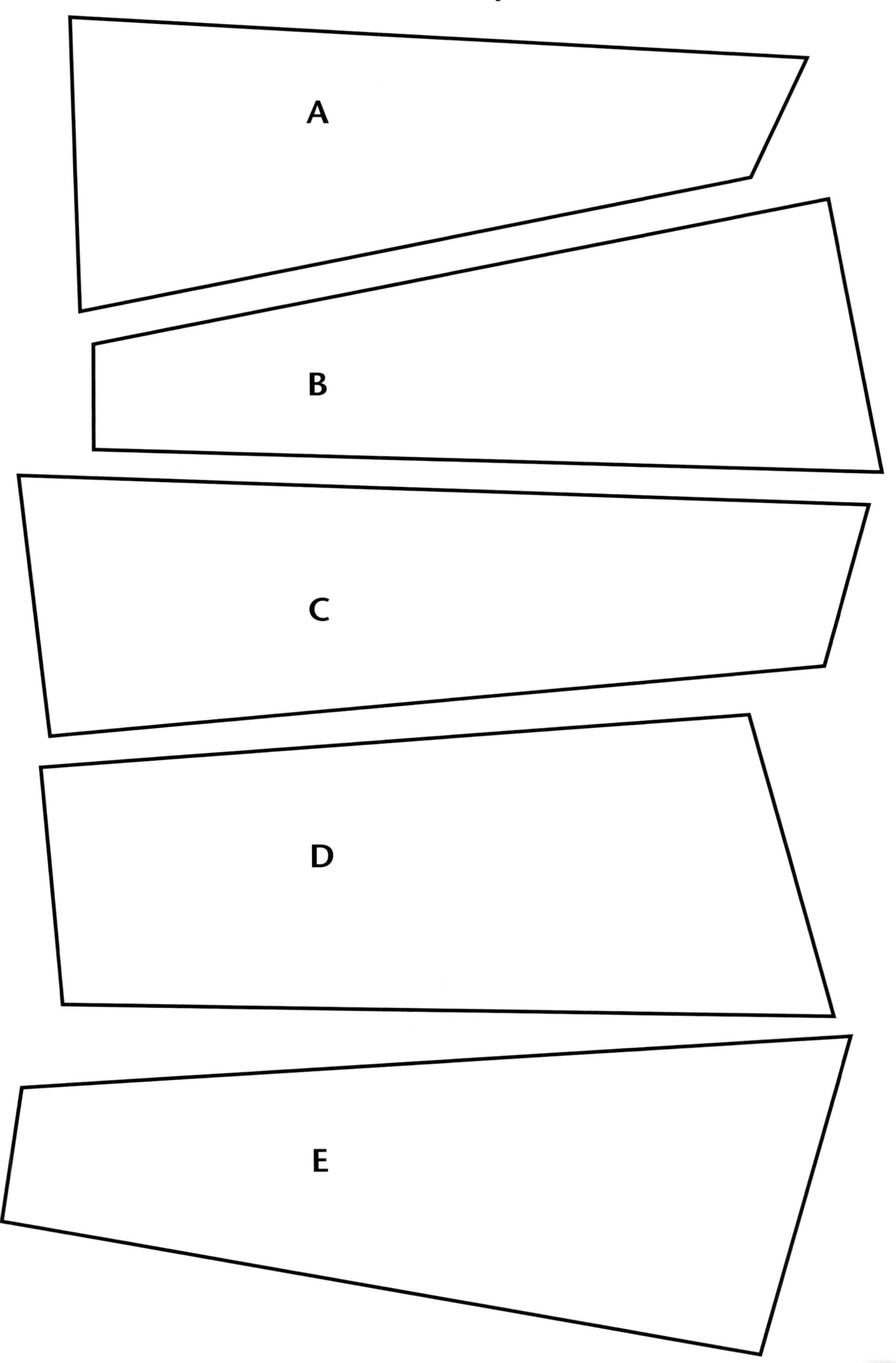

In an English Country Garden

Few things say 'England' the way a traditional cottage garden does; this one is crammed with different flowers in a riot of bright colours.

Many of the quilts in this book were inspired in some way by songs, and this is one of them: there's a traditional folk song which asks how many flowers, insects and birds are found 'in an English country garden' – the idea seems to be that there's such an abundance, it's impossible to list them all. The origins of the song are hidden in the mists of time, and there are dozens of different versions of the lyrics, but most versions include daffodils, hollyhocks, forget-me-nots, roses and lupins, as well as heartsease and phlox.

Flowers have always held a special place in the British heart. Witness our habit of giving baby girls the names of different blooms: Lily, Poppy, Daisy, Iris; Rose, Jasmine, Primrose, Violet; Heather and Erica; Briony and Honeysuckle. Gilbert and Sullivan created Buttercup, the singing dairymaid (sounds like a Country and Western star), and who could forget Hyacinth Bucket ('It's pronounced ***Bouquet***!')? More generalised plant names include Fleur, Florian (a rare male one), Fern, Blossom; the Welsh name Blodwen means 'white flower.' Herbs and spices make their appearance too: Rosemary, Sorrel, Basil (another male one), Saffron – and see page 108 for tree names that appear on the cradle roll. It's interesting to see how these names have waves of popularity through the years; maybe soon we'll see a swathe of infants called Montbretia, Tarragon or Snapdragon.

Particular flowers are often considered to have symbolic meanings – both in folklore and in religion; this probably came to its height in the Victorian idea of The Language of Flowers. Kate Greenaway wrote and illustrated ***Language of Flowers*** in 1884, and there were many other books on the subject. If you both knew this language, you and your secret lover could send messages to each other in plain sight, by carrying or giving a bouquet containing a particular mix of blooms, or perhaps by wearing a single flower as a buttonhole. Roses generally signified love, and this idea lives on in the association of roses – particularly red ones – with Valentine's Day. Perhaps we could update this idea: a posy of bramble flowers and holly could suggest 'I'd like a Blackberry for Christmas' etc ...

There are plenty of other folk songs that feature flowers. Many begin their story on a spring or summer day in the countryside; the abundance of blooms provides a beautiful natural bower, and also offers the opportunity for all kinds of imagery; the lover can compare his (or, occasionally, her) love to all the delightful blossoms (her skin was like soft rose-petals, his eyes were like cornflowers, etc etc). The flowers in songs are often symbolic, too. A great Scottish favourite is ***The Flowers of the Forest*** (***The Floo'ers o' the Forest***, in Scots); the tune dates back to at least the beginning of the 17th century. The 'flowers' of the title refer to young Scots men cut down in battle; the tune is held in such reverence that many pipers will only play it at funerals and memorials, rather than for entertainment. In traditional songs such as ***The Flower of Killarney*** and ***The Rose of Allendale***, the flowers in the titles are beautiful girls.

The planting of a flower garden always seems to be about so much more than simply creating something beautiful, and in itself appears to symbolise home. I love cottage gardens where every square inch is ablaze with different blooms and foliage, so I crammed as many flower representations into my quilt as I could. Hollyhocks, delphiniums, poppies, daisies (ordinary and Michaelmas), forget-me-nots, daffodils and roses create the garden, along with a couple of butterflies to help pollinate the blossoms. Down the side of the quilt, the floral lettering says 'in an English country garden.'

Inside information

There's a lovely website hosted by Jenny Bailey, who has spent several years cataloguing and photographing the seasonal garden flowers, plants and trees, as well as birds, butterflies and other visitors: www.english-country-garden.com

For further reading: Kate Greenaway's ***Language of Flowers*** *is still available in facsimile, and in 2011 author Vanessa Diffenbaugh was partly inspired by this volume to write her modern novel* ***The Language of Flowers****.*

Materials

Most of the fabrics are cotton, and I've also used guipure lace flowers and leaves and 'silk' blooms (the kind of flowers used in bridal head-dresses etc). The flower garden is built up on a cotton batik background featuring a design of leaves, and the butterflies are sequinned appliqué motifs. The lettering is cut from about a dozen different tiny flower prints.

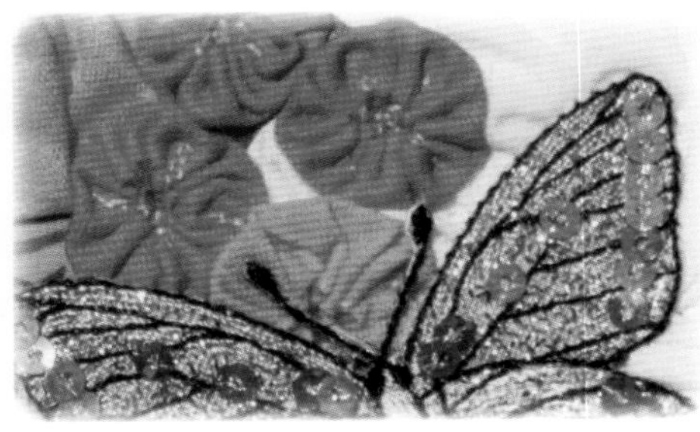

Techniques

Suffolk Puff flowers in different sizes create the large hollyhock heads, while the delphiniums are built up from painted artificial flowers. The roses are made by folding lengths of ribbon, and other techniques include fusing, lace appliqué, fabric painting, machine embroidery and cutwork, machine appliqué and quilting.

Backing and binding

A green Fossil Fern print gave me a soft-looking fabric for the backing. I cut the edges in an irregular wavy line, to give a naturalistic feel, and then bound them with a very narrow double bias edging.

PROJECT

Lace Flower Gardens

I created these little floral panels using flower motifs cut from guipure lace, painted with fabric paints and then appliquéd onto layered sheers and silks. Create your own rough-edged design, which you can then use to decorate a notebook, journal, handmade book, photograph album etc. Guipure lace flowers are often sold by the metre; simply cut them up into individual blooms, then either use them as they are (some motifs come ready-coloured), or tint them with fabric paints or fabric pens.

finished size: 7 x 5in (18 x 13cm), but you can vary this to fit your own journal or notebook

You will need:

- silk or cotton background fabric, 7 x 5in, in a colour to tone with your journal cover and lace motifs (if you want to decorate a particular book, make this piece 2in smaller than the book front in each direction)
- several different sheer fabrics in colours to tone with your flowers/ book cover, the same size as the background fabric
- flat wadding, the same size as the background fabric
- a selection of different guipure lace flowers and/or leaves
- fabric paints or fabric-painting pens (optional)
- sewing/quilting threads to match the coloured lace motifs (plus green, if you want to quilt stems and leaves etc)
- any extra beads, charms, butterfly motifs etc you want to add to your work
- glue

Instructions

1 Colour/tint the lace motifs with fabric paint if you wish, and fix the paint according the manufacturers' instructions (**a**).

TIP

If your lace motifs aren't 100% cotton, put a non-stick ironing sheet between the motifs and the iron as you fix the paint. Or you could experiment with fixing the motifs in the microwave – that's the way I do it these days!

2 Lay the wadding on a flat surface and cover it with the background fabric. Cut the sheer fabrics into rough squares and rectangles, and layer them up on top of the background fabric to create an attractive pattern (**b**). Pin the layers together to secure them while you add the motifs.

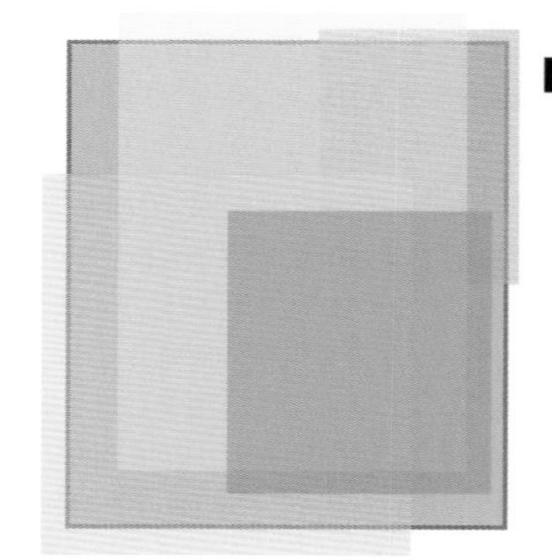

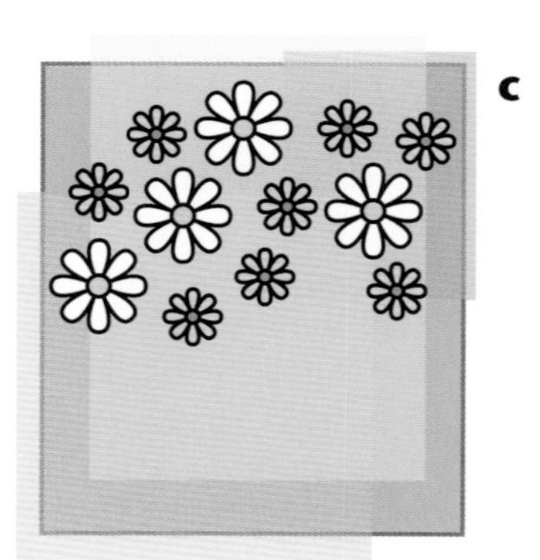

3 Lay the motifs out in a pleasing design (**c**); once you're happy, pin the motifs in place.

4 Use free machining or little hand stitches to attach the motifs to the background; quilt in stem or leaf motifs if appropriate (**d**).

d

5 Add any beads, charms etc to the design, then glue the finished panel to the front of your journal or notebook (**e**).

e

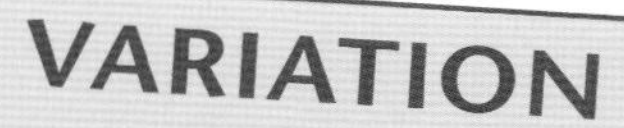

For a special wedding present, use white or cream flower motifs and match the colours of the fabrics to those used for the celebration (the bridesmaids' dresses, the bouquets and buttonholes, or the groom's waistcoat, for instance). You could always add the initials of the bride and groom in the quilting, or stitch them on with seed beads. When the panel is finished, stick it onto the front of a bought wedding photograph album.

The High Seas

Our rich maritime tradition – real and fictional – provides a wealth of nautical inspiration.

Throughout history, the lure of the sea has been irresistible for our island inhabitants. From time immemorial, we've set sail – for trade, for exploration, to provide food, and to conquer or repel other nations. Ancient Celtic tales tell of the voyages of Brendan and Columba, in the 6th century. Famous British seafarers include Raleigh and Drake in the Elizabethan era (see page 39). Raleigh was constantly searching for El Dorado, as well as helping to colonise Virginia; he also captained the first in a long line of ships called *HMS Ark Royal* (the flagship of the British fleet during the Armada campaign in 1588). Nearly four hundred years later my father served on one of the modern versions, an aircraft carrier that would have made Raleigh's eyes pop out.

Captain Cook, another giant of exploration, made the first European contact with Australia and was the first recorded person to sail around New Zealand. Our best-known sailor ever, though, is Lord Nelson – famous for captaining the *Victory,* and for winning (and dying at) the Battle of Trafalgar. Modern sea voyagers include Sir Francis Chichester (the first person to sail solo around the world using the clipper route), and Ellen MacArthur, who for three years held the record for the fastest circumnavigation. The British Antarctic Survey has been doing invaluable work at the bottom of the world for over 60 years. Notorious British pirates include the English Blackbeard (Edward Teach), Irishwoman Grace/Gráinne O'Malley, the Scot Captain (William) Kidd, and the fictional Captain Hook and Long John Silver.

BELOW: the Ark Royal, *photographed in 1957 with a replica of the* Mayflower

Above: this group of sailors includes my grandfather, back right
Below: the house on which this blue plaque appears is now owned by Chris' brother!

SIR ARTHUR HENRY ROSTRON
KBE RD RNR
U.S Congressional Gold Medal
CAPTAIN OF THE RMS CARPATHIA WHO RESCUED ALL 706 SURVIVORS FROM THE ILL FATED SS TITANIC 15TH APRIL 1912
LIVED HERE 1926 to 1940
PRESENTED BY SOUTHAMPTON OCEAN LINER EXHIBITION

British literature abounds with sea-stories and voyages, both real and fictional: ***Hornblower; Kidnapped; Treasure Island; Gulliver's Travels; The Voyage of the Dawn Treader; The Sea, the Sea; The Voyage of the Beagle; We Didn't Mean to go to Sea; The Chronicles of Ingo***. ***Robinson Crusoe*** was based on the real-life experiences of Scottish castaway Alexander Selkirk, who spent over four years on an uninhabited island after being marooned there by his captain. This idea itself spawned a very popular long-running radio programme, ***Desert Island Discs***, conceived by Roy Plomley; just in case there's anyone left in the world who doesn't know the format, a guest is asked to choose eight pieces of music, a book and a luxury to keep them company if they too were cast away.

Many iconic artworks have been inspired by the sea, from Turner's ***Fighting Temeraire***, through Alfred Wallis and the rest of the St Ives and Newlyn schools, to Maggi Hambling's ***Scallop*** memorial to Benjamin Britten on the beach at Aldburgh. Lifeboats are another crucial aspect of maritime life; the best-known rescue was performed by Grace Darling, daughter of a Northumberland lighthouse-keeper. She and her father rescued 13 people from the wreck of the *SS Forfarshire*. Apparently I was almost born at sea, the crossing from Northern Ireland to Liverpool when my mother was nine-and-a-bit-months pregnant being particularly turbulent ...

Probably most days we use or hear phrases that come from life at sea. Spinning a yarn, burning our boats (see p125), plumbing the depths, fathoming something out, no room to swing a cat, moonlighting. Sometimes we push the boat out, splice the mainbrace and drink like a fish, and then become three sheets to the wind; someone probably then puts their oar in and tells us to pipe down, which takes the wind out of our sails and puts us straight in the doldrums. Probably been sailing a bit close to the wind; oh well, we can't clutch at straws – no point spoiling the ship for a ha'porth of tar, or making a hue and cry. All hands on deck; let's toe the line, learn the ropes, and make everything ship-shape for a bit of plain sailing – time and tide wait for no man, and we're all in the same boat ... and so it goes on.

Image by Tim Bell, reproduced courtesy of The National Museum of the Royal Navy

Above: Nelson's flagship, the Victory
Below: the Needles lighthouse on the Isle of Wight

Above: Grace Darling's tomb in Bamburgh churchyard; note the oars.

On the quilt I've portrayed some of my favourite parts of British nautical history. At the top a ship's wheel is next to a lifebelt (representing the lifeboats) from Gilbert and Sullivan's ***HMS Pinafore***. A small roundel features a photograph of Ernest Shackleton's ship *Endurance*, while a sexy mermaid figurehead decorates the prow of an ancient sailing ship; mermaids were notorious for luring sailors off the straight and narrow with their songs. Fish celebrate our seafood heritage, and a leaping dolphin is framed in a porthole. The decorative knot is a Turk's Head, and the blue plaque marks one of the homes of Admiral Jellicoe. The large Mariner's Compass design hovers above an 1818 King's Shilling (the traditional wage given to a sailor enlisting into the navy) and an anchor. The message in flags is the beginning of Nelson's famous signal *'England expects every man to do his duty,'* while the symbol crossed out next to it relates to his famous comment *'I see no ships!'* At the bottom of the quilt a pirate map shows where the treasure is buried, and the Owl and the Pussycat are setting out to sea in their beautiful pea-green boat.

Inside information

The homepage of our modern navy is www.royalnavy.mod.uk/. If you'd like historical information, there is a Royal Navy Museum in Portsmouth Dockyard (www.royalnavalmuseum.org/), where of course you can also see the Victory *and* HMS Warrior. *The photograph of* Ark Royal *is reproduced courtesy of Peter Swarbrick at www.shipspictures.co.uk*

Materials

Almost all of the fabrics used in this quilt are cotton prints and plains, with the addition of a few synthetics and metallics; some of the fabrics are enhanced with fabric paint. I used decorative braids on the lifebelt and the flags, around the ship's wheel border, and to weave the Turk's Head; the lettering on the lifebelt is embroidered by hand. The King's Shilling and the Endurance photograph are fused onto thick interfacing; buttons, beads, sequins and charms complete the embellishments.

Techniques

I used many different techniques for the various roundels, including machine appliqué, cutwork, fabric painting, machine quilting, stained glass patchwork, foundation-piecing (for the Mariner's Compass), and printing from the computer onto fabric.

Backing and binding

The larger roundels are bound with bias binding to complement each design; the smaller ones are edged with machine satin stitch. The backs of the roundels feature various different fabrics; several of them sport a maritime flag print, and the Owl and the Pussycat have a starry sky. The back of the King's Shilling shows the obverse of the same coin, and the treasure map is backed with the same print that I used on the front.

PROJECT

Nautical Herb Cushion

The cheerful colours and prints that I've chosen for this cushion create the impression of nautical bunting – emphasised by the little triangular prairie points I've slipped under some of the braids. The design on the front is built up using a decorative version of stained glass patchwork; instead of using the same braid or bias binding for all the lines, I've used a mixture of ribbon, braid, ricrac and broderie anglaise, and bias binding in different widths and colours. Lines of machine embroidery and individual fabric motifs add the final embellishments.

finished size: 14in (35cm) square

You will need:

- two 15in (38cm) squares of bright nautical-print cotton fabric
- toning fabrics for the different parts of the design:
  - one 3½in (9cm) square for patch A
  - one 5in (13cm) square for patch B
  - one 8in (20cm) square for patch C
  - one 10in (25cm) square for patch D
  - one 10in (25cm) square for patch E
  - 7 x 12in (18 x 30cm) for the triangles (if you prefer your triangles plain rather than textured, you can use a smaller piece: 6 x 4in/15 x 10cm)
- assorted ribbons, braids, bias bindings, broderie anglaise etc in your chosen colourscheme; you can use any of these for the straight 'leading' lines, but you will need something with a bit of stretch or give (eg bias binding, ricrac, gathered lace) for the curved lines
- sewing threads to match the nautical fabric, and to match your ribbons and braids
- 15in (38cm) square of flat wadding
- 2½in (6cm) squares of cotton fabric for the prairie points (optional)
- extra braids, embroidery threads, fabric motifs, beads etc for embellishment (optional)
- polyester stuffing
- dried herbs, lavender or pot-pourri, plus two 6in (15cm) squares of muslin (optional)
- paper scissors, pencil

Instructions

1 Use a photocopier to enlarge the templates on page 33 by 141% (from A4 to A3) and cut out the different parts of the design. Use templates A-D as guides to cut out the relevant fabric patches (**a**); you don't need to add any seam allowances.

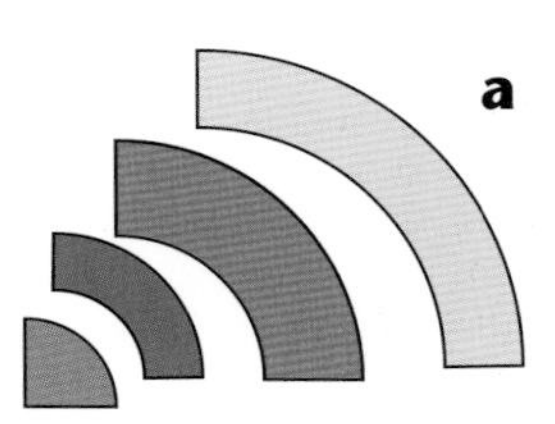

2 Lay the square of wadding on a flat surface and position one of the nautical-print fabrics on top, right side up. Lay fabric square E on top, also right side up, so that there's an even border of fabric all the way around (**b**). Lay the other fabric patches (A-D) in position on top (**c**) and pin in place; all the raw edges should butt up.

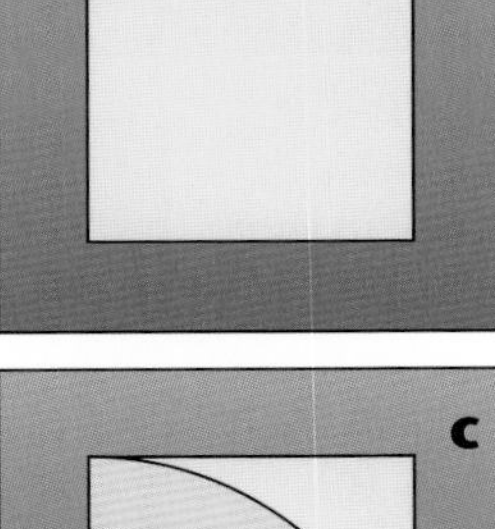

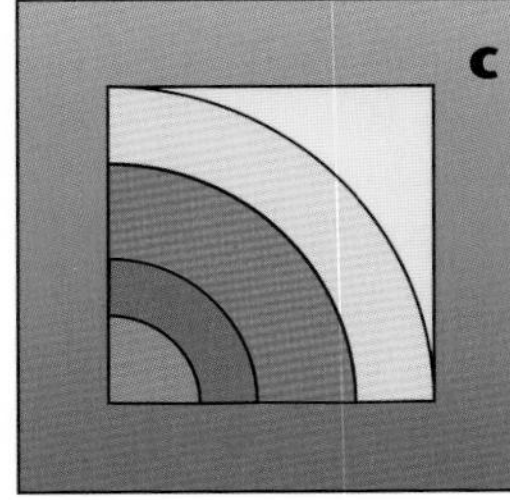

3 If you'd like to use flat patches for the decorative triangles on arc C, use template G to cut three triangles from the appropriate fabric (**d**). If you'd like to add texture to your triangles, use template F to cut three fabric

d

triangles. You can then pleat, gather, fold or scrunch these larger triangles until they are the same size as template G; trim the edges of the triangles to neaten them if necessary.

TIP

If you've scrunched or folded your triangles to create texture, you might find it useful to fuse them onto patches of iron-on interfacing before you trim and position them – this will help to hold the folds or gathers where you want them.

4 If you would like to use any prairie points, create them from the small squares of fabric by following the sequence shown (**e**); fold each square in half (wrong sides together), then fold in each edge to the centre and press. These little folded triangles can then be slipped under any of your 'leading' lines before you stitch them down (**f**).

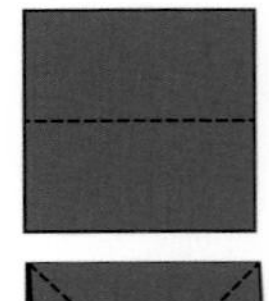

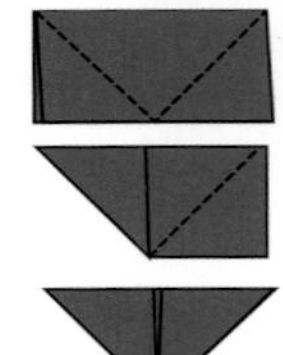

e

f

5 Pin the triangles in place so that they create an even pattern across arc C (**g**). To hold all the patches in place while you add the leading lines, use a medium machine zigzag (about 2-2.5 length and width) around the raw edges.

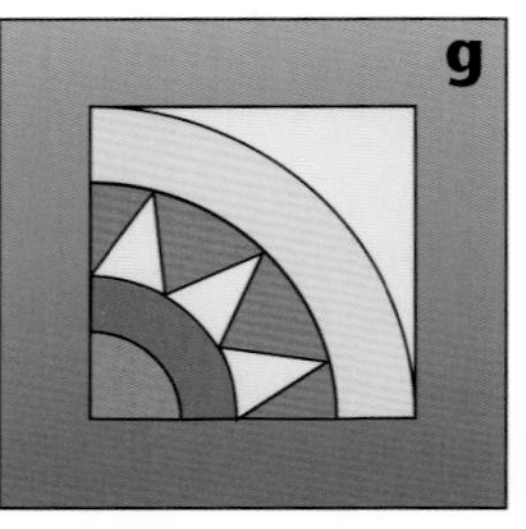

g

6 Add short lines of ribbon or braid to the edges of the three triangular patches (**h**), stitching them down by hand or machine. Once these lines are secured, pin and stitch the lines around each of the four arcs (**i**). If you want to add any knotted cords, as I've done on arc B (**j**), add this before you go onto the next step (so that the raw ends can be sealed under the final leading line).

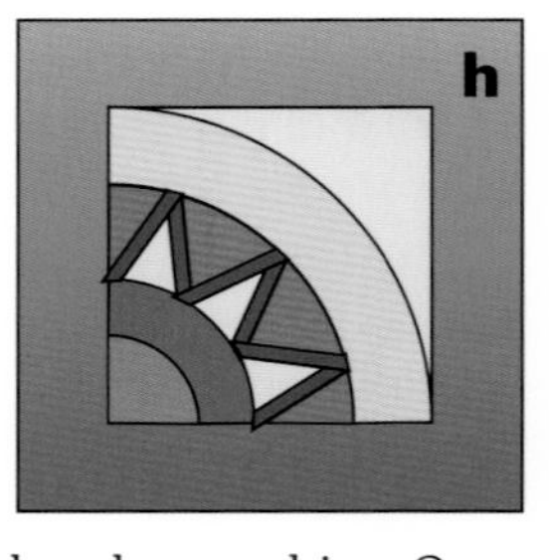

h

i

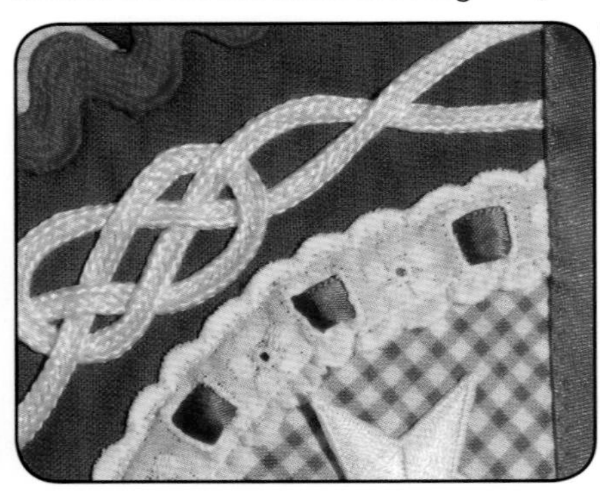

j

7 Now add a single line of ribbon or braid all around the edge of the square design (**k**); begin and end the line at one corner, folding the ribbon or braid crisply at the other three corners and neatening the raw ends by folding them under each other. If you wish, decorate any or all of these lines with embroidery by hand or machine.

k

8 Put the appliquéd square and the backing square right sides together, and stitch a ½in seam around the edges; leave an opening of about 6in (15cm) in the middle of one edge for turning (**l**). Clip the corners (if you wish you can clip the wadding up to the stitching line, but it's not essential), then turn the cover right side out and press the edges.

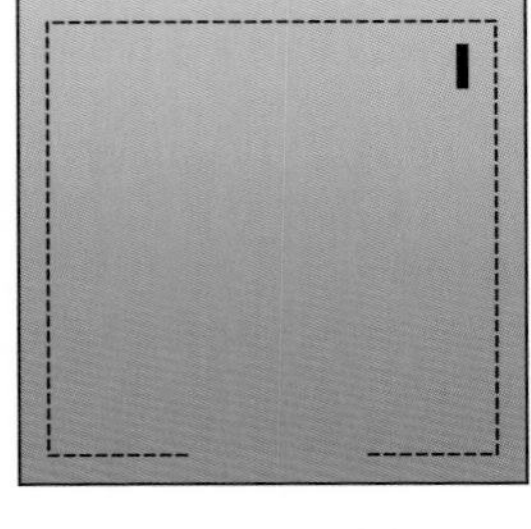

l

9 To make the scented insert, put a handful of herbs/pot-pourri/ lavender in the centre of one square of muslin and then put the other muslin square on top; stitch around the raw edges by machine (**m**), using straight stitch or zigzag.

m

10 Stuff the cushion (not too firmly, so that you don't distort the design on the front); once it's quite well filled, push the scented insert into the middle of the stuffing. Fold in the raw edges of the opening, and hand-stitch it closed using ladder stitch.

VARIATION

This design works well in all kinds of different colourschemes; you don't need to stick to the nautical theme! I've used the same templates to stitch a Christmassy version, using rich greens and reds set off with silver, and also a Scottish herb cushion in shades of lavender and green bordered by tartan silk.

Lighthouse on the Channel Island of Alderney

Nautical Herb Cushion templates; enlarge by 141% (A4 to A3)

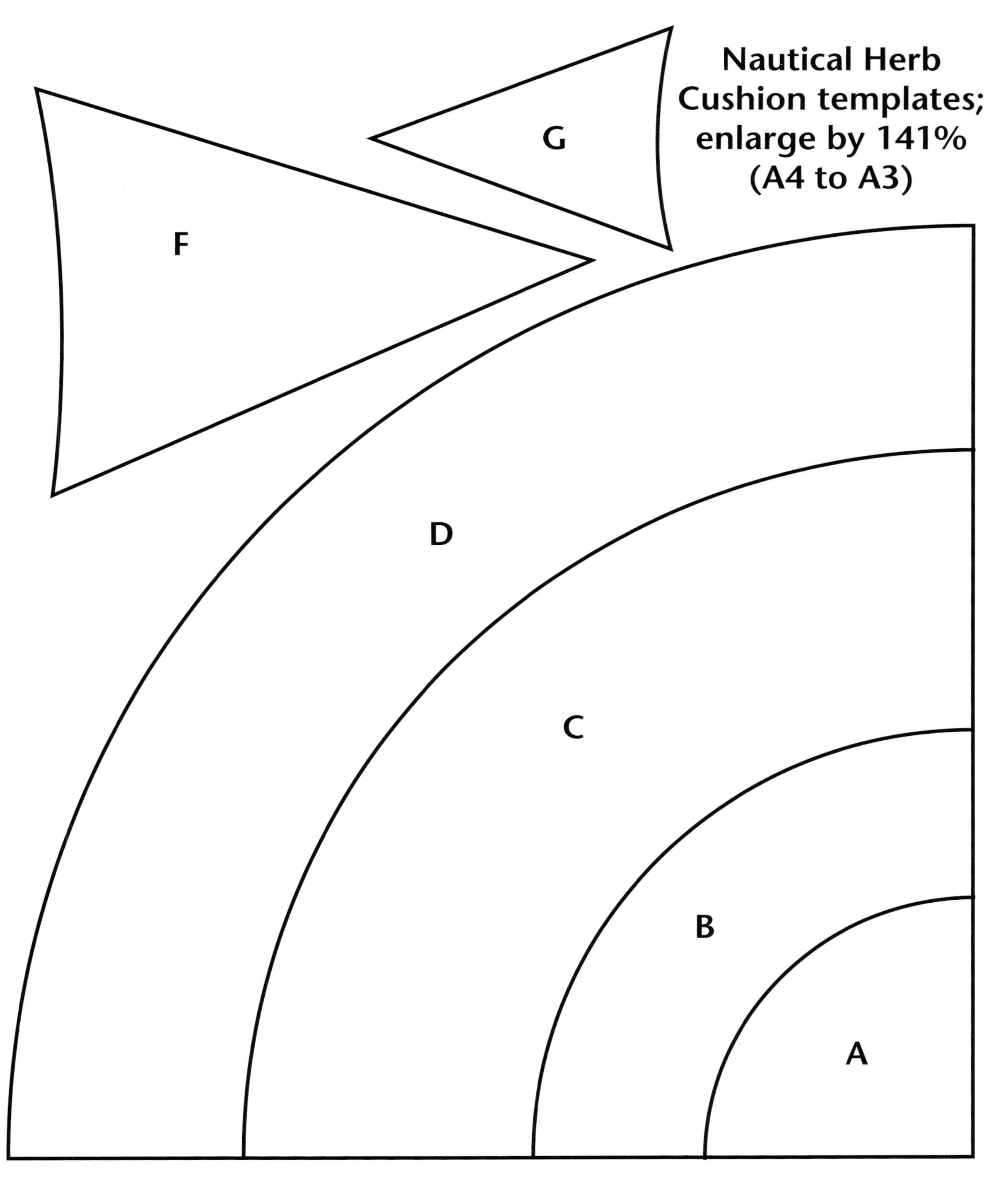

2011 And All That

There's more to this scene from the Bayeux Tapestry than meets the eye ...

If you had to list the most memorable dates in British history – you know, the really important ones that everyone knows – 1066 would no doubt be right at the top. In fact in many people's cases, mine included, it would just about **comprise** the list. So what was so significant about 1066? Surely there were battles going on all the time throughout our history? Why was this one so important?

The Saxon church at Bosham (complete with Rhennish Helm spire) appears in the Bayeux Tapestry – Harold prayed there before the Battle of Hastings

On September 28th 1066, William of Normandy began invading England. This was a tricky time for the English king, Harold II, because his almost-namesake Harald III (king of Norway – do try to keep up) had also picked that year to invade. Harold's forces had been busy fighting off the Norwegians at the Battle of Stamford Bridge in Yorkshire, so although victorious were rather battle-weary. By the time they'd marched down to the south coast they were also pretty tired (not to mention probably hungry and irritable).

The famous/infamous Battle of Hastings took place on October 14th. Harold was killed, and victorious William, henceforth known as William the Conquerer (or William I of England), began a completely new chapter of English history; the Normans were to have an untold influence on the language, architecture, culture and even the surnames of the British Isles. ***The Domesday Book*** (pronounced Doomsday) is a survey that William commissioned of his new lands; it's an unparalleled source of information on life in Norman England.

Another reason the Battle of Hastings is so famous is because of the Bayeux Tapestry, one of the best-known textiles in the world. Strictly it's not a tapestry, as it's not woven; the design is embroidered in wool on a linen ground. The scenes depict events leading up to the Conquest, and in particular the Battle of Hastings; although it's French, the tapestry retains a great affection in English eyes because it depicts such a monumental event in our history.

The Bayeux Tapestry is just one of several large textile works commemorating historical events or traditions. The Guernsey Tapestry depicts 1,000 years of life on that island. The Overlord Embroidery is a tribute to the people who took part in the 1944 D-Day landings in Normandy. The Prestonpans Tapestry commemorates the journey that Bonnie Prince Charlie ('the Young Pretender') made from France to win the Battle of Prestonpans in 1745. And the Quaker Tapestry, housed at Kendal in the Lake District, tells the story of Quaker life and beliefs.

As the original tapestry depicts an extraordinary event in British history, I decided to use mine to commemorate another equally astonishing thing: England winning the annual Ashes cricket series against the Australians in 2010, on English soil – then winning **again** in 2011, on Australian soil! Miraculous happenings indeed … marked by Halley's comet (believed to foretell momentous events), appearing on the quilt, just as it does on the Bayeux tapestry.

And cricket, of course, is an English institution. It hasn't led to quite as many everyday idioms as seafaring (see p29), but there are still plenty of them: playing with a straight bat, on a sticky wicket, it's not quite cricket etc. The title refers to a volume in our glorious heritage of nonsense literature, ***1066 and All That***, written by W C Sellar and R J Yeatman, first published in book form in 1930. The subtitle says it all: *A Memorable History of England, comprising all the parts you can remember, including 103 Good Things, 5 Bad Kings and 2 Genuine Dates.* It's a minestrone of all the half-remembered facts from our history lessons.

So I have blended all these great English institutions into one quilt. The style, obviously, is taken from the Bayeux Tapestry, decorated with pig-latin. From the top:

- HIC EST STRAUSS REX – *here is King Strauss* (England captain, with bat held aloft)
- AUDENTES FORTUNA VIVAT – *fortune favours the brave*
- HIC PONTING REX INTERFECTUS EST – *here King Ponting* (Australia captain) *is slain*; he's lying on a pile of stumps, having been hit by a cricket ball, and is saying CRICKET NON EST – *it's just not cricket*
- FINIS CORONAT OPUS – *the end crowns the work*
- At the bottom, the urn which holds 'the Ashes' is safely installed at CASTELLUM LORDS, *the castle of Lord's Cricket Ground.* The building protecting it is decorated with the ground's famous Old Father Time weather-vane – just visible in the 1984 photo at the top!

Chris aged around 6, padded up and ready for action …

Inside information

Read more about the Bayeux Tapestry at www.tapestry-bayeux.com/. An English copy, stitched in the 1880s, can be seen at the Museum of Reading (www.bayeuxtapestry.org.uk/).

For details of the other wonderful textiles, see www.guernseytapestry.org.gg/; www.ddaymuseum.co.uk/overlord.htm; www.prestonpanstapestry.org/; www.quaker-tapestry.co.uk/. I won't even bother to try and explain 'the Ashes;' for inside information, go to www.lords.org/history/the-ashes/.

Materials

For the background I chose a coarse-weave cotton fabric, in a neutral colour that reflects the background of the Bayeux Tapestry. The subtle tones of the original gave me the colour-scheme for my quilt, but created in fabric paint and stranded embroidery cottons instead of wool.

Techniques

Rather than using laid work for the design, I decided to use fabric painting; I then hand-embroidered round each patch in chain-stitch, using a contrasting colour. A few of the smaller shapes (eg the motifs on the shields) are edged with backstitch in a toning colour to create a strong outline. Because I was working on fabric already layered with backing and wadding, the embroidery quilts the work as well as embellishing it.

Backing and binding

The loosely-woven fabric gave me the opportunity to fringe the edges of the quilt, to carry on the slightly homespun feel of the design; I used another panel of the same fabric for the backing, and fringed that too.

PROJECT

Fleur-de-Lys Bowl

After the Norman Conquest, many French influences and symbols came to Britain to stay; one of the most common was the fleur-de-lys (or fleur-de-lis), a stylised lily flower, historically associated with the French monarchy. For this decorative stitched bowl, I've designed an outline fleur-de-lys motif; five repeats of the shape create the sides, attached to a pentagonal base. I created a decorative fabric by couching different threads and fabric scraps onto a plain background, but if you prefer to keep things simpler, just use a plain or print cotton fabric. The bowl is stiffened with firm interfacing; you can use pelmet stiffener, but I find that the best ones are heavyweight Fast2Fuse™ and FlexiFirm™.

finished size: diameter roughly 12in (30cm), height 5in (13cm)

You will need:

- two strips of fabric, each measuring 30 x 6½in (76 x 17cm); if your fabric is strongly directional, and you need to trace all the fleur-de-lys shapes the same way up, you will need a slightly longer strip of fabric and interfacing.
- one strip of heavyweight fusible interfacing, 30 x 6½in (76 x 17cm)
- large reel of thread to match or contrast with your fabric
- decorative threads and fabric scraps, plus sewing threads, for embellishing the fabric (optional)
- two 7in (17cm) squares of template plastic
- pencil, paper scissors
- long, strong pins

Instructions

1 Trace the fleur-de-lys shape (template A) onto one square of template plastic, and the base (template B) onto the other; cut the shapes out along the marked lines (**a**).

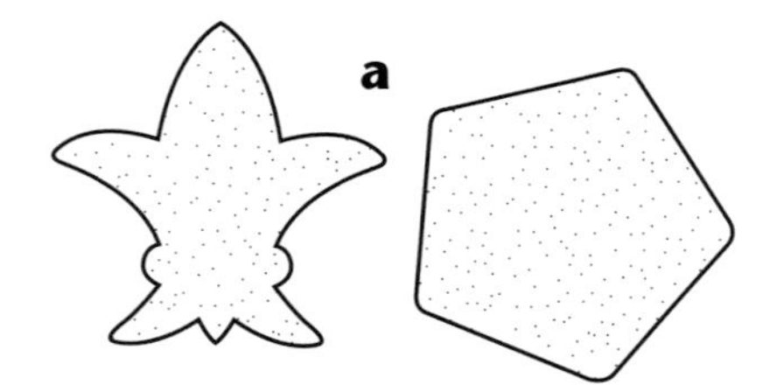

2 Lay one strip of fabric right side down on the ironing board, then position the fusible interfacing on top. Cover this with the second strip of fabric, right side up, and use an iron to fuse the fabric strips firmly onto the interfacing.

3 If you are embellishing the fabric strip, do so now. I laid lots of coloured fabric snippets on one side of the fabric, then stitched them down with random lines of machine straight stitch; I couched decorative threads on top, then turned the fabric strip over and did the same on the other side.

4 Trace round the fleur-de-lys shape five times on the strip, top to tail if your fabric isn't directional, and then trace round the base shape once (**b**). Cut all the shapes out along the marked lines (**c**).

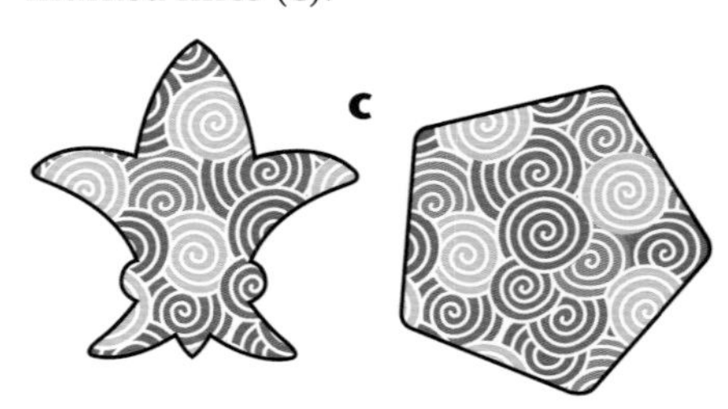

b

5 The secret to a good finish is your satin stitch. Set the machine up to a width of about 3.5 or 4, and set the length to satin stitch. If you don't have a particular setting for satin stitch, set the length to the smallest setting that still allows the fabric to feed through without snagging. Use the offcuts from the fabric strip to practise getting the stitch in just the right place on the cut edge of the shapes.

TIP

If you have a Bernina, thread the bobbin thread through the little hole on the arm of the bobbin case before you put it into the machine; this fractionally tightens the bobbin tension, and produces a really handsome satin stitch. (If you have a different make of machine, you won't have this feature, but you should still be able to make a good-looking stitch.)

6 Work a line of satin stitch all around the edge of each shape, including the base (**d**). You may well find that you have small gaps in the stitching; if so, go round it a second time, keeping the stitch settings the same (I usually do it twice as standard).

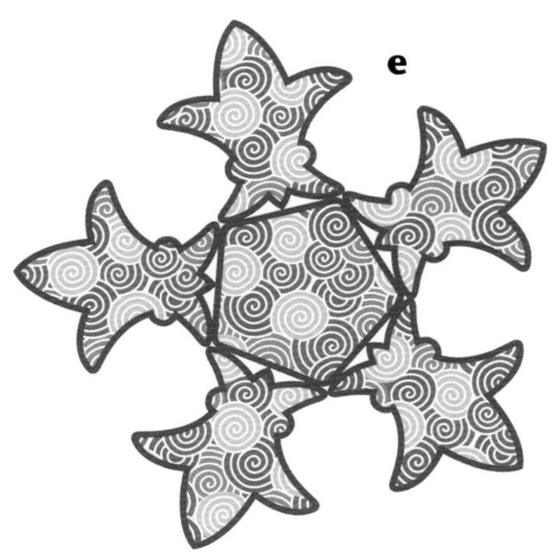

7 Lay the base on a flat surface, and position the fleur-de-lys motifs around the edges as shown (**e**); the central points, and the bottoms of the outside curves, will just 'kiss' the straight edges of the base. Pin the shapes together, using the pins horizontally towards the base (**f**).

8 Set your machine to a zigzag – width about 2, length about 1 (the measurements aren't critical). Beginning with one of the places where the shapes just touch, work two or three stitches forwards, then back, then forwards, then back. Lift the needle (don't bother to cut the thread) and move to the next place where the shapes touch; do the same. Continue round the base, stitching in the same way until each fleur-de-lys is attached in three places (**g**). Snip off all the loose threads.

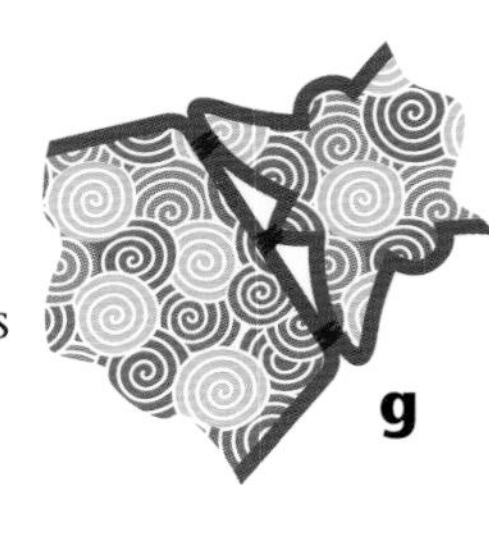

9 Now position the shape under the machine so that the base is behind the machine foot. Beginning with one pair of tips at the bottom of two fleurs-de-lys, pull the points together and use the same method to stitch them. Work round all the lower points in the same way; as you work, allow the base to curve up behind the machine foot, which will allow the shapes you're joining to lie flat under the foot.

10 Do the same with all the joins between the upper points; snip off the stray ends, and your bowl is ready to take its place of honour on your table or sideboard.

VARIATION

I've used regal golds and bronzes to capture a bit of the Norman feel; other colours that would give you a royal effect include purple, emerald green, ruby red and royal blue. Or you could go for pastels, or perhaps a pretty cotton print for a completely different effect.

Left: a typical Norman-style church doorway
Below: recreational cricket à la 1805, in Charterhouse Square, London

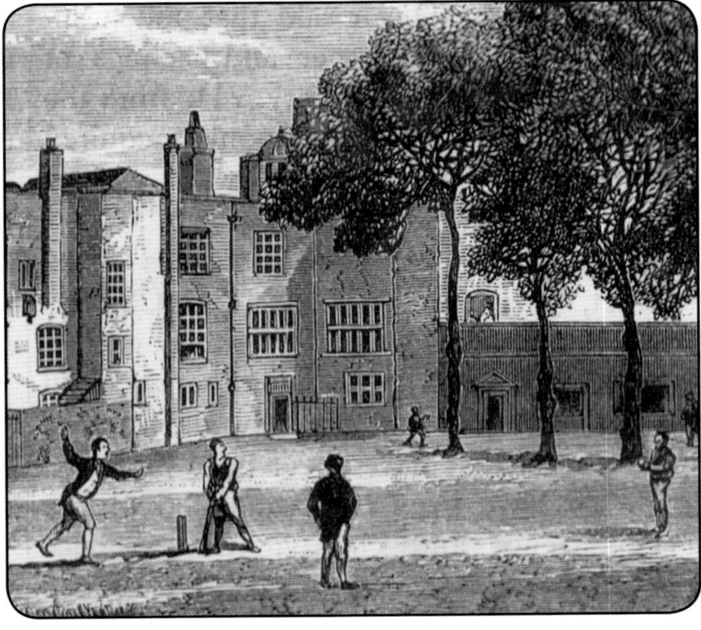

Fleur-de-Lys Bowl templates; full-size

Elizabeth

An idea for a quilt featuring the two Queen Elizabeths became a celebration of Elizabeths generally …

Every Briton my age or younger has only known one monarch, Queen Elizabeth II; we all live in the second Elizabethan age. Although our monarchy has historically been patriarchal, with a male heir to the throne always taking preference over even an older female (this is all set to change in the next few years, of course), we have had two Queen Elizabeths, both of whom have have had extremely long reigns. When I began working on this series of quilts, I decided to create one which would explore both the differences and the similarities between these two monarchs and their reigns, separated by 500 years; in the centre of the quilt I've merged their two signatures.

Image by Gail Lawther, reproduced with the kind permission of The National Trust

Above: window at Melford Hall, Suffolk, where Elizabeth I was entertained in 1578; Below: front page of Worthing Gazette's *Coronation special*

Both Elizabethan ages have been times of great change. Elizabeth I of England (also sometimes known as Good Queen Bess, The Virgin Queen or Gloriana) was born in 1533. She was the daughter of Henry VIII – **that** must count as

Jordan & Cook

Worthing Gazette

Coronation Number
16 PAGES

It was a television-and-showers Coronation Day here in Worthing

FIRST IT WAS SO QUIET, THEN SO

TV parties kept people indoors

And this was the C-day spirit

Shirley was procession heroine

Chancel screen

'With all my heart I shall strive to be worthy of your trust'

Fireworks

Winning window

SERVICE HAD

NINETY PI

coming from a dysfunctional family – and Anne Boleyn, and after assorted succession shenanigans she reigned from 1558 until her death in 1603: 45 years. Even after her death, Elizabeth I was considered to have created a Golden Age. During this first Elizabethan era, new worlds were being opened up: great adventurers such as Sir Walter Raleigh and Sir Francis Drake were undertaking voyages to previously unknown lands. To symbolise this 'conquest of the world,' portraits of the Queen often show her holding or resting her hand on a globe, or standing on a map of the world. Elizabeth's reign is also famous for the flowering of English drama; of course Shakespeare (see p113) was an Elizabethan, and other contemporary playwrights include Christopher Marlowe ('Kit') and Ben Jonson. The first theatres in the country were built during this time, including the original Globe.

The first Queen Elizabeth never married nor had children, hence her title of The Virgin Queen – although whether that epithet is technically correct has been a matter for endless conjecture down the ages! Her best-known quotation probably silenced anyone who felt she was disqualified from being a good monarch because of her sex: *'I know I have the body of a weak and feeble woman, but I have the heart and stomach of a king, and of a king of England too.'* Certainly by staying unmarried she retained an enormous amount of power, and began to be seen as something more than human, almost as a goddess. As a result, the cult of Gloriana grew up around her. This image was fed by sumptuous portraits showing the queen eternally young (face plastered in white make-up to hide the lines, red wig covering sparse hair), dressed in priceless jewels; this opulence has inspired my bejewelled version at the top of the quilt.

The "Crown Jewels," guarded by pikemen, are borne past the Town Hall where the Mayor, Councillor R. A. Mitchell, reviewed the parade.

At first there were two effigies in this tableau. One of t... lapsed, so Shirley Budd took over the robes for the re... journey.

...d outside the Pier Pavilion kept in good spirits and had ...s it passed by on its way to Homefield Park via the Town Hall.

A light touch to the procession was provided by Worthing Excelsior Cycling Club. They entered a group under the title "Cycling throughout the Ages." Their machines ranged from boneshakers to modern racers and the riders were cheered all along the route.

Fifty thousand blooms went into this model of the *Queen Elizabeth* in flowers made by Wo... and West Sussex Growers' branch of the National Farmers' Union. Cornflowers, carnations, and arum lilies were used. Members worked every night of the week to complete it.

Another page from Worthing Gazette's *Coronation issue, dated June 3rd 1953, showing some of the local celebrations*

Queen Elizabeth II has also reigned over a time of astonishing change. Born Her Royal Highness Princess Elizabeth of York, she became Queen on the death of her father, King George VI, in 1952, and in contrast to her namesake she is the monarch of several countries (the exact number depends on whether you count the United Kingdom as one or four), and also head of the Commonwealth (the remnant of the enormous historic British Empire). As I write this paragraph she has just celebrated 60 years on the throne – becoming our second-longest-reigning monarch (after Queen Victoria). Elizabeth II's coronation was the first to be televised, and during her reign people have set foot on the moon, computers have been invented (and taken over our lives), and test-tube babies have become commonplace.

In contrast to her namesake, the current Queen Elizabeth has seen – and overseen – many times of austerity. When she married, Elizabeth needed ration coupons to buy the fabric for her wedding gown (designed by Norman Hartnell), and post-war rationing didn't have its final death-throe until after she became Queen. Since that time there have been various other financial recessions, and I have reflected this much less opulent Elizathan era in a much plainer portrait, inspired by the head of the monarch that appears on stamps and coins.

For the border above the first Elizabeth I took popular motifs from cross-stitch samplers of the time: carnations and hearts. Then I began looking for a suitable motif for the second Elizabeth, something to reflect the computer age. The thought came to me that everything we see on a computer screen is actually pixellated if you look at it very closely – just like a cross-stitch sampler. And what better symbol of the computer age than the unsophisticated aliens that launched a thousand video games: the first, the best, Space Invaders?

For some reason, while I was working on the design of this quilt I decided it would be interesting to incorporate references to other famous Elizabeths, too – real and fictional – who have played an important part in British life, so their names decorate the border. Here are the chosen 25, from the top:

- Elizabeth Garrett Anderson, the first woman to qualify as a doctor in Britain, and England's first female mayor
- Lizzie Siddal(l), favourite model and muse of the pre-Raphaelites (husband Rossetti was responsible for deleting the second 'l' from her surname)
- Elizabeth Pargetter of radio soap ***The Archers*** ('An everyday story of country folk')
- Betty's Tea Room, a famous Harrogate establishment
- Elizabeth Allen – Enid Blyton's ***Naughtiest Girl in the School***
- Violet Elizabeth Bott, tormenter of the eponymous hero in Richmal Crompton's ***William*** books. (catchphrase and favourite threat: *'I'll thcream and thcream 'till I'm thick!'*)
- Eliza Manningham-Buller, former director-general of MI5
- Elizabeth Taylor (although we lent her to the States, she was English born and bred)
- cook Elizabeth David, who introduced the British to such 'foreign' delights as Parmesan, olive oil and courgettes
- Lizzie Dripping, a 1970s children's TV programme; the title is slang in the Nottingham area for someone who tells tall tales
- Elizabeth Butler-Sloss, the first woman judge in the Appeal Court
- author Elizabeth Goudge, whose book ***Green Dolphin Country*** unwittingly began my early fascination with New Zealand (and the Channel Islands)
- Lizzy Bennet from Jane Austen's ***Pride and Prejudice***; my favourite literary heroine
- Betty Boothroyd, first woman Speaker of the House of Commons
- prison reformer Elizabeth Fry
- Elizabeth von Arnim, author of ***The Enchanted April***
- Betty's Hot-Pot, signature dish of Coronation Street's Betty Turpin, played for over 40 years by Betty Driver
- poet Elizabeth Barrett Browning, married to Robert
- Elizabeth Pepys, long-suffering wife of diarist Samuel; her first name is sometimes spelt with an 's'
- Bess of Hardwick, 16th century countess; while her (fourth) husband helped to keep Mary, Queen of Scots captive, the two women worked on needlework projects together
- Elizabeth Mackintosh, real name of the reclusive author who wrote under the names of Josephine Tey and Gordon Daviot
- 19th century novelist Elizabeth Gaskell
- contemporary novelist Elizabeth Jane Howard
- Elizabeth Bowes-Lyon, mother of our current queen
- Eliza Doolittle, cockney flower-girl in Shaw's play ***Pygmalion*** and Lerner & Loewe's musical ***My Fair Lady***; also, the stage name of London singer-songwriter Eliza Caird

And I can claim a modest part in the long line of British Elizabeths, too: it's my middle name.

Inside information

www.elizabethfiles.com, hosted by Claire Ridgway, says on its strapline that it tells 'the real truth' about Elizabeth I; it's certainly a mine of information on every aspect of her reign and influence, and includes details of related books as well as a gallery of different portraits of the monarch.

As a sign of the times, the British Monarchy has its own official website: www.royal.gov.uk.

Materials

For Good Queen Bess I used several different cotton, synthetic and metallic fabrics, as well as silver bias binding, lace and braid. The rest of the quilt uses cotton fabric as a background, and the cross-stitch panels are worked in stranded cotton and metallic thread on Aida fabric. The whole quilt is embellished with beads and jewels.

Techniques

QEI's face is embroidered by machine and lightly painted, and the main patches of the design are appliquéd using stained glass patchwork. QEII's head, the signatures and the border are painted in various shades of silver; around the head I've added pale pink machine quilting, and stitched 60 pink pearl beads – one for each year of her reign. After I'd machine-pieced the two head panels, the cross-stitch borders and the signature section, I used machine appliqué to set the pieced section inside the border, then outlined the pieced centre with silver bias binding.

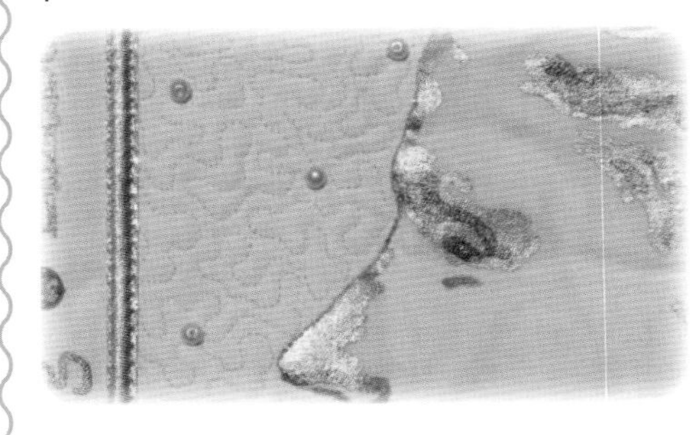

Backing and binding

As carnations feature on the front of the design, I felt that this pretty pink carnation print tied in very well with the themes. To reflect the opulence of the first Queen Elizabeth, I added an extra border of beaded silver braid which shows up well against the dark pink binding.

PROJECT

Gloriana Table Runner

This sumptuous table-runner celebrates the exquisite cross-stitch samplers stitched during the reign of Queen Elizabeth I – sometimes known as Gloriana. These samplers often featured flowers, hearts, crowns etc, and carnations were a particularly popular motif. I've translated the carnations and hearts that I used for the main quilt (see page 39) into an appliqué design, enlarging the motifs but keeping the stepped edges to echo the feel of the original counted-thread patterns.

The appliqué shapes are fused onto the background with bonding web (so no need to worry about turning under the edges!), then edged with a little machine zigzag to hold them in place; you can then decorate the design with extra quilting and embellishments if you wish.

finished size: long runner approx 56 x 12in (142 x 30cm); (for a shorter runner, see the Variations box)

You will need:

- one 56 x 12in (142 x 30cm) piece of background fabric, either cotton or silk; I used white
- one 56 x 12in (142 x 30cm) piece of flat wadding
- one 56 x 12in (142 x 30cm) piece of backing fabric
- firm fabrics for the appliqué pieces:
  - 24 x 9in (60 x 23cm) for the petals (I used a pale-pink/silver print)
  - 4in (10cm) square for the flower centres (I used dark pink)
  - 15in (38cm) square for the stems (I used a pale blue/silver print)
  - 5in (12.5cm) square for the pink hearts (I used a mid pink)

  - 5 x 3in (12.5 x 8cm) for the silver hearts (I used a bonded silver fabric that doesn't fray)
- double-sided bonding web:
  - 24 x 9in (60 x 23cm) for the petals
  - 4in (10cm) square for the flower centres
  - 15in (38cm) square for the stems (the heart shapes will fit onto the scraps left from these pieces)
- sewing threads to match all your appliqué fabrics
- 4yd (3.5m) binding for the edges of the runner; I used a silver bias binding to produce a ½in-wide edge on the front of the work
- if you'd like to embellish your table runner, suitable hand or machine embroidery/quilting thread(s), buttons, beads, jewels etc
- pencil, short ruler (for drawing the shapes), long quilt rule (for positioning them), paper scissors
- small, sharp-pointed scissors

Instructions

1 Use pencil and the short ruler to trace petal template A three times onto the paper side of the relevant bonding web piece; three tracings will give you enough petals for four flowers! In the same way, trace stem/leaf template B four times onto the 15in square of bonding web. Trace flower centre template C once onto the 4in square of bonding web (this will give you all four flower centres). In the spaces left on your bonding web pieces, trace the complete heart template D once (this will be used for the four pink hearts), then trace two more single hearts from the same template (these will be used for the two silver hearts). Cut all the shapes out roughly, outside the drawn lines (**a**).

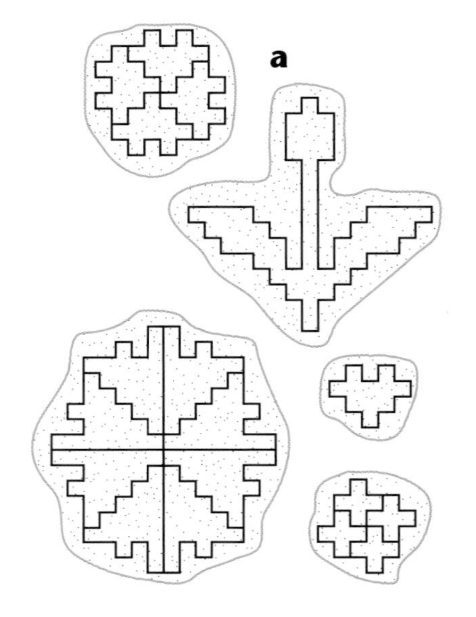

TIP

Using the short ruler is quicker and easier than trying to trace all the lines freehand, and will give you much straighter lines to cut along.

2 Fuse the bonding web shapes, rough side down, on the wrong sides of the relevant pieces of fabric; cut out all the shapes along the marked lines, to create the individual petal, flower centre, stem and heart patches (**b**).

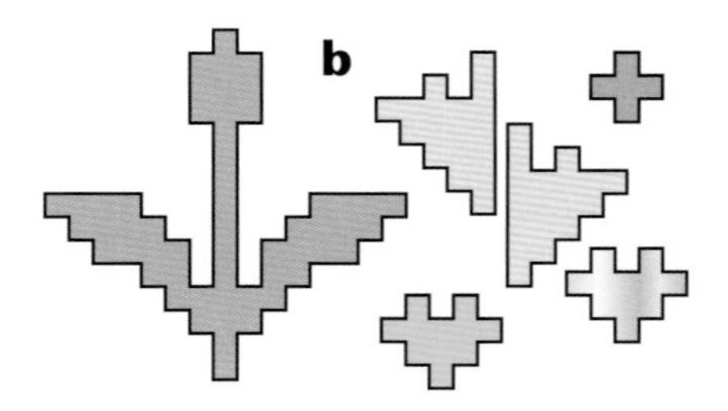

3 Fold the background fabric in half lengthways and then widthways; press the folds lightly to mark the centre point of the fabric, and unfold.

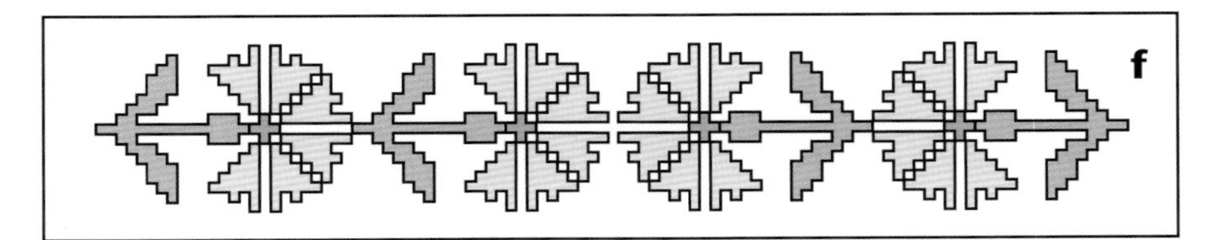

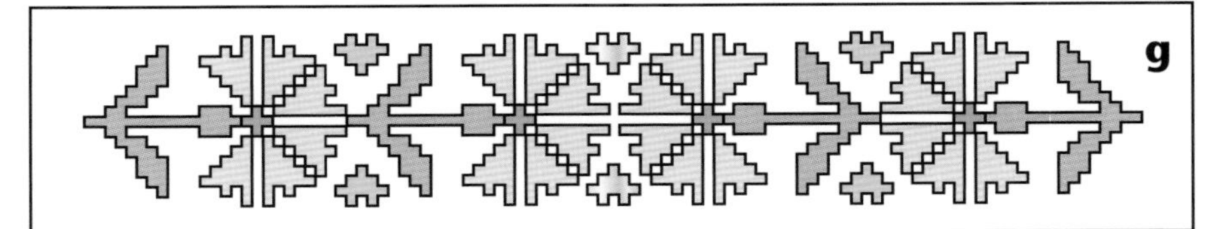

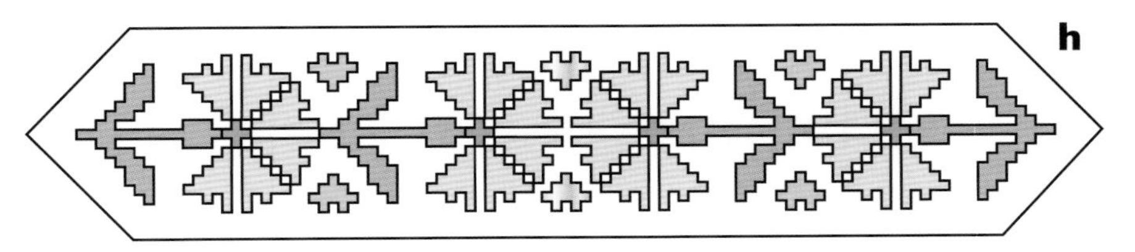

4 Working on the right side of the fabric, and beginning from the pressed cross-shape marking the centre of the runner, position the first two carnation heads. Peel the backing papers off the shapes (petals and flower centres) and position the top petal pairs so that they are ¼in each side of the short centre line, and ¼in each side of the long central lines (½in apart in total), as shown (**c**). Check that these first petals are level with each other, then position the other petals and flower centres to create the two flower heads (**d**); pin in place.

5 Now position and pin the stem/leaf patches of these two flowers, lining them up with the flower centres as shown (**e**); once you're happy with the positions, press the first two carnations in place. Add the next two carnations the same way, below the first ones (**f**); the petals of these lower flowers just touch the stems of the upper flowers at the corners. Now add the heart shapes between the flowers as shown (**g**); use your long rule to check that the tops of the hearts align with the outside edges of the flower petals.

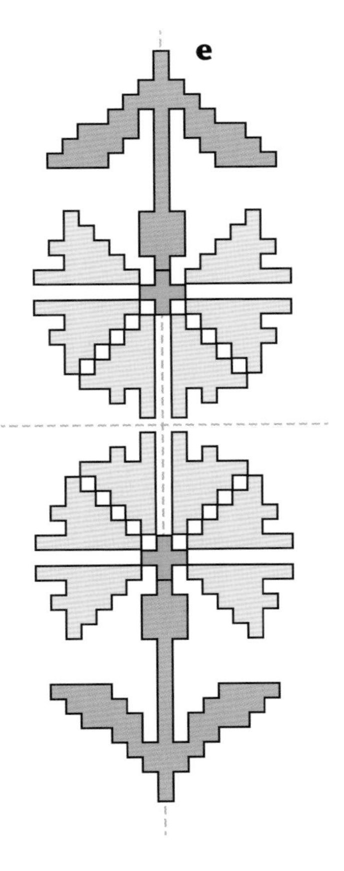

6 Press the background fabric to remove the central creases. Lay the backing fabric on a flat surface, right side down, and position the wadding on top so that the raw edges align; position the appliqué design on top, right up, and secure the three layers using your preferred method (see p136). Working from the centre of the quilt outwards, work a small machine zigzag stitch around the edge of each appliqué piece in matching thread (this is where a knee lift, if you have one, comes into its own ...).

7 Fold the corners of the table runner under at 45°, to echo the angles of the flower stems, and press; make sure that the folds are even, and remember that you need to allow for the width of the binding. Once you are happy with the angles, trim the three layers along the folds (**h**), using a rotary cutter and ruler.

8 Bind the edges of the runner (see p136), folding the binding crisply at the corners and points. Add any further quilting you fancy, either by hand or machine, and embellish the design with beads, jewels etc if you wish.

VARIATION

If you don't want to create such a long table runner, stitch a half-length version. Cut the background fabric, wadding and backing fabric to 31 x 12in (79 x 30cm), and decorate it with only two carnation designs – obviously for this version you will need smaller pieces of appliqué fabric, less bonding web, and a shorter binding strip. Create the central design just as in the instructions, but make and appliqué just the two flower motifs rather than four – then follow the instructions to trim and bind the edges.

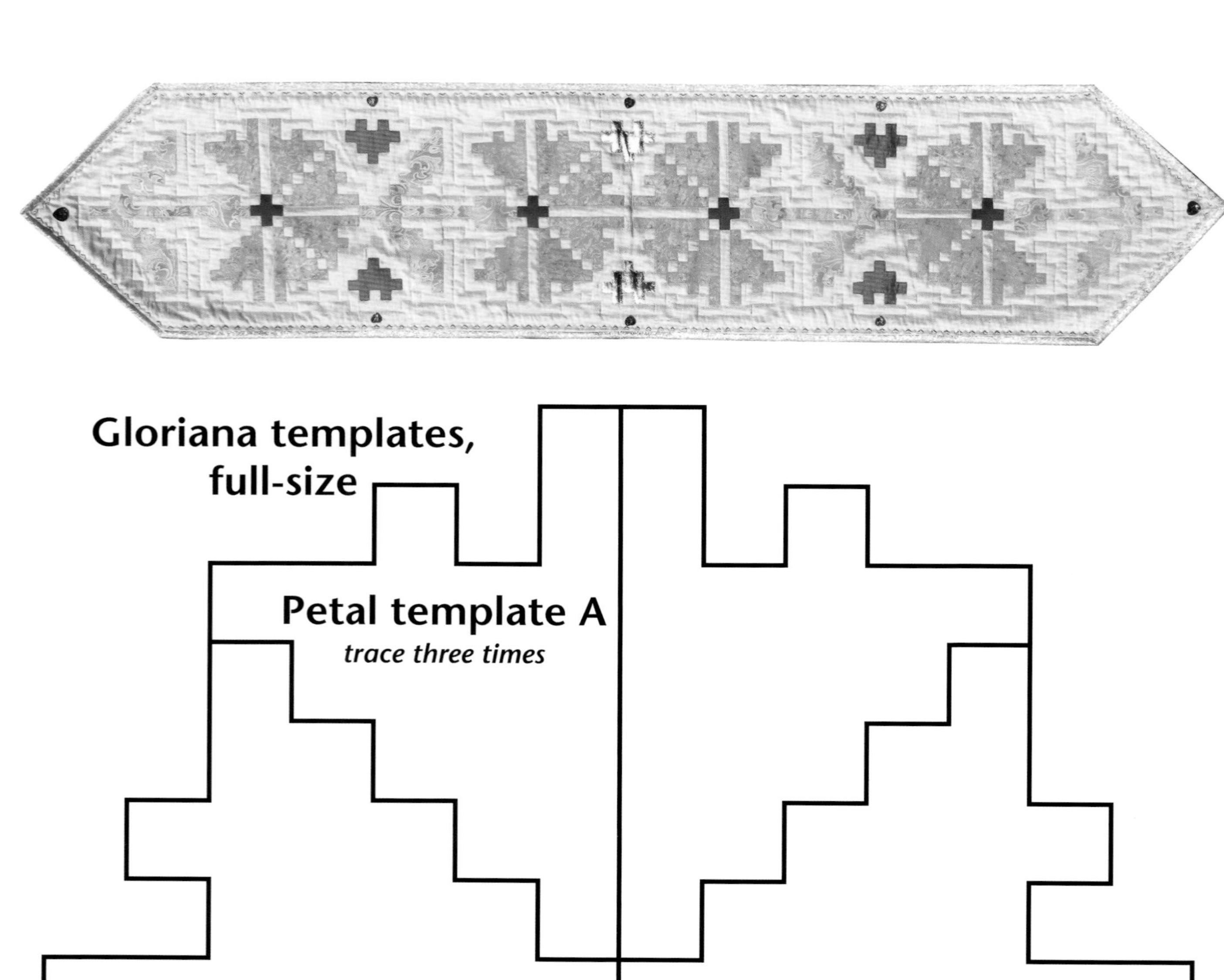

Gloriana templates, full-size

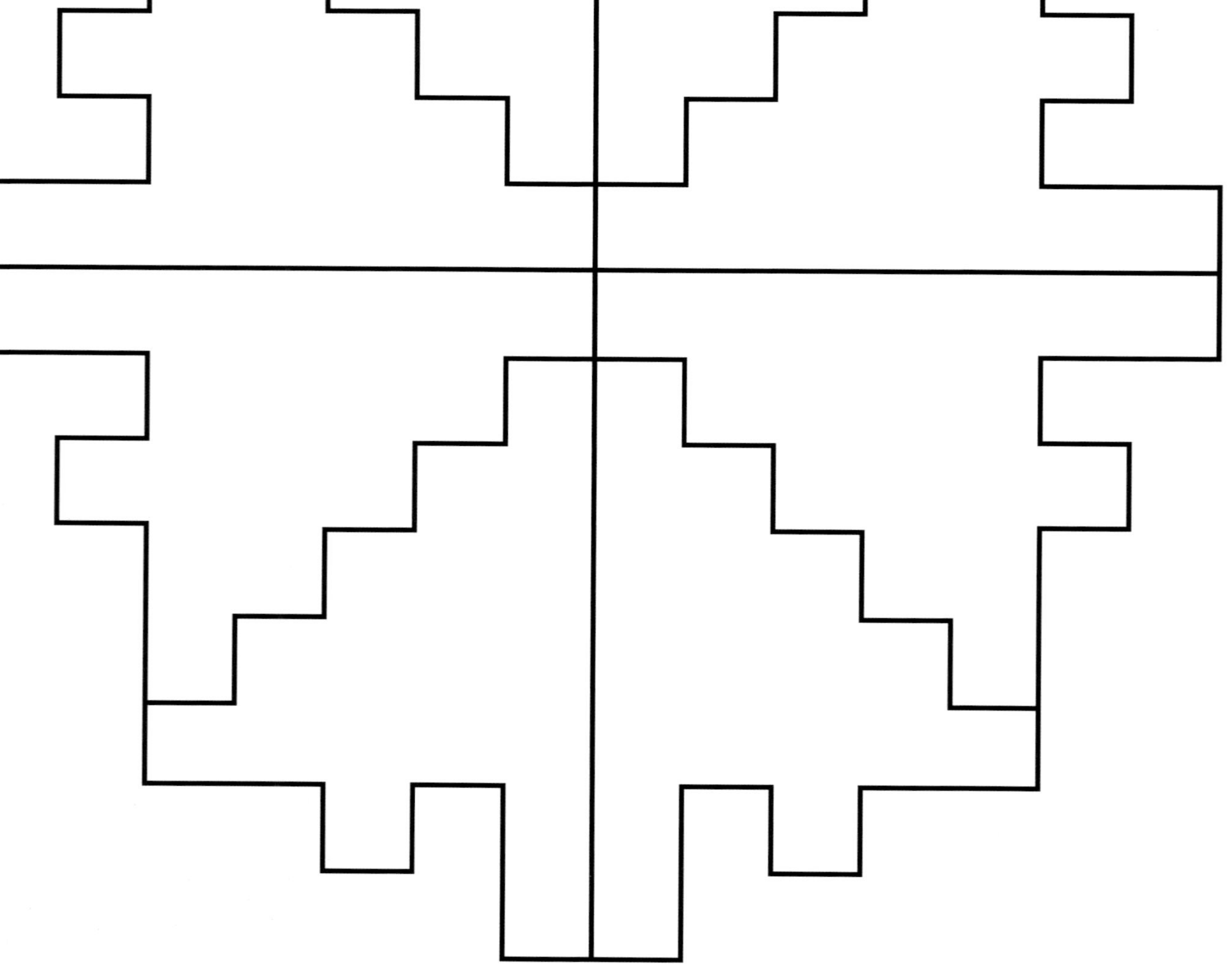

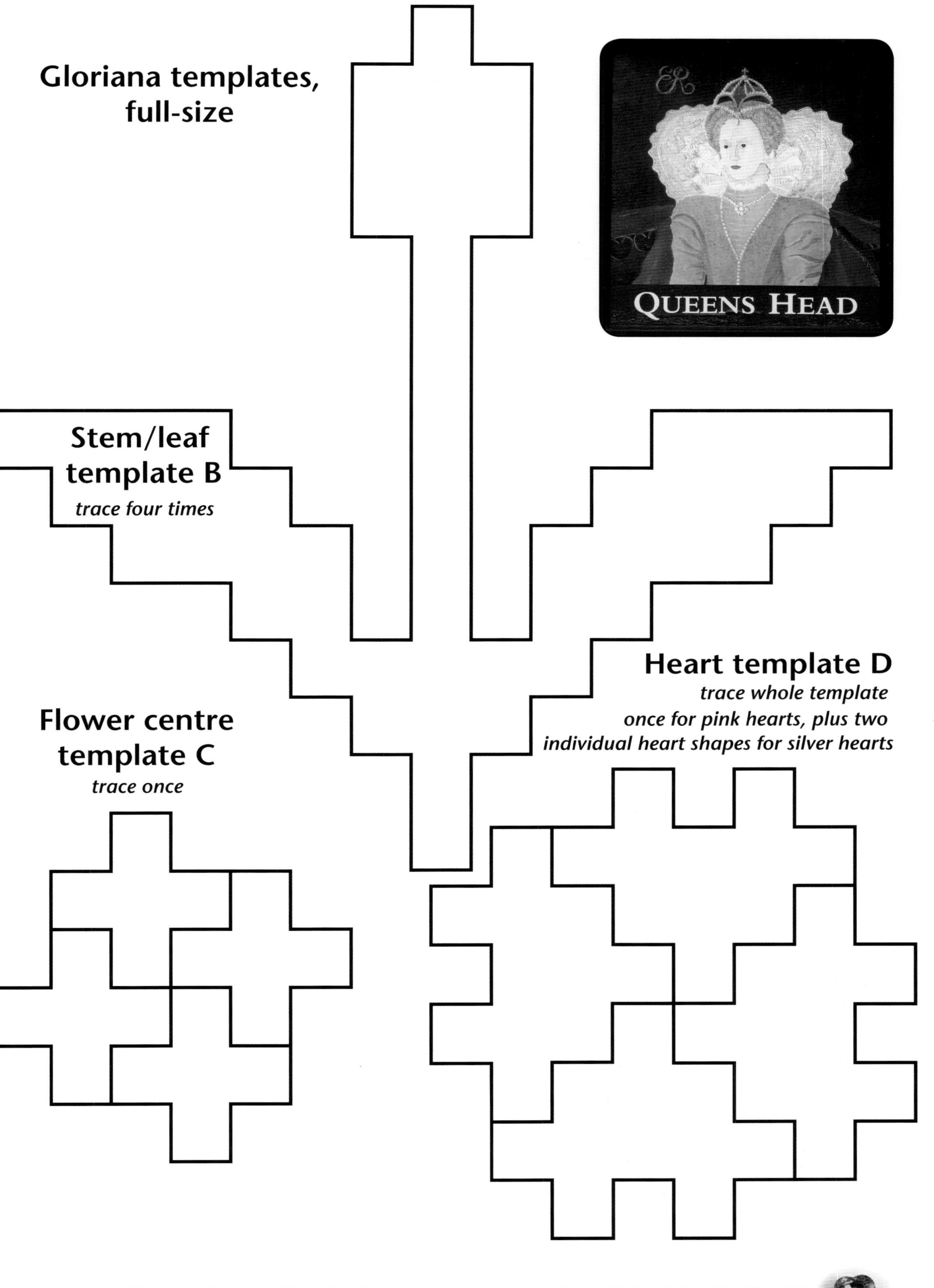
Gloriana templates, full-size
QUEENS HEAD
Stem/leaf template B
trace four times
Heart template D
trace whole template once for pink hearts, plus two individual heart shapes for silver hearts
Flower centre template C
trace once

The Fab Four

The iconic faces of the Lads from Liverpool became the image of the Swinging Sixties.

In 1963, when I was 8, I came back from several years living in Malta. When I began going to the local school in Cornwall, the other children in the playground could only talk about two things, and I didn't know what either of them was: the first was Daleks, and the second was The Beatles. Needless to say, I was soon enlightened on both subjects …

The Beatles emerged at just the right moment in history. For the first time, things that until then had only been available to the discerning few were becoming freely available to the (possibly undiscerning!) masses. High fashion was suddenly accessible for everyone off the peg. For teenagers all over the country, Carnaby Street, the King's Road, and the Biba shop in Kensington became destinations for weekend pilgrimages. Even the concept of the teenager was new – until then, when children weren't at school they dressed in smaller versions of their parents' clothes.

American girls on the famous pedestrian crossing outside Abbey Road Studios

After the years of post-war austerity, suddenly people had disposable incomes, and children had significant amounts of pocket money; and we used that to develop and feed into our own youth culture. The Swinging Sixties, with all their connotations of social and sexual revolution, were in full sway; pop (short for 'popular' – literally meaning 'of the people') culture was born.

Pop music, as it became known, was the backing track for all this change; and the kings of pop were the mop-topped Beatles. They became a worldwide phenomenon, and spread the influence of British pop culture still further; and because they were working-class, and came from Liverpool, their success emphasised that their music was for **everyone**. Pop art, which fed into the fashion and music worlds, was the first fully 'accessible' art form – as with the clothes, pop art was cheap, bright, disposable, ephemeral. We covered our bedrooms with posters (Athena poster shops were hugely popular), and our school books with bright stickers; album sleeves became an artform in their own right. And when a new trend arrived, we could easily and cheaply replace our art, clothes, music, jewellery, hairstyles.

The strong lines and bright colours of Pop Art segued naturally into Op Art – geometric abstract designs which created optical illusions.

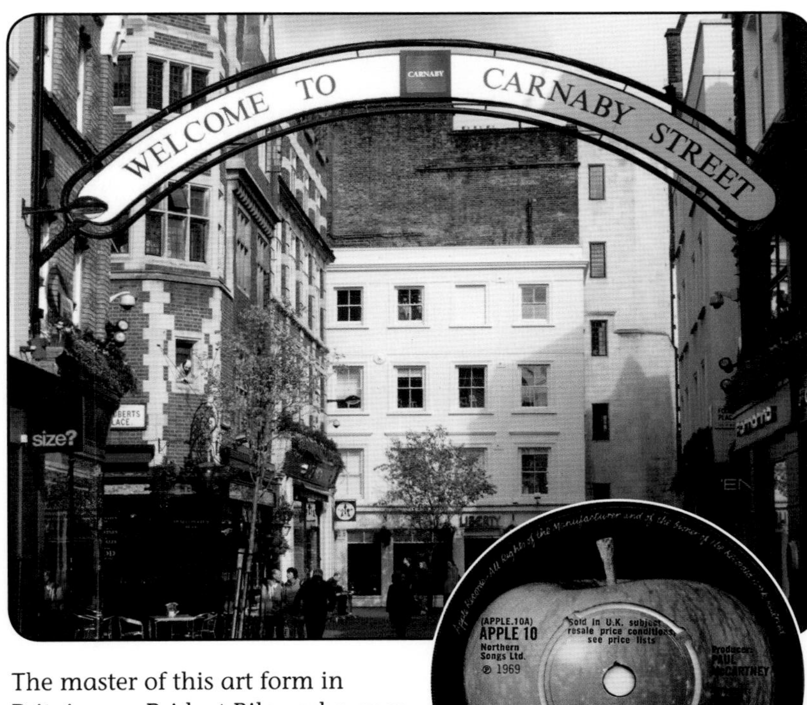

The master of this art form in Britain was Bridget Riley, who once described the 60s as 'the party at the end of the war;' fabrics inspired by her paintings were in turn used in high-street fashions. As the 60s trickled into the 70s, experiments with mind-altering substances became commonplace (also heavily influenced by those four lads from Liverpool); partly as a result, Op Art itself was then reborn as Psychedelic Art, keeping the bright colours and abstraction, but melting them into random curves and swathes.

The trend towards flowing lines revived an interest in Art Nouveau designs; in particular the typeface Arnold Bocklin, inspired by (and named after) the Symbolist painter who died in 1901, went astral. In fashion, hemlines moved downwards and ethnic influences ruled. The new 'flower children' went barefoot, wore Indian-style headbands, and dressed in long flared jeans and coloured cheesecloth or psychedelic prints. In the world of music, the very celebrity industry they had helped to create meant that the Beatles were eclipsed by new names and new styles, but their influence on our culture – for good or bad! – was immeasurable.

I've blended the Pop Art, Op Art and Psychedelic trends in the quilt. The Fab Four are the stars of the design, with their names created in the Arnold Bocklin typeface. The two-tone style of the faces reflects the iconic monochrome portraits taken of the boys by Astrid Kirchherr, photographer girlfriend of Stuart Sutcliffe who is often referred to as 'the fifth Beatle,' but I've done them in 70s-style psychedelic prints. Quant-type daisies in bright pop colours have been softened into more flowing flowers, and the quilting styles have echoes of Op Art.

Inside information

There are hundreds of books available on the Fab Four (collectively and individually), but the only authorised biography is ***The Beatles*** *by Hunter Davies; it was first published by Heinemann in 1968, and has been updated various times since. For a good collection of Beatles info, go to www.thebeatles.com. For stuff on the 60s and 70s generally, try the relevant sections of www.retrowow.co.uk, where you can learn everything you ever wanted to know about the gadgets, toys, cars, fashions, television, food – and, of course, the music – of those decades.*

Materials

Cotton fabrics throughout. The coloured background fabric features the Beatles logo that appeared on Ringo's drum set, and I've picked four psychedelic prints in acidic colours for the main motifs.

Techniques

Each head/lettering motif was fused onto a white background, then machine-quilted in a spiral of wavy stitching, working out from the centre to create an Op Art effect. Each panel was then tacked to the background, and the curved edges neatened with a bias strip of the same coloured fabric – very basic stained glass patchwork, using invisible machine appliqué. The background itself is machine-quilted with a geometric design of random straight lines; all the quilting was done in invisible thread, so that the stitching didn't visually interrupt the fabric prints.

To create the flowers, I bonded bright cotton fabrics onto thick interfacing then cut out the flower shapes and edged them with machine satin-stitch. They're appliquéd by machine around the centre oval, so that the petals stand proud of the quilt.

Backing and binding

A second Beatles-print fabric makes the perfect backing for this quilt. I sculpted the edges to suggest the kind of bubble-writing that was wildly popular in the 60s, and to echo the Pop/Op art theme I cut bias strips of a bright polka-dot fabric and used it to bind the curved edges.

PROJECT

Woven Bags

Op art delighted in creating the effect of movement, by juxtaposing contrasting colours in strong geometric grids – straight or wavy. In this project I've created several little op art bags, echoing those patterns of the 60s; the bag is perfect for holding jewellery, make-up or a travel sewing kit. The foundation of each bag is a little woven mini-quilt; if you're new to woven quilts, you'll soon see ways that you can adapt the technique to larger projects. For a really Bridget-Riley-type effect, work in black and white plains or prints, or choose another equally contrasting colourscheme.

finished size: each bag is roughly 8 x 6in (20 x 15cm)

For each bag, you will need:

- two contrasting pieces of cotton fabric for weaving, each piece 8 x 16in (20 x 40cm)
- two pieces of double-sided bonding web, each piece 8 x 16in (20 x 40cm)
- flat wadding, 9 x 17in (23 x 43cm)
- cotton lining fabric, 8 x 16in (20 x 40cm)
- machine quilting threads to match your two fabrics, or to contrast with them (eg you could weave with black and white fabrics, then quilt with red)
- 1yd (1m) bias binding for binding the edges in a toning or contrasting colour, ¾in finished width (ie, when the raw edges have been folded under)
- pencil, ruler; quilt rule/mat/rotary cutter (if you're cutting your strips straight rather than wavy)

Instructions

1 Fuse a piece of bonding web onto the wrong side of each piece of 'weaving' fabric, making sure that you put the rough side of the bonding web against the fabric.

2 Now it's time for two decisions (don't panic: nothing earth-changing!) First of all, decide whether you want your weaving to use straight edges or wavy: if you decided on straight, you'll draw your pencil lines using a ruler; if you decide on wavy, then you'll draw the lines wavy (sounds logical, doesn't it?) Now for the second decision: decide whether you want the strips to be parallel with the edges of the rectangle or at 45°. Parallel lines will give you the effect of a straight weave; angled lines will create the effect of a bias weave.

3 If you're going for a straight weave, draw straight or wavy lines (as appropriate) on the paper side of the bonded fabric pieces; the lines on one piece will be parallel with the long edges, and the ones on the other will be parallel with the short edges (**a** and **b**).

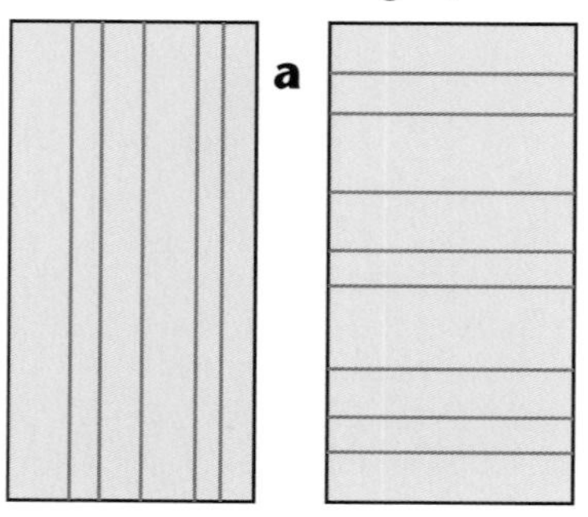

a

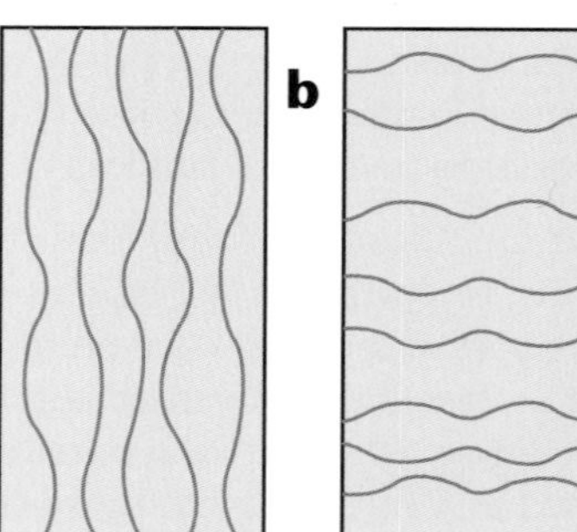

b

4 If you're going for a bias weave, do the same on the fused pieces but draw all the lines at a 45° angle – angling the lines one way on one piece, and the other way on the second (**c** and **d**).

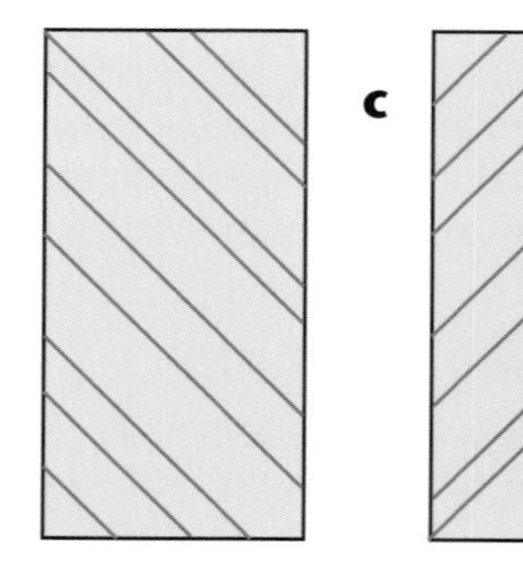

c

5 Number all the pieces in order, then cut along the marked lines to create two sets of weaving strips (**e**).

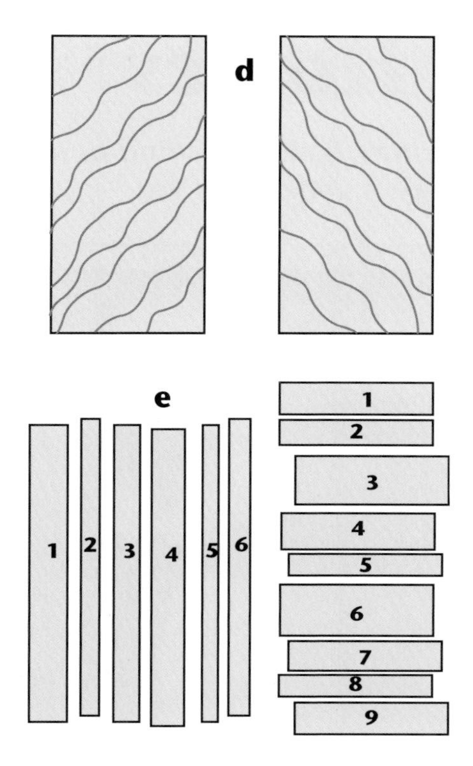

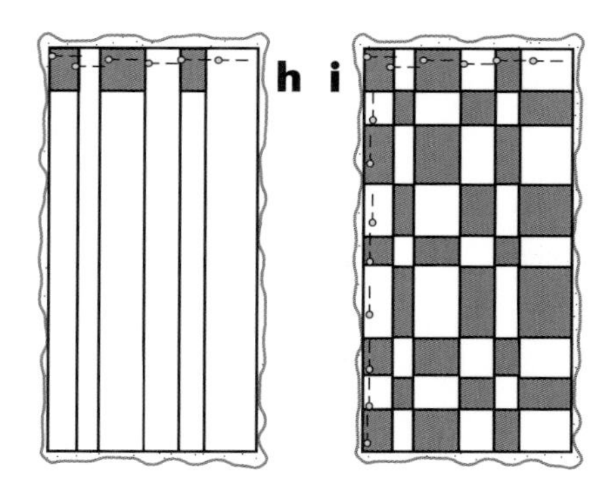

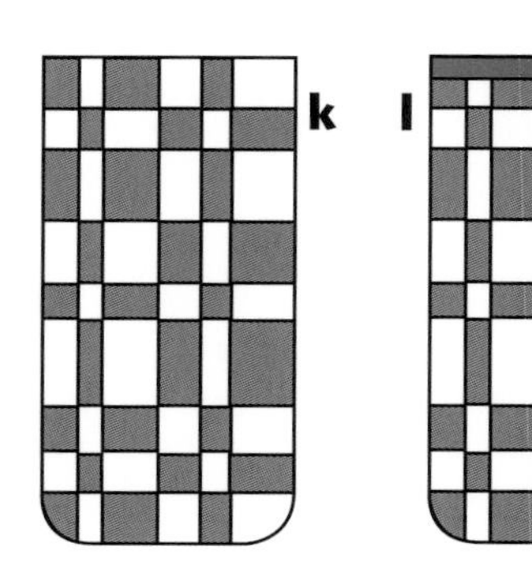

TIP

Numbering the strips will help you remember which order to weave them in – they all tend to look the same once you've cut them up!

6 Lay the rectangle of wadding flat. If you're doing a straight weave, lay the long set of strips in order on top of the wadding, right side up. Peel the paper off the strips one at a time, laying each strip back in position again once you've removed the paper. Pin one end of each strip to the wadding to hold it in place (**f**). If you're doing a bias weave, do the same with all the strips of one fabric (**g**).

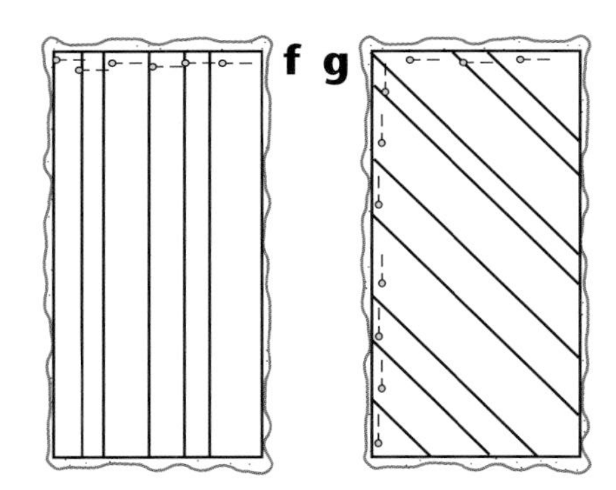

7 Lay all the contrasting strips out in order on the table. Working with one strip at a time, peel the paper off and weave it in and out of the first set of strips, and pin it into place (**h**).

Continue in the same way with all the other strips, pushing them all up nice and close against each other, until the woven design is complete (**i**).

8 Press the front of the work with a warm iron to fuse the strips into place. Lay the lining rectangle flat, right side down, and pin the woven design to it, right side up. Work your own choice of machine-quilting pattern across the design (**j** *below*); one of the simplest ways of doing this is simple series of slightly wavy stitching lines.

9 Trim the rectangle down so that it measures a neat 8 x 16in (20 x 40cm) – if it ends up a little smaller, it doesn't matter. At one end of the rectangle, round the corners of the woven design (**k**). Bind the other end with a strip of bias binding (**l**); you don't need to neaten the ends of the binding strip, as the raw edges will be hidden by the final strip of binding.

10 Fold the bottom 6in (15cm) of the quilted rectangle upwards, and fold the top edge downwards so that the curved end forms a flap at the front of the bag (**m**); press to set the folds, then bind the outside edge (**n** and **o**), folding the raw ends inside the binding strip at the bottom of the bag to neaten them.

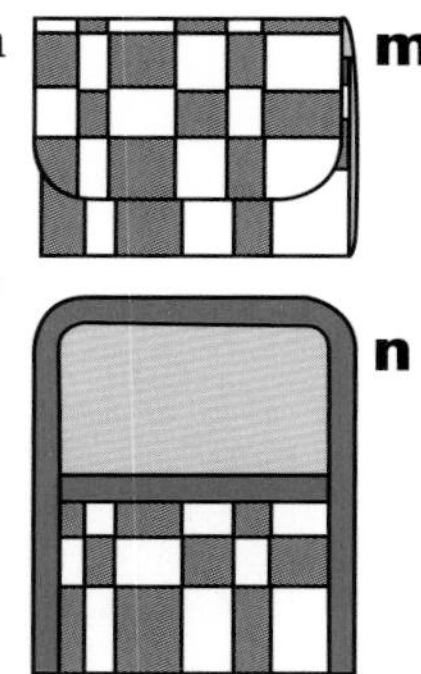

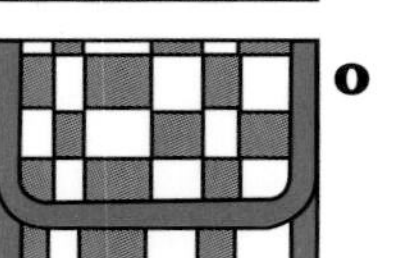

VARIATION

As long as you have two fabrics that will enable you to see the woven effect of the bag, they can be any kind of print or plain: try two interesting dyed/batik fabrics, two shaded fabrics, or two different toning prints.

j

Stately Homes

Throughout our land, ornate buildings stand as reminders of days gone by.

Britain is enormously rich in stately homes; when we visit one of these palatial buildings, it's often hard to believe that it was the home of just one family. OK, so the attics were stocked with maids, grooms, housekeeper, cook, parlourmaids, footmen etc, plus their work-spaces, but these only took up a small proportion of the space: the rest would be a vast maze of ballrooms, dining rooms, sitting rooms, 'retiring' rooms, halls, bedrooms, galleries, nurseries, smoking rooms, libraries, dressing rooms etc. Who on earth inhabited these palaces?

The answer, of course, is: our upper classes. One thing that fascinates visitors to Britain is our class system. There's no doubt that, these days, social class means less than it ever has done: there's also no doubt that it's been the backbone of our history for centuries. The upper class was generally produced by a self-sustaining cycle of birth, money, occupation and education; at the top of the pyramid were (and still are) royalty, followed by the nobility (people with hereditary titles). Under these were gentlemen and ladies, generally defined historically as people who didn't have to work for a living because they had inherited money. Inheritance has always been crucial, as it shows that you come from good old stock: hence the mistrust of people who have made their money through business (the *nouveau riche*), or who have been ennobled recently.

As in many other countries, people could improve their social status by increments, usually beginning with what was often referred to as a 'good' marriage – for a young lady of breeding, this meant that you could carry on living in the manner to which you were accustomed, or (oh joy!) move up the food chain. It was still considered quite scandalous, though, if there was a significant difference in the background of the two marriage partners. In a similar way, you could move down the social spiral (oh horrors!) by 'marrying badly.' We only need to look at Jane Austen's novels to see the importance of making the right marriage.

At the lower end of the social scale were the working classes: the clue is in the name – these were people who had to work to make a living. A great deal of their work, inevitably, involved maintaining the lifestyle of the upper classes. The middle classes bridged the divide between the two extremes; if they worked, it was in a profession such as law, the armed forces, politics, the church or finance – occupations that didn't involve manual labour. In the stately homes, a strict hierarchy was maintained among the servants; people such as butlers, governesses and housekeepers were considered (or considered themselves) superior to the manual workers.

At its worst, the class system bred a dreadful arrogance in the upper classes. For centuries, we drummed into our young gentlemen that **nobody** could know better than them how to run a business, a family, an estate, a country or even a planet. We also told our young ladies that **nobody** could know better than them how to run a household, a charitable organisation, a fund-raising event or a village fete. Question: how on earth did such a small country gain an empire on which, for many years, the sun never set? Answer: because we believed not only that we could, but that we ought to. This arrogance sometimes led to people of noble birth running amok, financially and morally: Hogarth's series of paintings ***The Rake's Progress*** portray this perfectly.

The grounds of this once-stately home outside Birmingham are now a public park, to be enjoyed by all!

At its best, upper-class families operated on a principle known as *noblesse oblige*: this basically means that if you are born with advantages, you have a responsibility to look after people who are less fortunate. The best landowners considered that they were responsible for the social, moral, physical and financial welfare of their dependents, just as they were for their own children. The upper classes were the first people to educate their daughters; not as intensely as their sons, of course, but every marriageable woman was expected to have several 'worthy' hobbies (eg botany or geology) alongside other accomplishments such as singing or playing the piano. Think of ***The Country Diary of an Edwardian Lady***.

This sense of responsibility also led to the upper classes playing a leading role in the very event that became their undoing: the First World War. Gentlemen donned their military uniforms and encouraged their servants and estate workers to do the same, so it's sometimes said that the war was won 'on the playing fields of Eton' – the idea being that our public schools taught our men to do their duty. Although we ended up the victors, the ensuing carnage killed nearly a million of our men, and left more than a million and a half wounded. As a result, some noble families lost their heirs and had to break up their estates (or have them inherited by ill or unsuitable younger sons, which generally led to the same result).

There was no longer the manpower to run the estates or the stately homes the way they had been run, and the remaining working-class men had lost their appetite for pandering to the whims of the upper classes. The nobility began to curb their excesses; fewer lavish dinner-parties, balls and shooting-parties. Modernisations such as central heating and labour-saving devices meant that fewer servants were needed, and new industries meant that working people had a slightly wider choice of occupation than before.

So, many of our stately homes are now visitor attractions, allowing all of us a glimpse into times gone by. The glory days are over: on my quilt, the building is beginning to crumble, and ivy is creeping in. Noël Coward's song ***The Stately Homes of England*** captures this decay of the upper classes perfectly, and I've used a portion from it on the quilt:

> *The stately homes of England,*
> *how beautiful they stand –*
> *to prove the upper classes*
> *have still the upper hand ...**

Inside information

For a guide to all Britain's stately homes open to the public (as well as various gardens, castles and other historic properties), visit www.stately-homes.com/.

Marianne North (1830-1890) was one well-bred young lady who earned a reputation as an outstanding botanical illustrator. In 1882 a gallery dedicated to her work was opened at Kew Gardens (www.kew.org/heritage/places/mariannenorth.html).

Materials

The whole quilt is stitched using cotton fabrics, with the addition of lace, ribbon and fabric paint.

Techniques

I've used machine appliqué to build most of the design: the decorative details on the windows are created with bias binding, ribbon, machine embroidery and lace. I used scraps of sheer fabric caught down with machine quilting to stitch the crumbling details on the walls and the paving, and fabric paint for the lettering. Fabric paint also adds depth to the statue; the sculpture, the urn and the Roman-style border fabric reflect the passion for Graeco-Roman design in many of our stately homes.

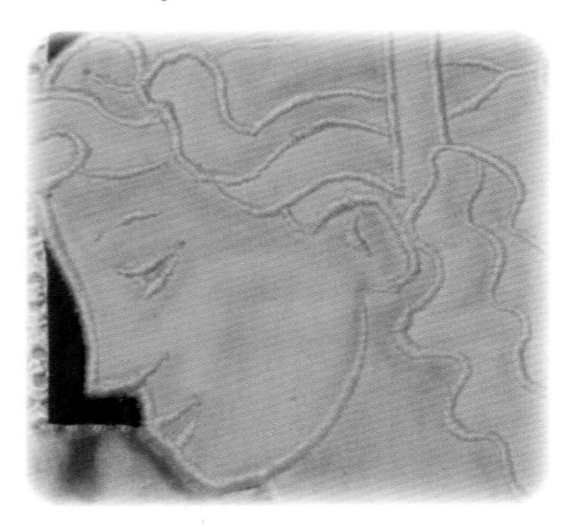

Backing and binding

The back of the quilt is the same marbled cotton that I used for the main building, and the simple binding is a darker tone of the same peachy-pink colour.

PROJECT

Topping Topiary

Design a pretty formal garden – without getting your hands dirty! This lovely line of topiary trees is created using simple fused appliqué plus a bit of machine stitching; the design comes together very quickly, and once all the pieces are in place you can quilt as you wish by hand or machine.

finished size: 35 x 21in (90 x 54cm)

Pot templates, full-size

You will need:

- background fabric 16 x 30in (40 x 75cm); half a metre gives you plenty for this piece
- contrasting border fabric:
  two 30 x 3in (75 x 8cm) strips
  two 21 x 3in (54 x 8cm) strips
- 35 x 21in (90 x 54cm) flat wadding
- 37 x 23in (95 x 60cm) backing/binding fabric
- six different green foliage fabrics in a variety of tones, one 6 x 10in (15 x 25cm) patch of each (or, if you want to make all your trees in the same fabric – perhaps an interesting batik – one 18 x 15in/46 x 38cm piece)
- plain or print fabric for the pots, 8 x 6in (20 x 15cm) (or, if you want to use a different fabric for each pot, six different 3½in/9cm squares)
- 18in (45cm) square of bonding web
- 10in (25cm) brown bias binding or braid for the tree-trunks, roughly ¼in (6mm) wide
- sewing threads to match your green fabric(s), pot fabric(s) and tree trunks, and for attaching the border pieces
- pencil, paper scissors
- chalk marker and long quilt rule
- your choice of hand or machine quilting threads
- extra strip of fabric for a casing, or ribbon/tape for hanging loops

Instructions

1 Trace all the full-size templates (tree templates A-H, and pot templates I-N) onto the paper side of the bonding web, and cut around the edges roughly (**a**). If you're using the same fabric for all the pots, you can cut them out in a group rather than individually (the same is true of the tree shapes, if you're using the same fabric for all the trees).

2 Fuse the shapes onto the wrong sides of the appropriate fabrics, and cut them all out along the marked lines (**b**).

3 Press the rectangle of background fabric and lay it right side up. Use the chalk marker and ruler to draw a line 1½in from each edge. Peel the backing

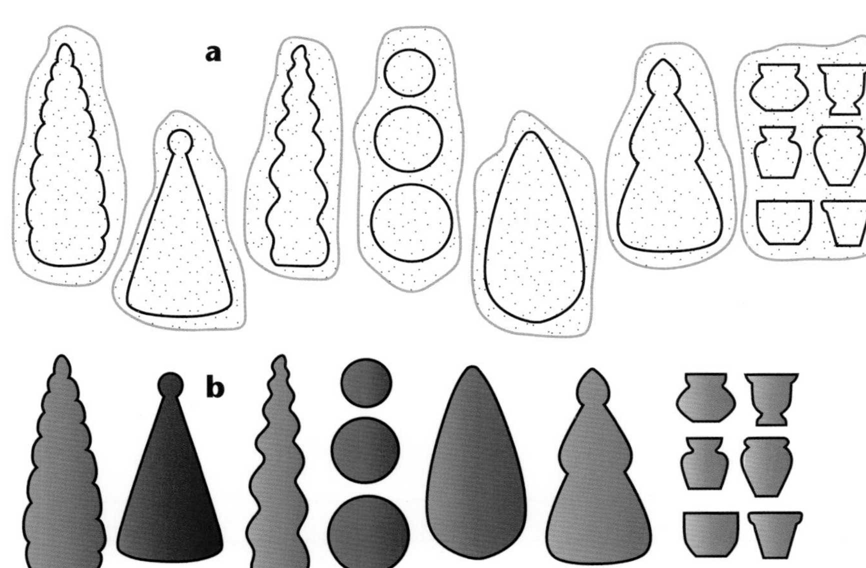

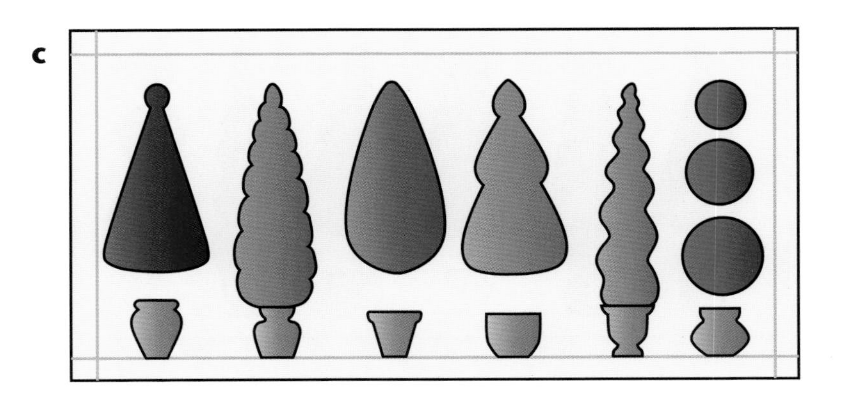

papers off all the cut patches, and position the trees and the pots so that they create a pleasing arrangement, keeping the tree shapes within the frame of chalk lines, and lining the bottoms of the pots along the chalk line at the bottom of the fabric (**c**). (You don't need to use the trees in the same order that I have – move them round to suit your own fabrics.) Once you're happy with the arrangement, pin all the shapes in place.

TIP

As you work on the quilt the chalk will rub off after a while, which saves you having to worry about removing the marked lines.

4 For each place where you want to add a tree-trunk, cut a length of brown tape/bias binding/braid long enough to tuck under the neighbouring tree/pot patches, and pin or fuse these trunk pieces in position (**d**). Now fuse all the tree and pot patches in place.

5 Using a small seam, add the two longer border strips to the top and bottom of the design; press the seams towards the darker fabric. Add the two shorter strips to the edges in the same way (**e**).

6 Lay the backing fabric on a flat surface, right side down, and position the wadding on top so that there's an even border of backing fabric around the edge. Lay the fused design on top of the wadding, right side up, and use a few pins to hold the layers together.

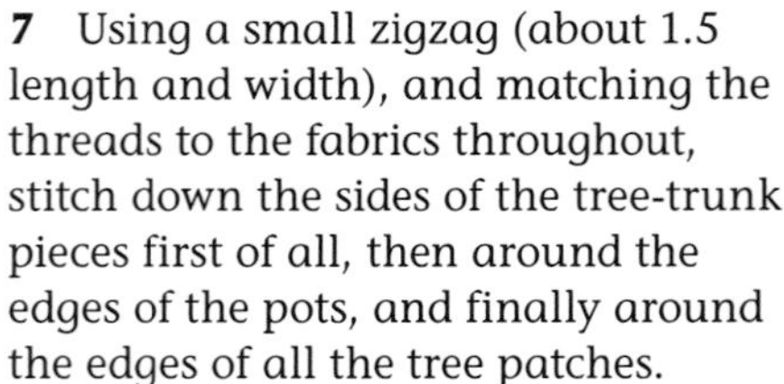

7 Using a small zigzag (about 1.5 length and width), and matching the threads to the fabrics throughout, stitch down the sides of the tree-trunk pieces first of all, then around the edges of the pots, and finally around the edges of all the tree patches.

8 Quilt the background as you wish by machine or hand. Once the quilting is complete, fold the excess backing fabric over to the front in a small double fold, and stitch the fold down by hand or machine.

9 Add a hidden casing at the top of the back, or hanging loops of ribbon or tape. Your indoor topiary is now ready to grace your own stately home!

d

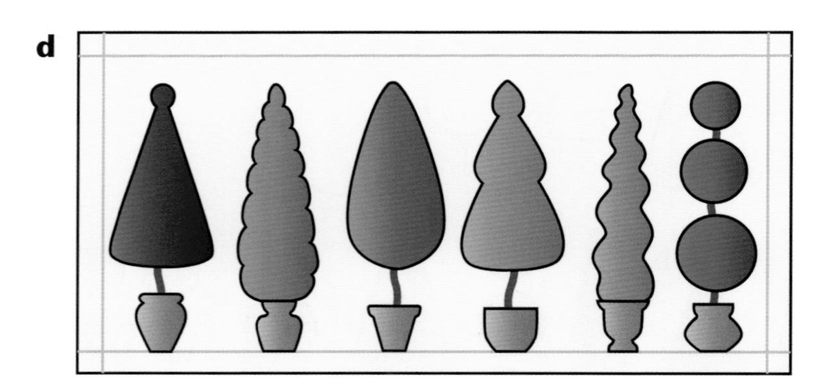

e

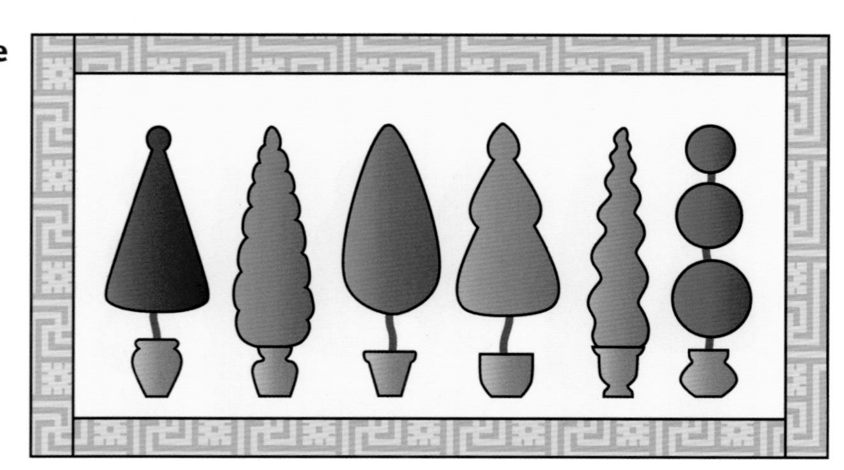

VARIATION

Why not stitch this design as a Christmas panel? Use seasonal prints for the trees, and perhaps gold prints for the pots, then decorate the trees with little baubles or a set of miniature Christmas light charms.

Tree templates, full-size

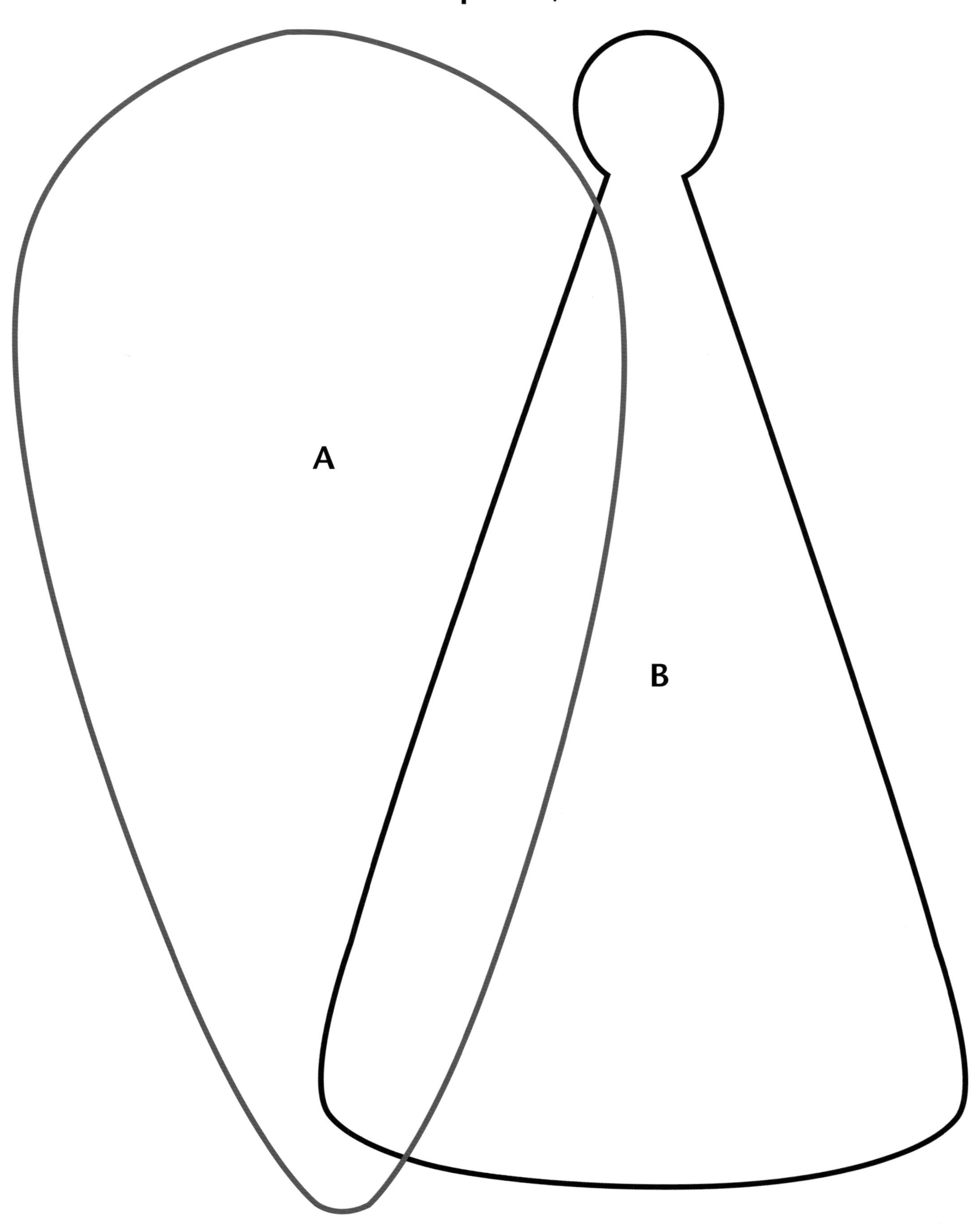

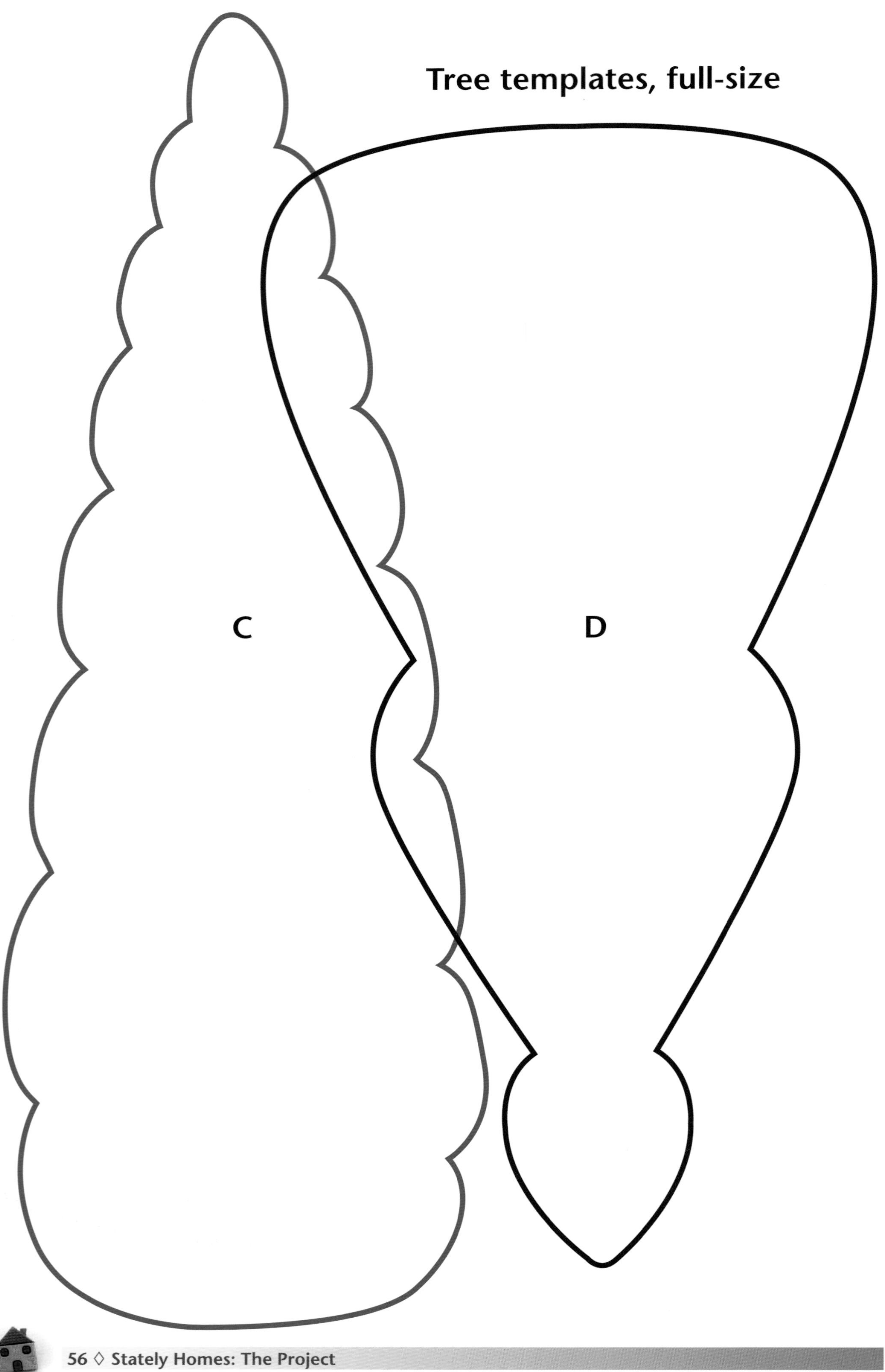
Tree templates, full-size
C
D

Tree templates, full-size

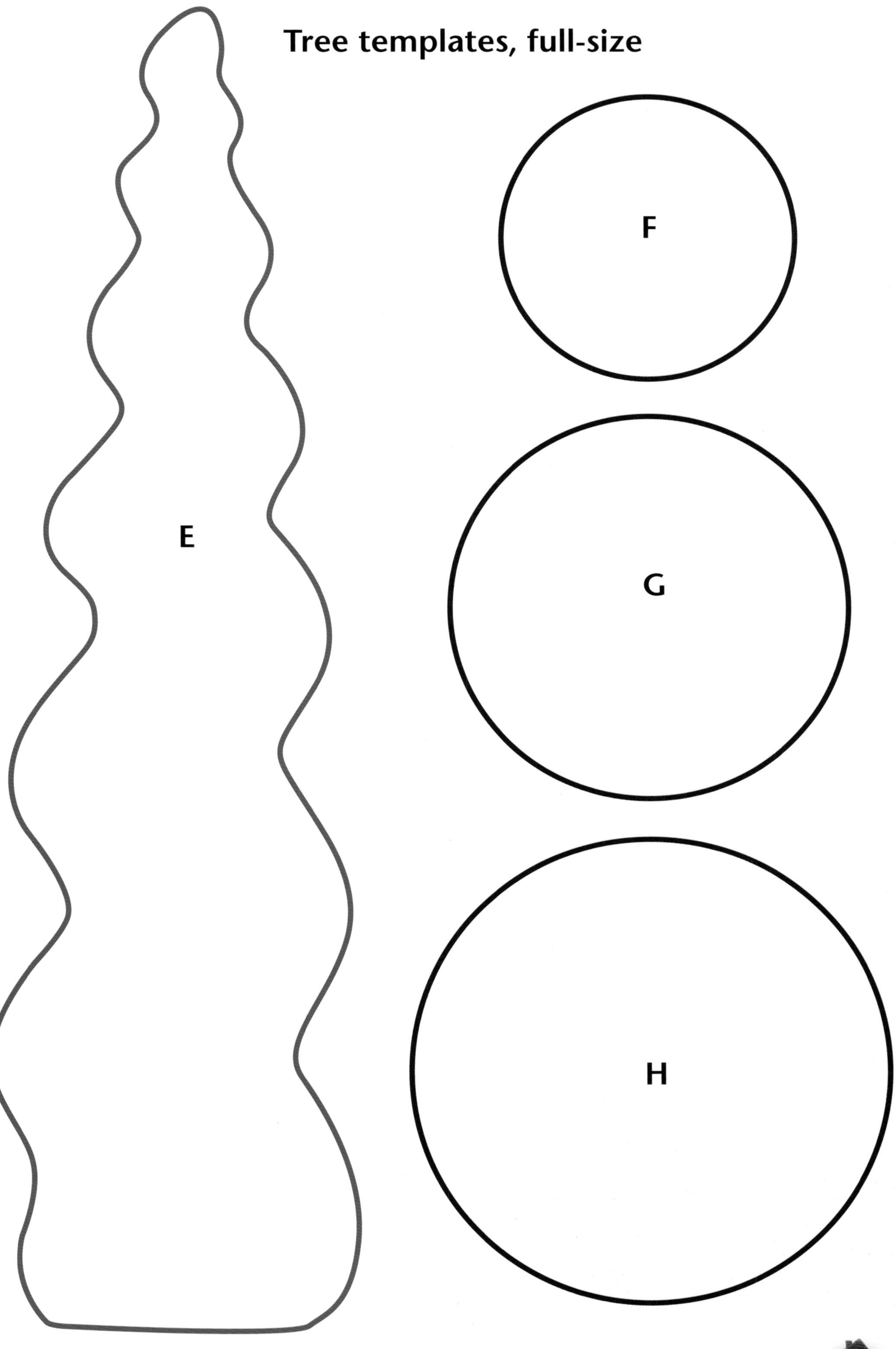

Ireland

St Patrick stands guard over the Emerald Isle.

Ireland is the third-largest island in Europe, separated from the mainland of England/Wales/Scotland by the Irish Sea. In the popular imagination, Ireland is peopled by little green leprechauns who are constantly dancing to Irish music while rainbows arc across the land (think ***Finian's Rainbow***). From the times we've visited, I can certainly confirm that the countryside is a patchwork of vivid greens, courtesy of the temperate climate and the soft rains that fall most days. These, of course, also produce the rainbows, so it's not all romantic invention. I can't personally vouch for the leprechauns, but a vital part of Irish life is the *craic* (pronounced 'crack') – an untranslatable word that generally refers to having a good time, and of course music and dance play important roles in this, as well as good conversation and being in good company.

Irish music is famed the world over, and – particularly since its revival through the ***Riverdance*** spectacular – so is Irish dancing. Traditional folk musicians such as The Dubliners and The Chieftains made their mark internationally, and were followed by people such as Sinéad O'Connor, Enya and Clannad. A particular favourite of ours is piper Troy Donockley, who has played with many different artistes as well as being a superb musician in his own right.

Ireland is home to many natural wonders: one is the spectacular Giant's Causeway, a mosaic of hexagonal basalt columns. It had always been one of my ambitions to go there, and we finally made it a few years ago. The Burren is an unusual karst landscape (where water has eroded rock into fissures); alpine flowers grow in the cracks in the rock, known as grikes. Connemara is famous for its marble, its ponies and its whiskey (the Irish version of the drink is spelt with an 'e', as opposed to Scotch whisky). The Blarney Stone is a massive bluestone block built into the walls of Blarney Castle; legend has it that if you kiss the stone (which involves a rather terrifying physical manoeuvre over a steep drop), you will get 'the gift of the gab.' This has led to our word *blarney*, meaning anything from flattery to hogwash.

Celtic culture in all its forms has influenced Irish life heavily: somewhere around the year 800AD the beautiful ***Book of Kells*** (now in Trinity College Library, Dublin) was produced. Croagh Patrick (see p13), also called The Reek, is a mountain overlooking Clew Bay, on which Patrick is reputed to have built a church; it's from the summit of Croagh Patrick that the saint apparently threw a silver bell that banished all snakes from Ireland. Certainly it's true that there aren't any, so **something** certainly sent them running. Or slithering. Patrick's fellow Irish monk, Columba, took Christianity to the north of England (see p125).

I wanted my quilted celebration of Ireland to be relevant to the whole island, and St Patrick seemed the best possible unifying force. This Celtic saint is a favourite patron saint of American churches, and features in many stained glass windows there; wherever he's depicted, he's often holding up a shamrock, the emblem of his homeland, so I've put one in his hand. I'm always happy for any excuse to include Celtic knots in my quilt designs, as I love them so much, so I've appliquéd one at the top of the quilt. Patrick often appears standing on a snake, or with several round his feet, so I've made the knot under his feet into a lovely glittery snake, complete with jewelled eyes.

There is an ancient prayer attributed to the saint, and it's become known as St Patrick's breastplate; I've incorporated part of it into the upper knot:

I bind unto myself today
the strong name of the trinity …
the three in one and one in three.

Like many of the scholar-saints, Patrick is frequently depicted holding a bible. I decided that, for such a learned man, the bible would pose no problem at all, so I've given him much more of a challenge: my version is holding ***Finnegan's Wake*** by James Joyce. (Someone once described Joyce's ***Ulysses*** as the author talking to himself, and ***Finnegan's Wake*** as him talking to himself in his sleep.) To fortify Patrick in his task, there's a glass of Ireland's most famous tipple, Guinness, ready beside him. He is standing on the hexagonal stacks of the Giant's Causeway, stitched in the Kelly greens of the Emerald Isle, and behind him is the turquoise sea. The bottom border is a repeat pattern of tiny coffin shapes – a memorial to the many sons and daughters of Ireland lost in the Potato Famine and the Troubles (see p6).

Below: the Coffin Ship *sculpture, by John Behan, looks out across Clew Bay towards America; it's a memorial to the victims of the Potato Famine*

Inside information

The St Patrick Centre in Downpatrick (where else?!) is full of information on the saint: www.saintpatrickcentre.com/. For a taste of the craic, you can listen to all kinds of music from the Emerald Isles at www.irishmusic.co.uk/; there's also an ***Irish Music*** *magazine (www.irishmusicmagazine.com/)*

Materials

I've used a mixture of cotton fabrics, brocades and metallics; fabric paint was also used for various parts of the design. Fusible bias binding in two different widths edges the fabric patches, and charms and jewels complete the embellishments.

Techniques

The ST PATRICK lettering, the words from the prayer and the saint's face are all created in fabric painting; the fabric patches were attached using reverse appliqué, then edged with machine satin stitch and stained glass patchwork. I used machine quilting around the top lettering, and along the horizontal lines of the design.

Backing and binding

Once I saw this shamrock-print fabric, what else could I use to back St Patrick?!

PROJECT
Emerald Isles

The constant washing of gentle rain gives Ireland the lush green fields that have led to its nickname, The Emerald Isle. The central panels of these large cushion-covers are created from crazy stained glass patchwork, using lush fabrics and ribbons in shades of Kelly green, and echo that patchwork of green fields. I've even added some (fake) emeralds! You don't have to do the patchwork in greens, of course; you can make it match your own decor, or stitch the design in Christmassy colours to make some seasonal throw-cushions.

finished size: each cushion-cover is approx 20in (roughly 50cm) square

For each cushion-cover, you will need:

- one 13in (33cm) square of foundation fabric – eg calico, sheeting etc; all of this will be covered, so you don't need to use anything fancy!
- plenty of large scraps of different fabrics in your chosen colourscheme for the crazy patchwork (I used greens, obviously …)
- four 17 x 5in (43 x 13cm) strips of contrasting fabric for the cushion border (I used a textured cream furnishing fabric), plus matching sewing thread
- two 21 x 14in (55 x 36cm) pieces of fabric to match the border, to create the cushion-back
- ribbons, lace, braids etc in different widths and textures to complement the patchwork fabrics, plus matching sewing threads. You will need one piece that is at least 1½yd (1.5m) long, for edging the square of patchwork
- one 21in (55cm) square of flat wadding
- one 21in (55cm) square of muslin, calico or sheeting
- if you'd like to embellish your patchwork, suitable embroidery threads, plus buttons, beads, jewels (fake or real …) etc and threads to match
- one 20in (50cm) square cushion-pad
- 13in (33cm) square of paper (newspaper is fine)
- pencil, long ruler, paper scissors

Instructions

a

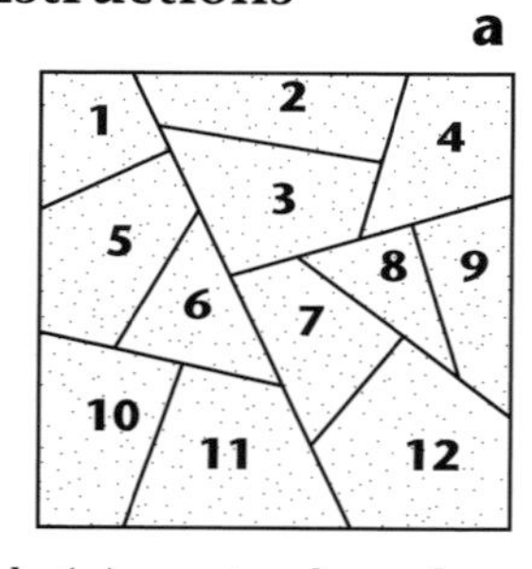

1 Use the pencil and ruler to divide the square of paper into different sections; you can use my lines as a guide (**a**), or simply make up your own design. The easiest way to begin is by drawing one long line across the square, and then subdividing it. Number all the different patches.

TIP

Numbering the pieces will help you remember which bit is which once you've cut the design up.

2 Once you're happy with the design, trace it onto the square of foundation fabric (**b**). Write in the numbers faintly; if you mark them too heavily, they may show through any pale fabrics.

b

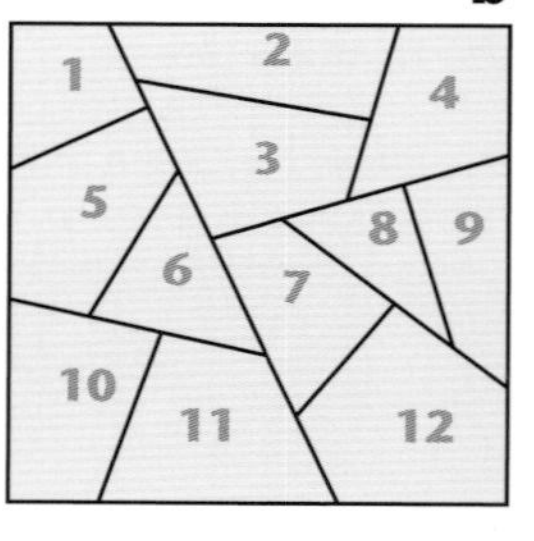

3 Choose which fabric you'd like for which part of the design; keep a good balance of tones and prints across the square. Cut up the paper design along the marked lines (**c**), then use these patches as templates for cutting your fabric patches (**d**); use each template right side up on the right side of the relevant fabric. You don't need to add any seam allowances on the fabric patches.

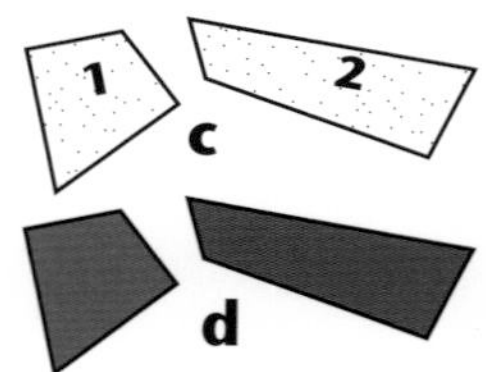

e

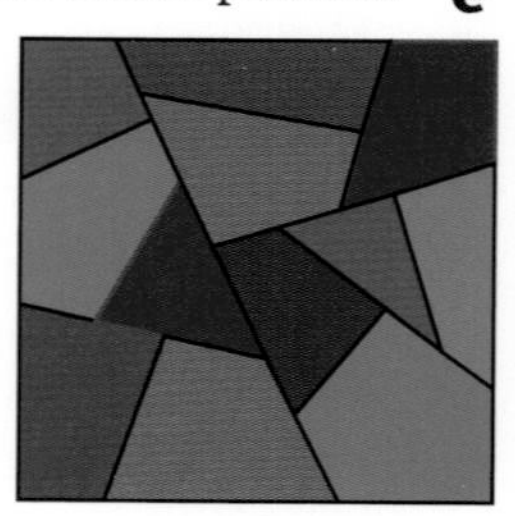

4 Pin the fabric patches in position on the background square (**e**), then use a large machine zigzag to tack the raw edges in place.

5 Using ½in (12mm) seams, add the first border strip to one edge of the square as shown (**f**); leave about 2in (5cm) unstitched at the top of the join, so that you can add the final strip easily. Add the second and third border strips (**g**), then the fourth one (**h**); once the final border has been added, you can complete the seam with the first border strip.

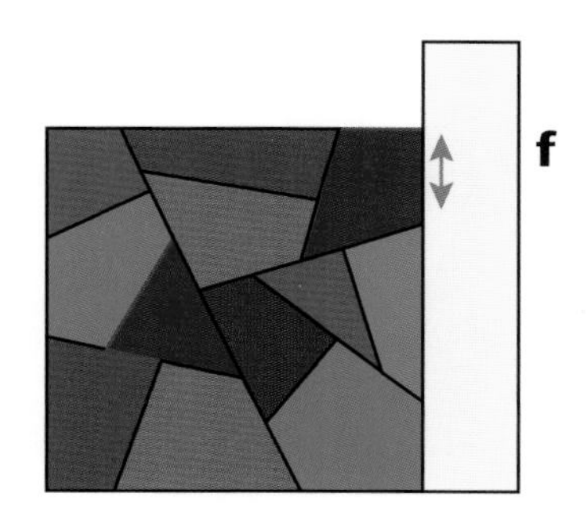

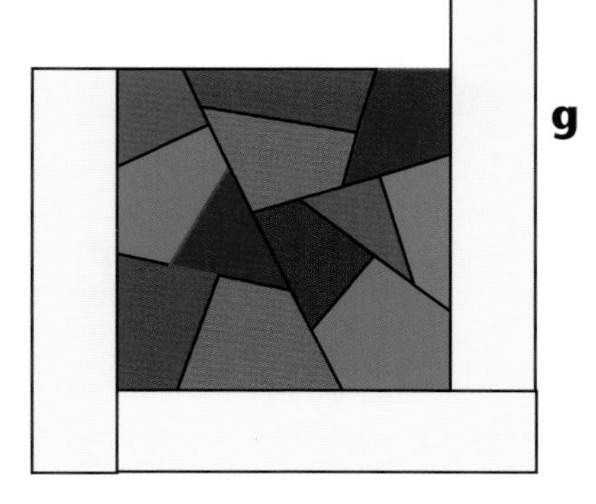

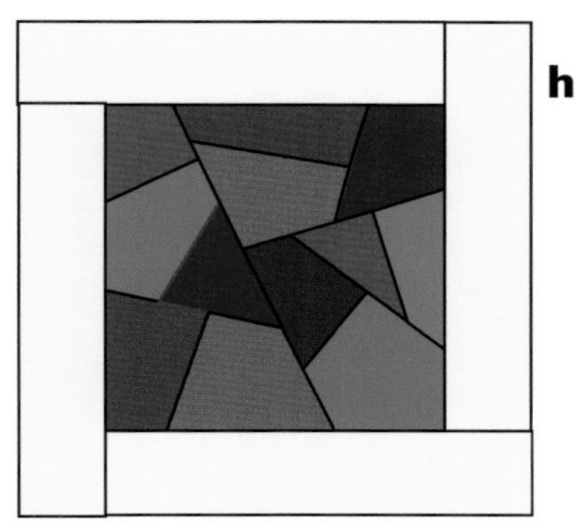

6 Lay the muslin, calico or sheeting square on a flat surface and cover it with the wadding. Position the design, right side up, on top. Add lines of ribbon, braid, lace etc to cover the joins between patches, stitching by hand or machine; you can layer two or more ribbons on top of each other if that creates a pretty effect. Begin with what I call the T-junctions (lines which go into other lines), and stitch the leading lines on these before you go on to the lines that cover them. Continue until you've covered all the joins between the patches (**i**).

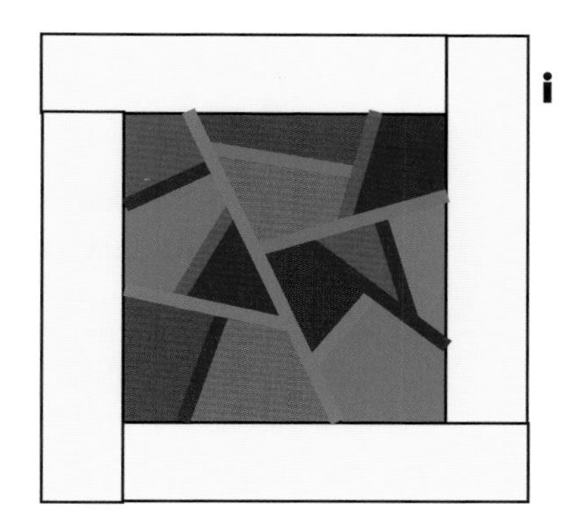

7 Add a line of ribbon or braid all around the central square (**j**), tucking the raw ends in neatly. (If you are using a thick ribbon or braid and find it difficult to finish off the raw ends, cover them with a bow or other embellishment.) Add any embroidery and embellishment that you wish.

8 To make the cushion-cover backings, fold under and stitch a small double hem on one long edge of each rectangle of backing fabric (**k**).

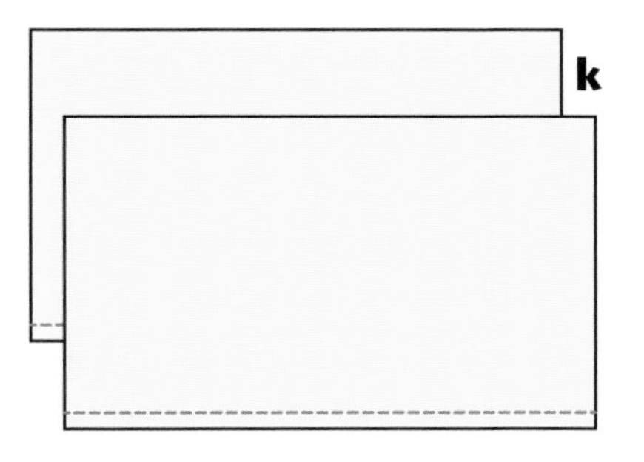

9 Lay the patchwork design right side up on a flat surface, then lay one backing piece on top, right side down, aligning the raw edges (**l**). Position the other backing piece so that the rectangles overlap, then stitch a ½in seam all around the edge (**m**).

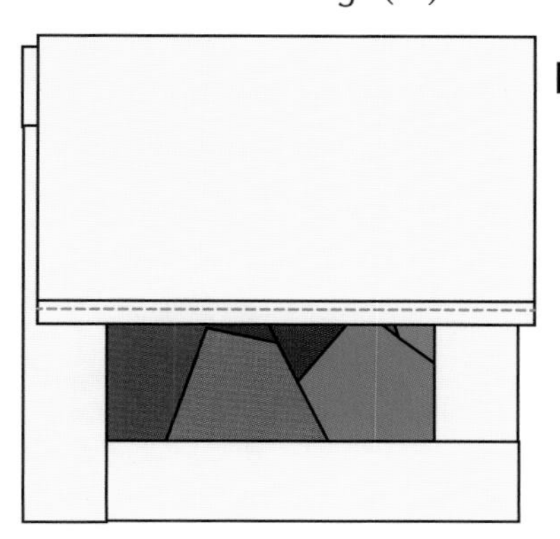

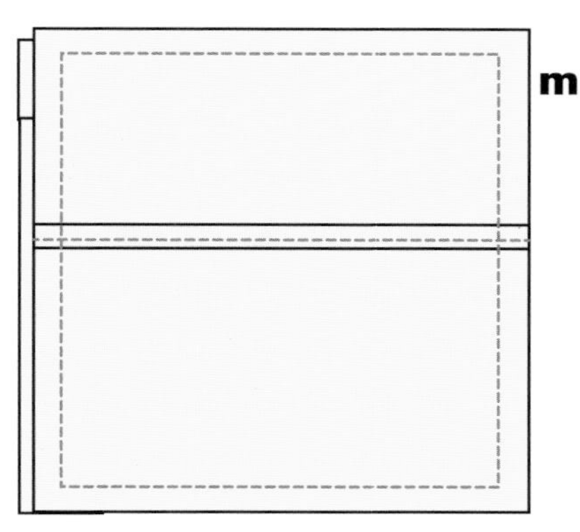

10 Clip the corners, turn out the cushion-cover, then press the very edges of the cover to set the seams. Stuff with the cushion pad, put in a comfy chair, then sit back and relax ...

VARIATION

This basic technique can be adapted to make a quilt or quilt panel of any size: make the central square larger to create a floor-cushion, or combine a whole batch of smaller squares with narrower sashing strips to make a full-size quilt.

A typical Irish peat bog

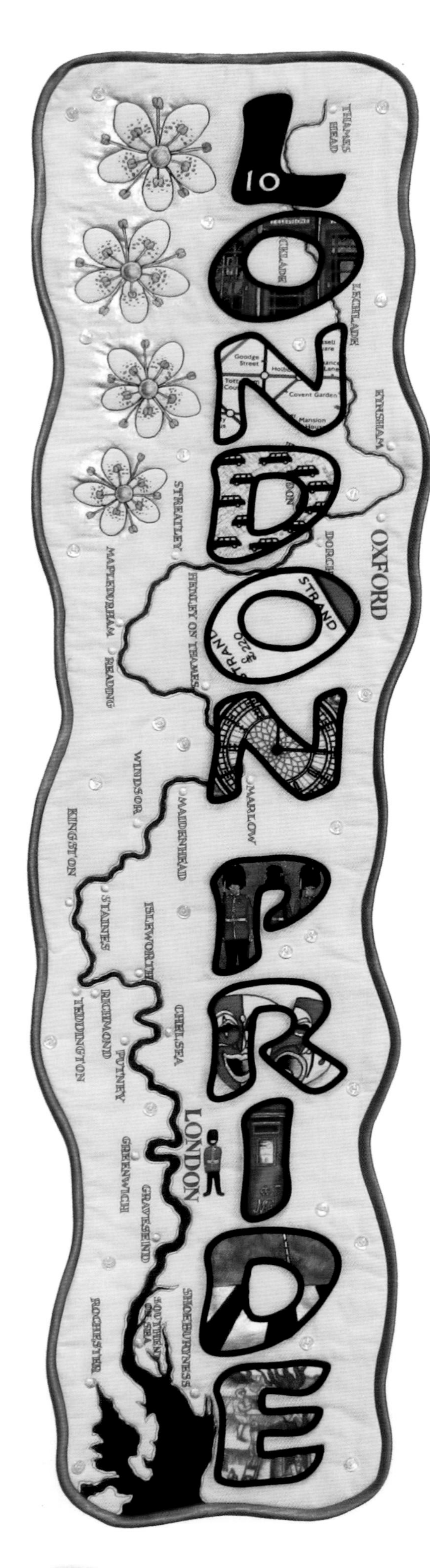

London Pride

Beefeaters, bearskins, bridges and Buckingham Palace; the lure of London is irresistible.

London's situation, near the mouth of the largest river in Britain, has made it a valuable trade site for millennia; the first known construction in the area dates back to around 4,500 BC. Much of what we now know as the City of London dates back to Roman times (see p109); the remains of their city walls can still be seen in places. The Romans called their settlement Londinium, and around the year 61AD it was stormed and destroyed by the Iceni tribe, led by the redoubtable Boadicea (or Boudica). By the 7th century, the Anglo-Saxons had developed a town they called Lundenwic, around the area that's now Covent Garden; Viking attacks (see p125) eventually forced the inhabitants to move back within the defences of the Roman walls.

Trade, political and financial activities grew steadily in the city from the middle ages onwards, and London became one of the most important ports in the world. Several years ago, when the Docklands area was being redeveloped, we visited the old Spice Wharves, where spices from India and the West Indies were unloaded; the timbers were impregnated with the scent, and produced the most amazing sensation of stepping back several centuries. In the area called Shad Wharf, many of the warehouses – now converted to smart flats – are named after the commodities they stored: Vanilla and Sesame Courts; Cardamon Building; Cinnamon Wharf; Ginger, Fennel and Caraway Apartments.

Above: Tower Bridge; Below: the Thames Barrier frames the Canary Wharf skyline

The city's world-renowned landmarks are almost too numerous to mention, but include Buckingham Palace, Harrod's, the Tower of London, London Bridge; Covent Garden Opera House and Market, the Houses of Parliament, St Paul's Cathedral, the National Gallery and the Albert Hall. London's Underground system was the first in the world, and its iconic topological Tube map (first designed by Harry Beck in the 1930s) has become the prototype of underground maps the world over. At Greenwich, home of the Greenwich Meridian – 0° longitude – you can stand with one foot in the eastern hemisphere and one in the western. The first ever A-Z map was created of London, by Phyllis Pearsall, in 1936.

London has been the inspiration for countless works of literature. Chaucer's pilgrims in ***The Canterbury Tales*** (see p78) set off from the Tabard Inn in Southwark; Dickens (see p96) set many of his books in different parts of London. Shakespeare's Globe Theatre (see p40) has recently been reconstructed on the banks of the Thames. Samuel Johnson wrote *When a man is tired of London, he is tired of life*, and the line *Earth has not anything to show more fair* is the first line of Wordsworth's poem celebrating the view from Westminster Bridge. Most of our national newspapers (I'll leave it to you to decide whether these also count as works of fiction ...) were born in Fleet Street, and even though they all dispersed to other locations in the 1980s, the term 'Fleet Street' is still used to refer to the British press.

Traditional songs about London abound. Of course, like every other important aspect of British life, it has its own nursery rhymes: ***Oranges and Lemons*** (*say the bells of St Clement's*): ***Pussycat, Pussycat, Where Have You Been***? (Answer: *I've been to London, to see the Queen.*) Interesting how several of these commemorate disasters: ***London Bridge is Falling Down***; ***London's Burning***. Other songs include ***Maybe it's Because I'm a Londoner***; ***Lambeth Walk***; ***A Nightingale Sang in Berkeley Square***; ***Sweet Thames, Run Softly***.

To be a true Cockney (traditionally an East End working-class Londoner), you are supposed to have been born within the sound of Bow Bells – difficult these days, as the original bells were destroyed in the Great Fire of London. Cockneys have their own culture, language and songs, and even their own 'royalty,' the Pearly Kings and Queens, whose costumes are decorated with pearl buttons stitched in elaborate designs. Cockney rhyming slang isn't used so much these days, but some examples have crept into the general English language: *apples and pears* (stairs); *have a butchers* (butcher's hook = look) *at this; dog and bone* (phone). There are also plenty of songs – ancient and modern – that are particularly associated with Cockneys, such as ***Down at the Old Bull and Bush*** and ***Knees Up Mother Brown***.

Above: Buckingham Palace; Below: the clock tower housing Big Ben

London has given its name to various aspects of life. For instance, a London Particular was a thick smog; before the days of the Clean Air Acts – coincidentally brought in after research by Chris' father – these could bring the city to a standstill. And London Pride is the name of a delightful little flower, a type of saxifrage. According to tradition, this flower quickly colonised bomb-sites after the Blitz, and so it became a symbol of the spirit of Londoners. This spirit of resistance was celebrated by Noël Coward (see p51) in his song ***London Pride***; the term has also been adopted as the name of a beer brewed by Fullers. I chose it, too, to form the letters on my London quilt; they feature, in descending order:

- No10 Downing Street ('probably the most famous front door in the world')
- traditional red phone boxes
- the Tube map
- London black cabs, the A-Z, and The Knowledge (the test cabbies have to take to demonstrate their in-depth knowledge of London's geography).
- a card from an early version of Monopoly (when you could buy a property in The Strand for £200!)
- the clockface of Big Ben – although strictly Big Ben is the name of the bell, not the clock or the tower.
- guardsmen wearing their bearskins
- comedy and tragedy masks, celebrating the city's Theatreland
- classic red postbox
- the most-photographed pedestrian crossing in the world, outside the Abbey Road Studios (see p46)
- the Great Fire of London

Inside information

*If you're planning a visit to London, try the official City Guide on www.visitlondon.com/ and the Time Out guide on www.timeout.com/london/. If you'd like to find out more about times past, Peter Ackroyd has written a detailed history of the city in **London: the biography**; you can also visit www.museumoflondon.org.uk/.*

Materials

Most of the fabrics on the quilt front are cotton, and the binding is satin; other materials include fabric paint and buttons.

Techniques

I used fabric paint to create the flowers, plus the course of the River Thames and the names along it; the background was then machine-quilted, and embellished with pearl buttons as a reference to the Pearly Kings and Queens. The letters are created in a mixture of fusing, printing onto fabric and painting, and I used stained glass patchwork to attach them to the background.

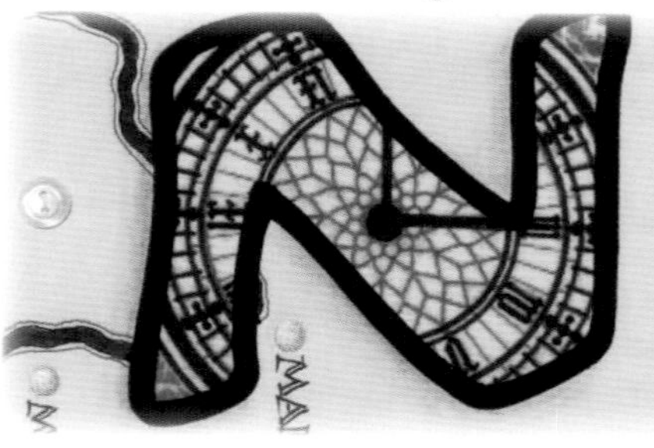

Backing and binding

Nutex's London Bus print reinforces the London theme, and a nice wide, bright red satin bias binding worked well with both the front and back of the quilt. As the shape of the Thames flowing through the quilt is so organic, I cut the quilt edges into random curves before I bound them.

PROJECT

St Clement's Quilt

Fuse and stitch a summery quilt top in a day or two – really! The method is easy fused appliqué; you can edge the motifs with machine stitching if you like (for instance zigzag, satin stitch or machine blanket stitch), or just leave them as they are and machine-quilt the whole design once it's assembled. I've used a mixture of machine blanket-stitch to edge the motifs, then big-stitch quilting in toning threads around the patches.

The inspiration behind this quilt is the nursery rhyme *Oranges and Lemons*, and it also relates to a famous London resident, Nell Gwynne. From an early age she was an orange-girl, selling fruit to the disreputable clientele of London theatres; she graduated to appearing on stage, where she caught the eye of Charles II and became his mistress for many years.

finished size: 25in (63cm) square

You will need:

- for the background patches; choose a selection of different citrus colours and tones:
- – four 8½in squares
- – four 4½ x 12½in rectangles
- – four 8½ x 4½ rectangles

  (I've put all the measurements in imperial, to ensure that the piecing works out correctly)
- for the appliqué motifs you'll need large and small scraps of fabrics in suitable colours (orange, yellow, lime green, leaf green); you will need an 8in (20cm) square for each of the largest motifs
- roughly 36 x 18in (90 x 45cm) bonding web, or the equivalent in smaller pieces
- if you'd like to edge your patches with machine stitching, suitable threads in toning or contrasting colours. (If you want to work satin stitch around the patches, you'll also need a tearaway foundation fabric or plain white paper)
- sewing thread for the piecing and to match the backing/binding, and your choice of hand or machine quilting threads
- 25in (64cm) square of flat wadding
- 28in (71cm) square of backing fabric in a colour to complement the other fabrics; this will fold over the edges of the quilt to create the binding.
- pencil, paper scissors
- extra fabric for a casing, or ribbon or tape to create hanging loops

Instructions

1 On the paper side of the bonding web, trace the following shapes:

- – one large lemon, two medium lemons and four small ones
- – four medium limes and five small ones
- – two large oranges, five medium ones, and four small ones
- – seven leaves
- – two inner orange segments
- – two outer orange segments

TIP

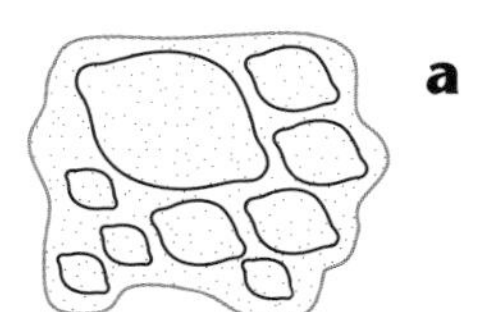

If you position all the same fruit shapes (eg all the lemons) near each other as you trace, you can cut and fuse them as a group.

2 Cut each group out roughly (**a**), and fuse them onto the wrong sides of the relevant fabrics; once they're fused, cut them out along the marked lines (**b**).

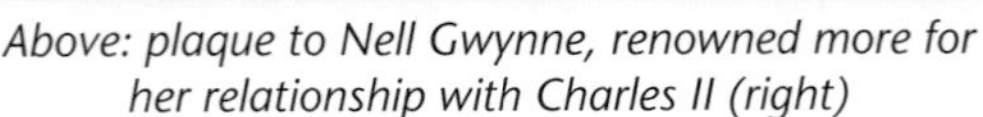
Above: plaque to Nell Gwynne, renowned more for her relationship with Charles II (right)

3 Lay the background squares and rectangles out in a pleasing fashion; as you can see, each quarter of the quilt consists of one square, one small rectangle and one large rectangle (**c**), but the individual patches don't have to be in the positions that I've put them. Join the patches to create four blocks (**d**), then join the blocks to create the quilt top (**e**).

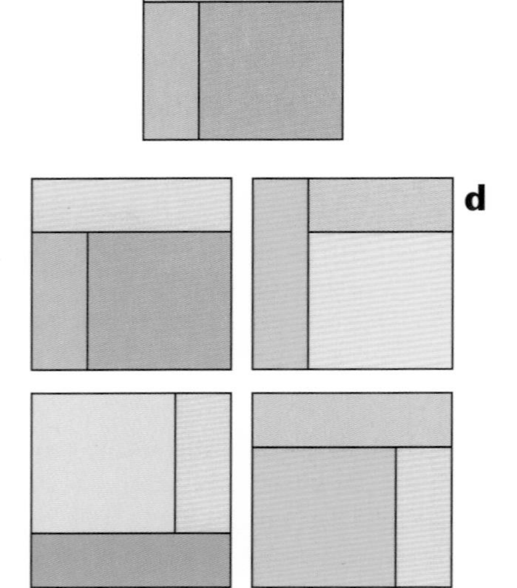

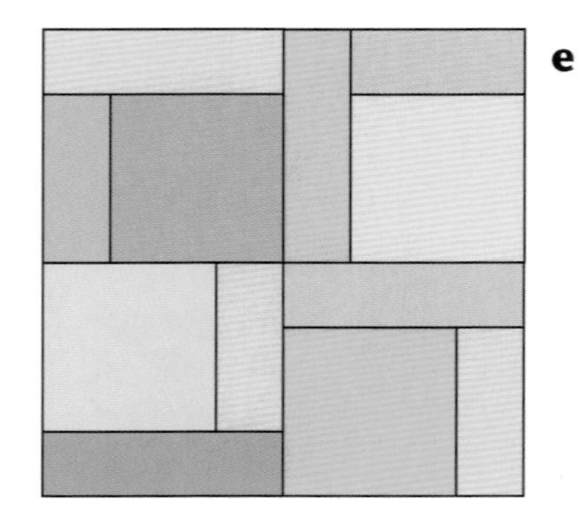

4 Peel the papers off the motifs and lay them out on the squares and rectangles to create a well-balanced design; once you're happy with the arrangement, pin the motifs in place and then fuse them in position (**f**). (The patches for the outer orange segments are fused on top of the inner patches.)

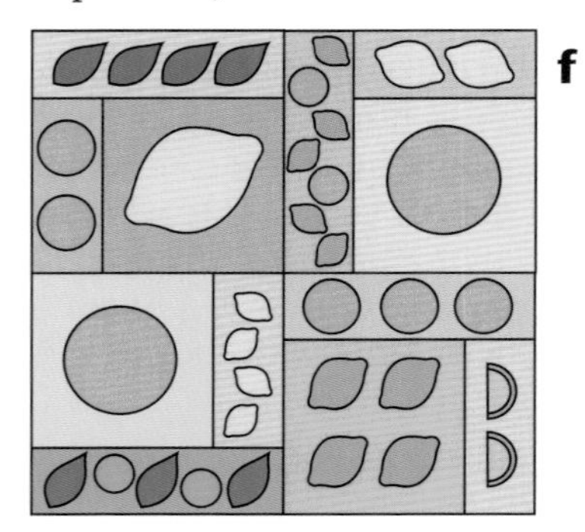

5 If you want to stitch around the motifs, this is the time to do it; I used a machine blanket stitch (**g**).

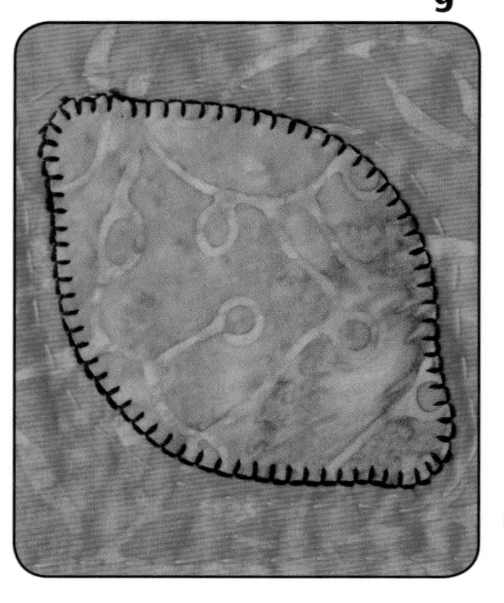

Trim the wadding to the same size as the quilt top if necessary, then lay the backing fabric on a flat surface, right side down. Position the wadding on top so that there's an even border of fabric all the way around, then lay the quilt top, right side up, on the wadding (**h**). Use your preferred method to secure the layers (see p136), then quilt the design as you wish by hand or machine.

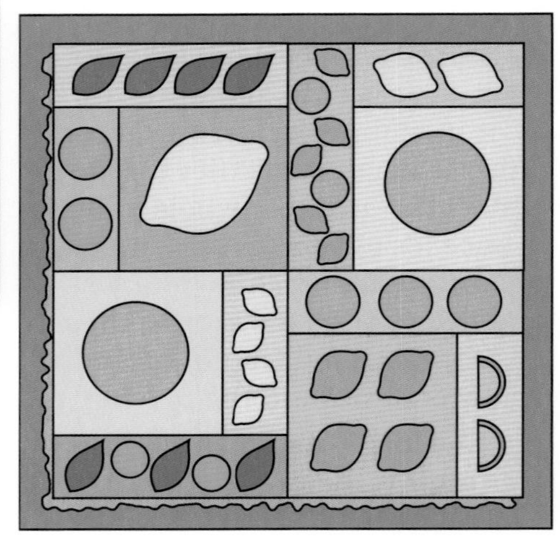

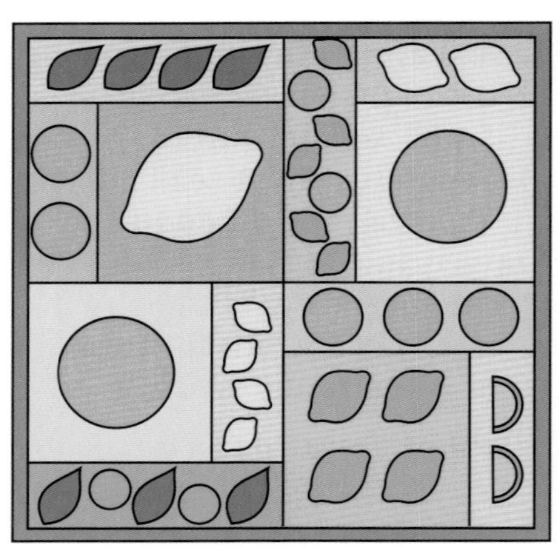

6 Fold the backing fabric over to the front of the quilt in a double fold (**i**), mitring the corners neatly. Stitch the folded edge by hand or machine. Add a casing on the back, or hanging loops of ribbon or tape.

VARIATION

This wall-hanging doesn't have to be square; if you prefer, you can stitch the blocks together into a long rectangle – either portrait or landscape format. The motifs would look lovely on cushion-covers for summer chairs; make one block for each cover, then add borders cut from a citrus-coloured print fabric.

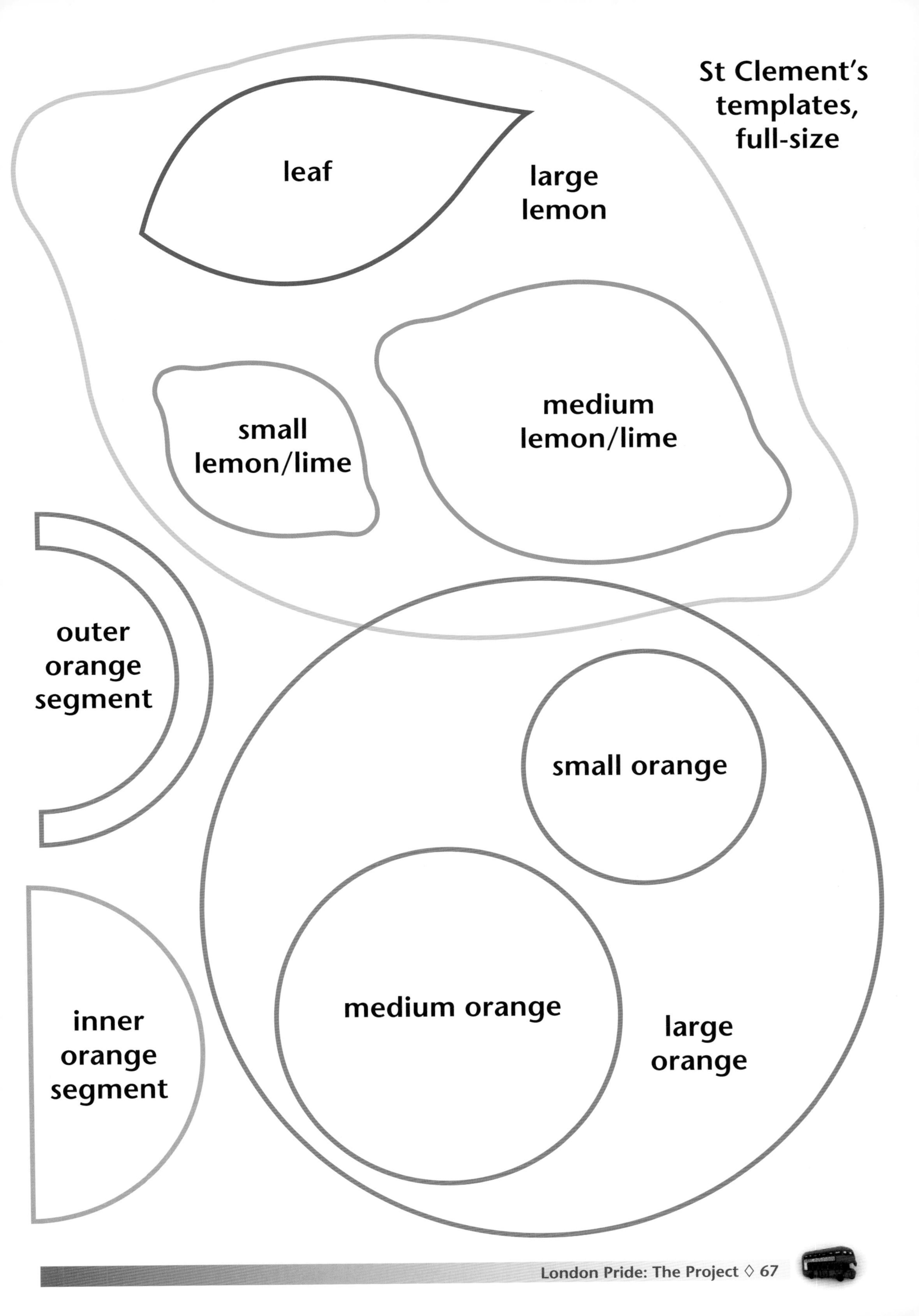
St Clement's templates, full-size
leaf
large lemon
small lemon/lime
medium lemon/lime
outer orange segment
small orange
medium orange
large orange
inner orange segment

The Heart of the Village

A celebration of two crucial parts of our heritage: folk arts, and the traditional pub sign!

Folk art is generally defined as art practised by peasants or labourers. In contrast to the fine arts, such as painting and sculpture, folk arts and crafts – while they may be very attractive – generally have a practical purpose: trug-making, basket-weaving, coracle making, smocking, quilting, patchwork. Many traditional arts and crafts, as well as occupations, have given us classic British surnames: Thatcher, Cooper, Carver, Fletcher, Chandler, Painter, Pargetter. Perhaps in future centuries families will bear the names Banker, Programmer, Couch-Potato?

ABOVE: detail of the Stoney Middleton well-dressing (see p4), used by kind permission of the village's well-dressing committee; TOP RIGHT: the village symbol of Abinger Hammer in Surrey

Villages are the custodians of our folk art, and also of our folk customs: morris dancing, beating the bounds, well dressing and maypole dancing, for instance. Some of these customs are extremely strange: every year in Gloucestershire, a cheese is rolled down Cooper's Hill and chased by the villagers; the winner gets to keep the cheese (perhaps the origin of the phrase the Big Cheese, see p87!). Gurning contests, a peculiarly English pastime, involve pulling your face into grotesque grimaces.

And the actual names of our villages are simply a delight – a pot-pourri of Gaelic, Norse, Anglo-Saxon, Old English and Norman roots, plus added local influences and words. Some prefixes or suffixes appear over and over again, eg –burgh, –burg, –chester, –cester and –caster, all meaning castle. Many Irish (and some Scottish) names begin with bally- or bal-, not surprisingly as it means farm or village. When I went to school in Cornwall we were taught the rhyme

by Tre, Pol and Pen
you will know Cornishmen,

because so many Cornish place-names begin with those prefixes: Polperro, Tregonning, Polzeath, Penzance etc. Some names, though, stand alone: Spital-in-the-Street, Curry Mallet, Wigwig, Higher Thrushgill, Appletreewick, Queen Camel, Epping Upland, and my all-time favourite, Huish Episcopi. Some sound rather dubious: the residents of Titty Ho in Northamptonshire must get tired of saying where they live, as must those who live in Thong (in Kent), and Butt Lane in Newcastle. Westward Ho! in Devon is the only British village name to end in an exclamation mark.

And, of course, the heart of any village is the pub. There are some common pub names that appear all over the country, such as The Red Lion, The King's Arms, The White Horse. Many pubs are named after the Marquis of Granby – because he provided money for demobbed soldiers to set up drinking establishments. Others relate in some way to alcohol production: The Malt Shovel, The Barley Mow. Other pub names are more unusual. Pubs called The Bishop's Finger originally only appeared in Kent; they related not to a cleric's digit, but to the fingerposts that marked the Pilgrim's Way (see p78).

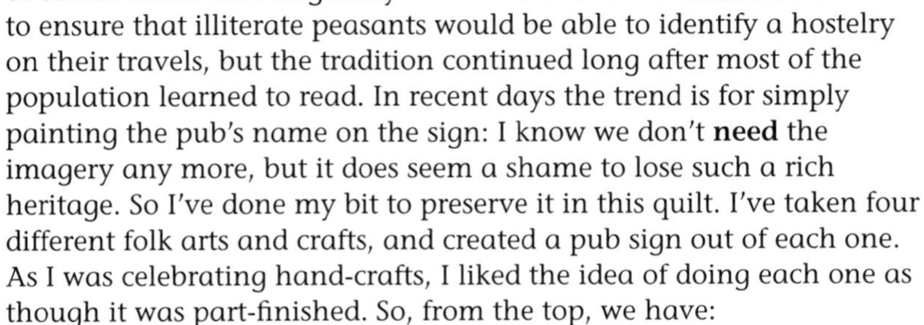

For centuries we've had a great tradition of painted pub signs; of course these were originally to ensure that illiterate peasants would be able to identify a hostelry on their travels, but the tradition continued long after most of the population learned to read. In recent days the trend is for simply painting the pub's name on the sign: I know we don't **need** the imagery any more, but it does seem a shame to lose such a rich heritage. So I've done my bit to preserve it in this quilt. I've taken four different folk arts and crafts, and created a pub sign out of each one. As I was celebrating hand-crafts, I liked the idea of doing each one as though it was part-finished. So, from the top, we have:

- The Pear Tree, done as a jigsaw puzzle. A London mapmaker, John Spilsbury, is credited with commercialising jigsaws around the year 1760.
- The Castle, painted in the style of folk painting known as Castles and Roses. This style is particularly associated with canal art, where the designs are painted on the side panels and bows of the narrowboats.
- The White Hart, created in a well-dressing style with flowers and leaves. Well-dressing is a Derbyshire custom that involves pressing flowers and leaves into soft clay to create pictures, which are then used to decorate the wellheads. As you might guess, the origins are in ancient folk religion, but the custom has been blended with Christianity in recent centuries.
- The Cross Keys, another popular pub name, depicted in traditional English patchwork. The shapes for English patchwork are made by tacking the fabric patches over paper templates; in years gone by old letters, bills of sale, catalogues etc would be used. I've left some of the patches on top of the design, and one of them includes an excerpt from Jane Austen's letter to her sister Cassandra, which asks her to bring more fabric for the quilt they were working on.

Inside information

*There's a recent book by Bob Mills called **British Folk Art**; you'll find details on britishfolkart.org.uk/. Compton Verney, owned by the National Trust, houses the UK's largest collection of folk art: www.comptonverney.org.uk/?page=collections/britishFolkArt.*

*For plenty of info on living on a narrowboat, go to www.canaljunction.com/; www.cheese-rolling.co.uk/ is the official site of the Cooper's Hill festival. **Well Dressing in Derbyshire**, by Roy Christian, is a colourful booklet packed with examples of the craft.*

Materials

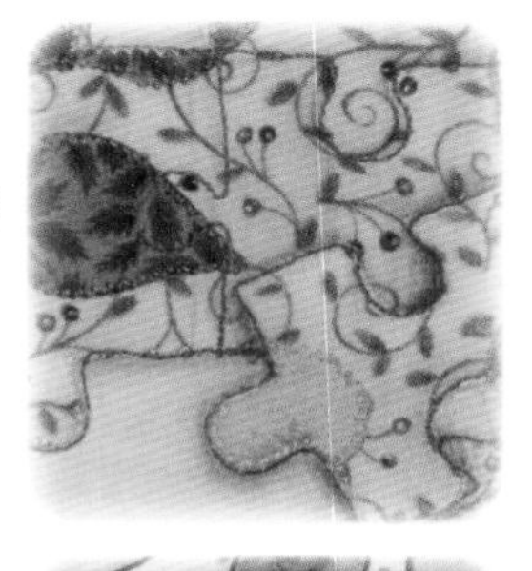

Most of the fabrics are cotton, but I've also used a bonded gold fabric on the keys, and black net to produce little shadows behind the 'spare' patchwork shapes – which are stiffened with tearaway foundation fabric. The well-dressing design is created in flower and leaf shapes, cut from guipure lace and coloured with fabric paint; I also used fabric paint for all of the Castle panel, and to create detail on the Pear Tree design.

Techniques

The Pear Tree panel was stitched using machine appliqué, and quilted by machine in red buttonhole thread to create the jigsaw-piece design. The Castle sign was painted, then contour-quilted by machine. I worked the outlines for the White Hart panels in a decorative machine stitch, then filled the spaces in with the guipure motifs. Finally, the patchwork background for the Cross Keys was stitched by hand; the keys and lettering were appliquéd by machine.

Backing and binding

The White Hart is backed with a suitable print in red, gold and white; the other panels are showcases for two fabrics from the Nutex Britannia range featuring British pub signs and pub drinks! The bindings are two different brown fabrics, to create the idea of wooden frames for the signs.

PROJECT

Cornucopia Quilt

Folk art often features fruit and grains, and on this quilt a veritable fruit salad is spilling out of a cornucopia – the symbol of plenty – surrounded by ears of wheat. The stencil-style design is achieved using shadow quilting (or shadow appliqué); the coloured patches are trapped between the white background and a sheer layer, then edged with hand stitching which also quilts the work. I used crystal organza for the top layer; this technique works well with muslin (American: cheesecloth) too.

finished size 42in (108cm) square

You will need:

- 42in (108cm) square white or pale cream background fabric
- 42in (108cm) square sheer white or cream fabric
- 42in (108cm) square flat wadding
- 42in (108cm) square backing fabric (this can be the same as the background fabric, or something different)
- cotton fabrics for the appliqué patches:
  - 16in (41cm) square of tan (basket)
  - 7in (18cm) square of purple (grapes)
  - 8in (20cm) square of ochre (pineapple)
  - 9 x 6in (23 x 15cm) of dark orange (pumpkin)
  - 2in (5cm) square of brown (pumpkin top)
  - 5 x 10in (13 x 25cm) of green/red (apples)
  - 6in (15cm) square of russet green (pears)
  - 7in (18cm) square of dark red (pomegranates)
  - 7 x 6in (18 x 15cm) of orange (oranges)
  - 5in (13cm) square of mid orange (tangerines)
  - 6 x 4in (15 x 10cm) of dark green (figs)
  - 5 x 4in (13 x 10cm) of purple/pink (plums)
  - 4in (10cm) square of yellow (lemons)
  - 2½in (6cm) square of lime green (lime)
  - 6 x 3in (15 x 8cm) of peachy-pink (peaches)
  - 5in (13cm) square of red (strawberries)
  - 4in (10cm) square of dark red (cherries)
  - 7 x 4in (18 x 10cm) mid green (cherry, apple and pear leaves)
  - 7 x 4in (18 x 10cm) darker green (pineapple and strawberry tops)
  - 31 x 20in (80 x 50cm) pale tan (wheat ears)
- sheet of dressmakers' tracing paper, at least 36in (92cm) square
- 1¾yd (1.5m) bonding web (buy this from an 18in-wide roll)
- pencil, long ruler, black felt pen
- sewing threads to match the fabric patches (or use white or cream throughout, if you prefer)
- 12in (30cm) x width of the fabric for binding the quilt

Instructions

1 Draw a grid of six by six 6in (15cm) squares onto the tracing paper, and follow the instructions on page 135 to enlarge the Cornucopia template (**a**). Number the parts of the basket, the grapes, the cherries, the strawberries, the sections of the pumpkin and the sections of the pineapple, as shown on the template. Write FRONT on this side of the tracing paper.

a

TIP

Use dressmakers' tracing paper so that the lines of the design show on both the front and the back of the paper; this helps when you're tracing the shapes onto the bonding web.

2 Turn the paper over, and trace all the different parts of the design onto the paper side of the bonding web; group the shapes for the same fruits (eg, all the cherries, all the figs) near each other, so that you can work with them as a group. Write in the numbers too. Cut each group out roughly, outside the marked lines (**b**).

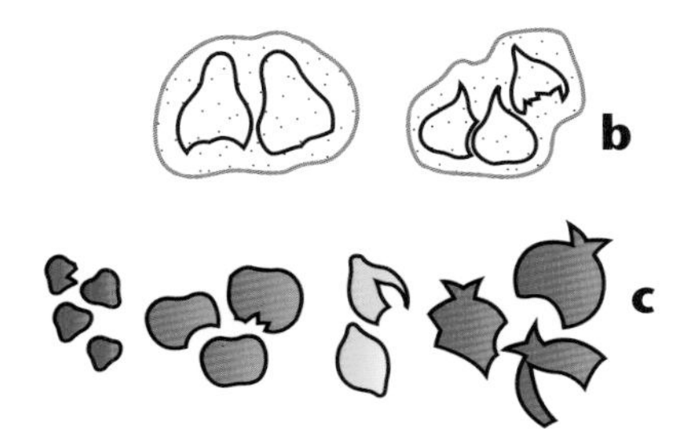

3 Fuse the bonding web shapes onto the backs of the relevant fabrics, and cut the shapes out along the marked lines (**c**).

4 Press the background fabric. Lay the full-size template right side up on a flat surface, and position the background fabric on top, right side up, so that there's an even border of fabric around the edge of the template. Pin the two layers in position; you should be able to see the template through the fabric.

5 Peel the papers off the back of the fabric patches and lay them in position on the background fabric; the numbers will help you to position the bits of pineapple, grapes etc on the correct parts of the design. Work on one part of the design at a time (eg, all the bits of the basket); when you're happy with the placing, fuse the patches in position, then go on to the next section of the design. Carry on this way until all the patches are fused in position (**d**).

d

6 Lay the backing fabric right side down on a flat surface, then cover it with the wadding; position the appliqué design on top, right side up, and cover this with the sheer fabric (**e**).

e

Use your preferred method to secure the layers (see p136). Beginning from the centre and working outwards, quilt around each patch (**f,** *overleaf*) using running stitch (if you're stitching by hand), or machine straight stitch.

7 Once all the quilting is done, trim the edges of the quilt if necessary. Cut the binding fabric into four strips, each 3in (7.5cm) wide x the width of the fabric, and join these into one long strip; follow the instructions on page 136 to bind the quilt.

Below: Maypole dancing in Sompting, 1914.
Image ref PC004032 West Sussex County Council Library Service, www.westsussexpast.org.uk

f

VARIATION

If you'd like a smaller quilt, just use the central cornucopia design without the ears of grain around the edges; this will give you a quilt roughly 30in (approx 75cm) square. You can also fabric-paint the design rather than using shadow quilting. The wheat ear shapes themselves would work well as a harvest motif; put several together in a sheaf, or use two to bracket a simpler fruit design.

Cornucopia Quilt template; enlarge to 36in (90cm) square

Caledonia

A celebration of all the good things found in the land of the thistle.

Scotland has been settled for many thousands of years; a neolithic farmstead on Papa Westray, in Orkney, is believed to be the oldest surviving house in northern Europe. By the time of the Roman occupation (see p109), the Scots were known as Caledonians, a name that apparently can be translated roughly as 'big tough people.' Living up to their name, they kept up a campaign of constant attacks; Hadrian's Wall was famously built to keep the Scots out of the rest of Britannia, as the Romans called the British Isles. When this 80-mile-long barricade kept being breached, the Antonine Wall was added, further up the country – but still didn't always do the job.

Scotland emerged as a sovereign state (as opposed to an informal alliance of tribes) in the middle ages, and remained that way until it became part of the United Kingdom under the Treaty of Union in 1707. Throughout Scottish history heroes (and occasional heroines) have emerged – particularly celebrated for repelling the English, or recapturing strongholds held by them. William Wallace (played by Mel Gibson in the film ***Braveheart***) was Guardian of Scotland for a spell, but was eventually executed by Edward I of England. Robert the Bruce (Robert I of Scotland) led a force against the English invaders for over 20 years; one of his most famous victories was the Battle of Bannockburn in 1314. The Abbey in Dunfermline, site of his tomb, bears his name carved in giant letters into the tower (see above). Mary Queen of Scots hoped to accede to the throne of England too, but this didn't go down too well with her cousin Elizabeth (see p39), who eventually had her executed. Rob Roy became a folk hero in the early 18th century as a kind of Scottish Robin Hood.

The patron saint of Scotland is St Andrew; according to legend, Óengus II, in the year 832, led a force of Picts and Scots against a strong force of Angles (I think I'm sensing a theme here …). On the eve of battle, during prayer, he vowed that if he was victorious he would appoint Andrew as the patron saint of Scotland. The next morning, apparently clouds arranged themselves across the sky in

The beautiful Falkirk Wheel, which dramatically joins two Scottish canals

an X shape, and this gave rise to emblem and distinctive colours of the saltire, the Scottish flag. Perhaps the best-known figurehead for Scottish independence, though, was Bonnie Prince Charlie, the Young Pretender. He was the focus of the Jacobite attempt to restore the Stuart line to the thrones of Scotland and England. Late one long midsummer evening we visited the site of his troops' final stand, on Culloden Moor; it was very moving seeing the Graves of the Clans, over which according to tradition the heather never grows, out of respect for the dead. After this defeat many distinctively Scottish symbols, such as wearing the tartan, were banned – and all bagpipes had to be surrendered as they were considered a weapon of war!

Scotland is also famous for its poets – both good and bad. Rabbie (Robert) Burns is sometimes called Scotland's Favourite Son. Some of his best-known poems are ***To a Mouse***, ***Tam o' Shanter***, and ***Auld Lang Syne***; this last one is sung at Hogmanay, the Scottish New Year's Eve celebration, a tradition which has spread well outside Scotland. Burns Night is celebrated on January 25th, his birthday, and Burns Suppers include a reading of his poem ***Address to a Haggis***. William Topaz McGonagall is rather a contrast: Wikipedia says of his poetry that it's 'widely regarded as some of the worst in British history.' Here's the ending of his best-known work, ***The Tay Bridge Disaster***:

> *'... for the stronger we our houses do build,*
> *the less chance we have of being killed.'*

Who can argue with that?

So, from all the history, natural beauty, wealth of poetry and folk songs, heroes and heroines – what was I going to choose to go on my Scottish quilt? The Scots sometimes get fed up with the 'touristy' vision of the country – all tartan, bagpipes, Loch Ness Monsters and shortbread; and yet those things too are part of Scotland. I decided to have a brainstorming session and simply write down all the things that I could possibly include: Evelyn Glennie, the Road to the Isles, Highland cattle, skean dhu, machair, oystercatchers, Muriel Spark, porridge, Eilean Donan, the Forth Bridges, reivers, Melrose Abbey, strathspeys, first-footing, Ben Nevis, spurtles, cullen skink, Scapa Flow, petticoat tails, House for an Art Lover, puffins, Loch Lomond, Sauchiehall Street ... There were so many, it was becoming ridiculous. So, the obvious answer was to include them all!

Inside information

To explore everything about Rabbie Burns, go to www.robertburns.org/. You can read more about (and of) McGonagall's poetry on www.mcgonagall-online.org.uk/.

Materials

The outer border of the quilt is created from satin, sheer and metallic ribbons in various different colours and widths; the inner section is cotton fabric, decorated with fabric paint.

Techniques

To create the outer border I wove the ribbons in a pleasing arrangement, layering some of the wider ones with sheer ribbons on the top for variety. To hold the weaving in position, and to quilt it, I ran lines of wavy machine stitching down the length of the woven strip, using variegated purple/green thread.

On the mauve central fabric I drew the outlines of the word CALEDONIA (an old name for Scotland, see p73), then filled the shape by writing in fabric pen all the items on my brainstorming list. Where there was the odd gap, I filled it with a little drawn thistle, and I highlighted a few areas with purple glittery fabric paint. I positioned the decorated fabric over the weaving and zigzagged round the edges; after I'd cut away the excess fabric outside the lettering, I then edged all the letters with a wide machine satin stitch, then machine-quilted just inside the letters using invisible thread.

Backing and binding

A dark tartan fabric makes a good backing for the quilt, and the binding is made from bias strips of another tartan; I rounded the corners of the quilt to echo the soft outlines of the lettering.

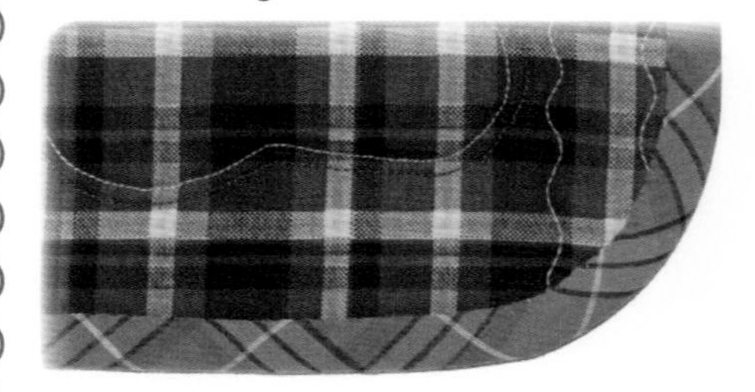

PROJECT

Scottish Landscape

The Caledonian hills and glens, often hidden in mist, are studies in greens, greys, browns and heather colours, perhaps with the sun glinting on a river or loch. I've captured these in an atmospheric landscape, built up from patches of tweedy fabrics in soft Scottish colours; pick muted beiges, browns, greys, lavenders and greens, with a touch of delicate blue-grey for the skies. Lovely slubby yarns create texture, and a friend donated some silk balls in matching soft colours (thankyou Rosemary!), which made great rocks at the bottom; a sheep appliqué provides the finishing touch.

finished size: 14 x 36in (36 x 90cm)

You will need:

- two pieces of loosely-woven background fabric, eg hessian, each one 14 x 36in (36 x 90cm)
- one piece of flat wadding 14 x 36in (36 x 90cm)
- rough-cut rectangles of about 25 different fabrics in soft landscape colours; I made each one 8-9in (20-22cm) long and 2-3in (5-8cm) high
- toning hand or machine embroidery threads
- textured yarns in colours to tone with the fabrics, plus threads to couch them down
- sewing thread to match the background fabric
- embellishments (sheep or flower buttons/charms, Scottish piper etc!)
- extra fabric strip for making a hanging sleeve

Instructions

1 On each edge of the woven background fabric, pull a thread about 1in (2.5cm) in from each edge as shown (**a**); this will create the area for the central design.

2 Lay the background fabric on a flat surface, and decide which fabric patch to use where. Begin with the pale blue pieces at the top, to depict the sky, then move down through the mauve and green patches to depict heather-covered hillsides; I put these pieces at angles to echo this idea of hills (**b**).

3 Add silvery/grey/white patches to create the idea of water, then move down into brown shades at the bottom, to produce earth and fields (**c**). Lay the patches out roughly, and reposition them as necessary, overlapping them in an interesting design; make sure that all the patches are well within the rectangle made by the pulled threads. Once you're happy with the layout, pin the fabrics in place.

4 Lay the backing fabric down on a flat surface, and cover it with the wadding; position the pinned design, right side up, on top. Work a few lines of tacking up and down the whole piece.

a

b

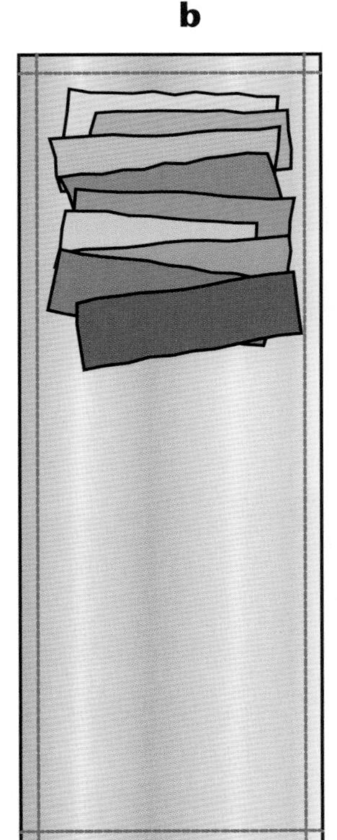

c

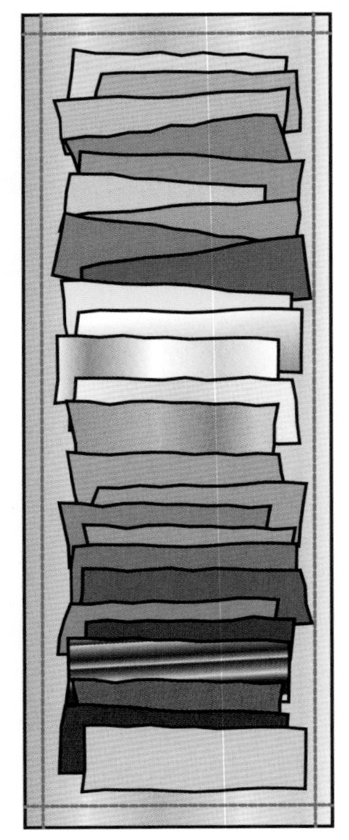

TIP

It's worth taking time to tack the pieces; if you leave the pins in, they'll keep getting in your way as you stitch the pieces down!

5 Embroider lines of decorative stitches across the design, either by hand or machine. I used a mixture of Cretan stitch, herringbone, feather stitch and large running stitches (**d** and **e**).

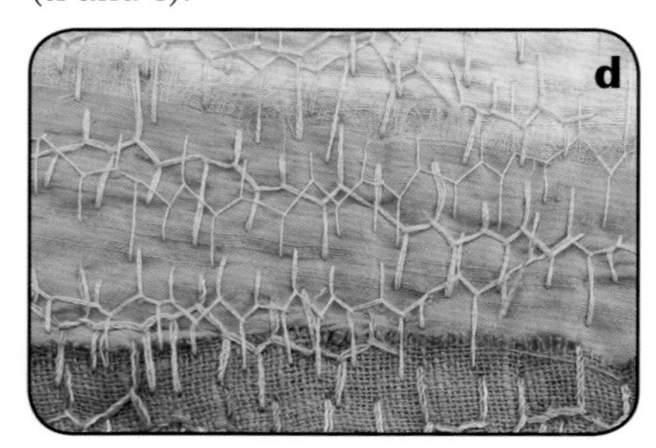

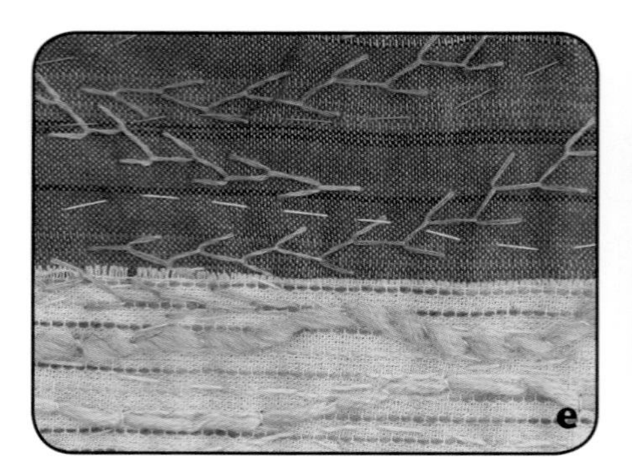

Take some of the lines out beyond the patches for variety, and finish some of them well within the patches. These lines appliqué the patches, embellish them and quilt them all in one go. Remove the tacking stitches.

6 Add lengths of textured yarns, catching them down by hand or machine (**f**); bunch them up in places, and let the lines wiggle for a naturalistic effect. Add any other motifs such as sheep, flowers etc (**g**).

7 Using a thread that matches the woven fabric, work a small zigzag stitch around the rectangle marked by the pulled threads. On the back of the work, carefully trim the backing fabric and wadding back to a few threads beyond the stitched line. Fray the edges of the panel back to ¼in (6mm) from the stitched line.

8 Add a casing at the top of the design, on the back, and slip a hanging pole through it.

VARIATION

This rough-edge appliqué idea works well for all kinds of landscapes, seascapes etc. Try using the same technique for interpreting a favourite landscape photograph; use the photo as a guide for picking your fabrics and threads, then build up the design and embellish it with suitable charms.

ABOVE: the Forth Road Bridge, and (below) the Forth Rail Bridge – or is it?!

Cathedral

Spanning a millennium of architecture, the cathedrals of Britain delight pilgrims and tourists alike.

It was a commission for a cathedral that was responsible for me becoming enthralled by textiles. When I was a young teenager I watched a documentary on the making of John Piper's tapestry for Chichester cathedral; it was woven in France in 1966, and the programme followed its progress from inspiration and design through to the finished hanging. I could hardly believe that something so breathtaking and vibrant could be created from thread. I'd already been playing about with fabric and thread for quite a few years, but that day the seeds were planted in my brain: it's possible to **stitch** pieces of art that are as breathtaking as the greatest paintings and sculptures.

Cathedrals have always been involved in commissioning great art – not only the contents of the buildings, but the buildings themselves. Our oldest cathedrals date from the 11th century, and the most glorious era of cathedral-building was during mediaeval times, when cathedrals such as Norwich, Wells (*above*), Hereford (*overleaf and p81*) and Salisbury were built. The Reformation poured a bit of cold water on the cathedral-building industry, as such flamboyant displays of wealth and opulence were frowned on as now seeming a bit Papish, but the industry was kick-started again by Christopher Wren in the late 17th century. Wren's masterpiece, St Paul's, was designed in neo-classical style; it was completed in a mere 35 years, and cost £700,000 (about £60 million in today's terms).

Coventry's Catholic cathedral is a symbolic building in many ways. The original Gothic version was fire-bombed by the Germans in 1940, and its shell still exists, next to the new building, as a poignant reminder of the war. The new cathedral was built in only six years, to a cutting-edge design created by Basil Spence; the metal spire, weighing one and a half tons, was positioned by helicopter in a matter of minutes.

Some random cathedral trivia:

• A cathedral is defined as the principal church of a diocese, which houses the 'seat,' or spiritual home, of a bishop; the word comes from the Greek *cathedra*, which means seat. Several buildings vie for the prize of being the smallest 'real' cathedral in Britain; one is Dunkeld in Scotland; another is Eglwys Gadeiriol Llanelwy (St Asaph Cathedral) in Wales.

• A city is classified as any conurbation that has a cathedral; the smallest in Britain is St David's, in Pembrokeshire, Wales, which is the size of a small village but does have a genuine cathedral. The smallest city in England is Wells, in Somerset, which is the size of a reasonable town but has a **massive** cathedral.

• Our northernmost cathedral is St Magnus, in Kirwall, Orkney; it dates from 1137, and features interesting polychrome (multicoloured) stonework. It includes a memorial to the hundreds of sailors who died when the *Royal Oak* was sunk by a German U-boat just off Orkney in 1939.

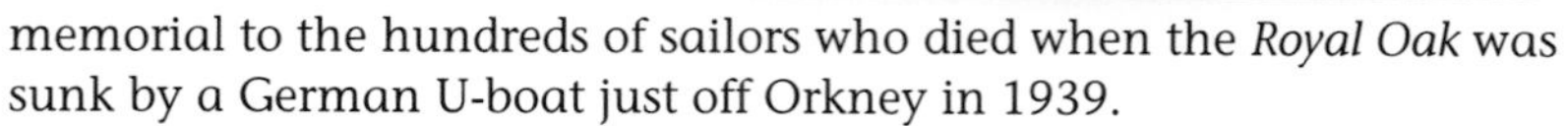

• Liverpool's Anglican cathedral is the largest in Britain (and the fifth-largest in the world). It was designed by Giles Gilbert Scott, who also designed our red phone boxes (see p62) and Battersea Power Station. Liverpool's Catholic cathedral is crowned with a unique lantern tower, designed by Frederick Gibberd; the cathedral's high altar is at the centre of the building, directly under the lantern.

• In 1170, Thomas à Becket was murdered in Canterbury Cathedral; ever since that time, people have made pilgrimages to his shrine – as celebrated by Chaucer in his ***Canterbury Tales***. Churches (including cathedrals) were traditionally places of sanctuary for criminals; if they were inside the building, they could not be arrested. (This is just one of the things that made Thomas à Becket's murder so shocking.) In Durham cathedral, the North Door has an imposing – and rather creepy-looking – door-knocker, a replica of the 12th century original; fugitives sought sanctuary by banging the knocker loudly to alert the officials.

• Fan vaulting is a particular glory of English mediaeval cathedrals; the soaring columns draw the eyes upwards, and the roof itself seems to float in the air. Gloucester cathedral has the earliest examples, dating from roughly 1351; the largest fan vault in the world is the roof of King's College Chapel in Cambridge.

I've tried to reflect some aspects of this magnificent history in my quilt. I've kept to the favourite mediaeval colour-scheme of scarlet, royal blue and gold with touches of emerald green, and picked up details from Gothic windows (including rose windows), floor tiles, decorative goldwork and ceiling bosses. Although I'm sure that grandiose human ambition had a hand in lots of the creations, ideally cathedrals were built for the glory of God, so I've incorporated that into the lettering: GLORIA IN EXCELSIS DEO.

Inside information

The BBC history site has a good basic introduction to cathedrals generally, and some of our most famous examples: go to www.bbc.co.uk/history/british/architecture_cathedral_01.shtml. For a comprehensive list of all the cathedrals in Britain, with links to all their websites, go to www.mybritain.com/cathedrals.htm; another good site is www.cathedralsplus.org.uk/.

Materials

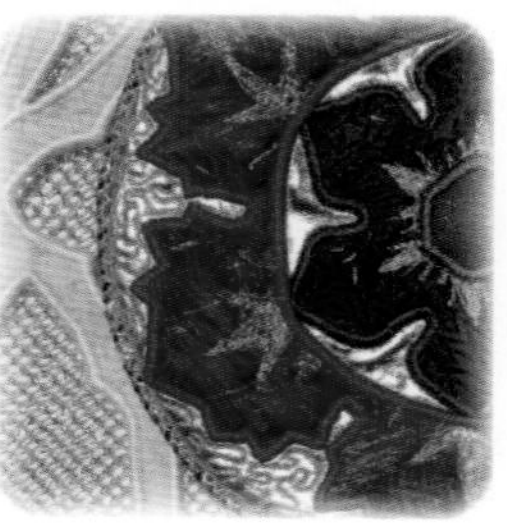

Most of the fabrics in this quilt are cotton, including various ones with gold overprinting to give the sumptuous effect I was looking for. I've also used gold fabric (including a gold mesh in the panes of the arched window), and various metallic embellishments, as well as gold, pearl and coloured beads. The ceiling boss and the gold motifs are stiffened with thick interfacing, and I used gold thread to edge and embroider various sections of the design.

Techniques

The gold motifs and arched window are created using machine cutwork. The other parts of the design were built up using standard and reverse machine appliqué, machine piecing, and English patchwork over papers. Embellishing techniques include machine quilting, foiling and hand-embroidered seeding stitches; the fleurs-de-lys at the top were stamped in gold fabric paint.

Backing and binding

The different parts of the quilt are bound in different ways, including conventional binding for the large Gothic tile, machine satin stitch for many of the motifs, and metallic braid circling the ceiling boss. I left the edges of several panels rough, to reflect the ancient history of the buildings. The ceiling boss is backed with a cathedral print.

PROJECT

Rose Window Wall-Hanging

My mother, who was also a quilter, used to stitch beautiful quilts inspired by the rose windows of our cathedrals, and I decided to make some of her designs live on through this quick-and-easy version. The lovely rich panel is very quick to assemble (the coloured patches are fused onto the background), then you can machine-quilt your design as you wish. You can make your panel all in one striking fabric as I have done, or or in any mixture of bold or subtle fabrics.

finished size: roughly 23in (58cm) square

You will need:

- If you're using one spectacular fabric (such as a bright batik or print) for all the different parts of the design, as I've done, you will need ½yd (50cm) of fabric. If you're using lots of different fabrics for the patches, you'll need 5-10 toning fat quarters or large scraps.
- 24in square of cotton background fabric; choose a good contrast to your fabric patches, either darker or lighter. (This fabric can be plain or mottled, or have a subtle print; choose something that doesn't detract from the fabrics you'll be using for the patches.) Note that a fat quarter isn't quite large enough for these 24in square pieces.
- 24in square of backing fabric (this can be the same as the front, or different)
- 24in square of compressed wadding (any of the flattish, felted-type waddings will do)
- roughly 30in piece of double-sided bonding web
- to bind the finished design you'll need a 100in (228cm) strip of contrasting fabric, 2in (5cm) wide, or four separate 25 x 2in (64 x 5cm) strips
- sewing thread to match the binding
- small and large fabric scissors
- paper scissors, pencil
- clear template plastic (minimum A4 size)
- your choice of quilting thread(s)
- rotary cutter, board and long quilt rule
- extra fabric strip for a hanging casing, or ribbon or fabric for hanging loops
- optional embellishments for your design can include beads, buttons, charms, jewels etc

Instructions

1 Trace templates A-D onto the template plastic and cut them out (**a**). Use these to trace 12 of shape A, 12 of shape B, 4 of shape C and one of shape D onto the paper side of the bonding web.

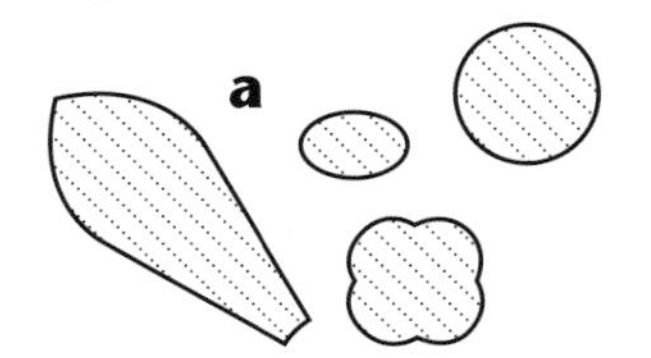

b

2 If you're using the same fabric for all the patches, don't cut the shapes out; simply fuse the bonding web onto the wrong side of the fabric. If you are using different fabrics for your patches, cut the bonding web shapes out roughly, outside the marked lines; you can cut them in groups if several shapes are going onto the same fabric (**b**). Once all your shapes are fused onto the relevant fabric(s), cut them all out along the marked lines (**c**).

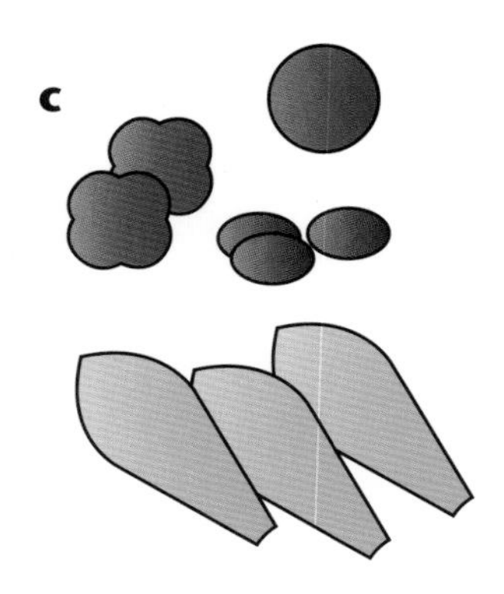

3 Press the square of background fabric, then fold it accurately in half and press (**d**), then into quarters and press (**e**). Fold this square accurately into three to create the ice-cream cone shape shown (**f**); the point of the cone is the centre of the folded square. Press all the folds to set them.

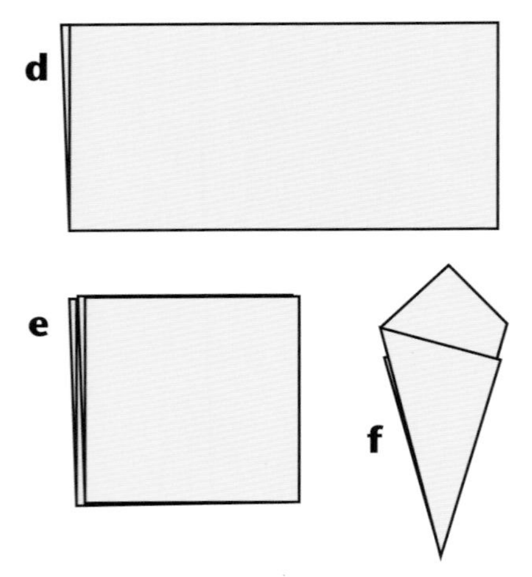

4 Unfold the background fabric and lay it on a flat surface (**g**). Peel all the papers off the backs of the fabric patches and follow the diagram to lay them out on the background (**h**); use the pressed folds to help you align the patches evenly. If necessary, use the quilt rule to check that the various patches are an equal distance from the centre.

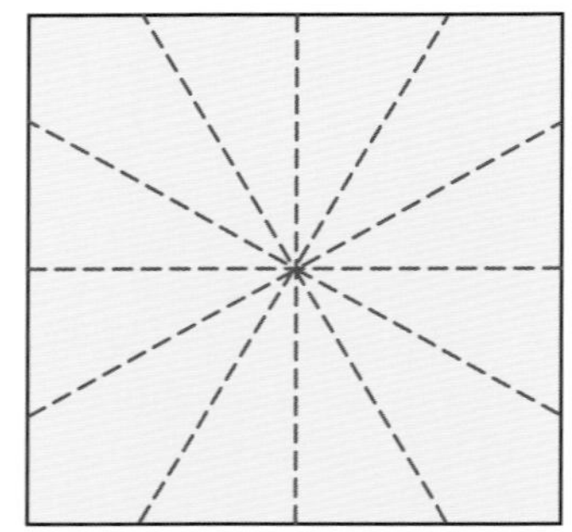

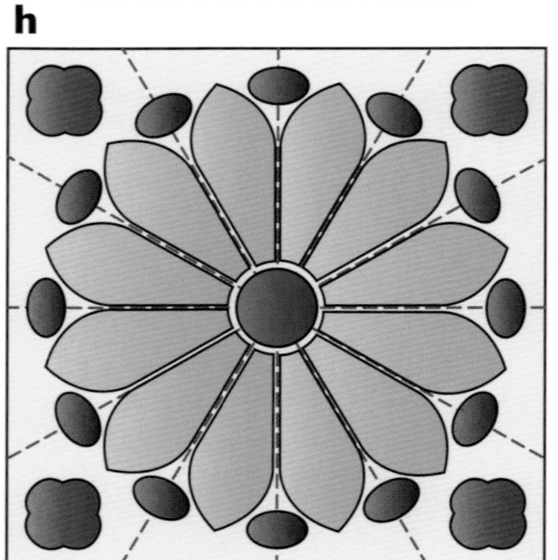

Once you're happy with the positioning, pin all the patches in place. Take the design to the ironing board; unpin a few patches at a time and fuse them in place, until your design is complete; this will also press out the straight creases you used as placement guides.

TIP

Position all the patches before you start pinning; if you pin lots of the patches in place and then decide to move them, you have to unpin them all and start again!

5 Lay the backing fabric right side down on a flat surface and lay the wadding on top, raw edges aligned; cover the wadding with the fused design, right side up (**i**), and use your preferred method (see p136) to secure the layers. Now stitch your chosen machine quilting design across the quilt; I used wavy vertical lines at uneven intervals. Just ensure that each patch has several lines of machining across it to guarantee that it is securely attached.

6 Trim the design down to an accurate square, then bind the edges (**j**) using either a continuous binding strip or four separate strips. To hang the quilt, add a hidden casing on the back, or stitch on hanging loops of ribbon or fabric.

VARIATION

This design also looks really good in Christmassy fabrics; once the pieces are fused in place and quilted, you can add all kinds of lovely seasonal embellishments such as charms, sequins and beads. Or use lots of different springtime, or summery, or autumnal fabrics to create the design – like a seasonal scrap quilt.

Detail of Lichfield Cathedral's facade

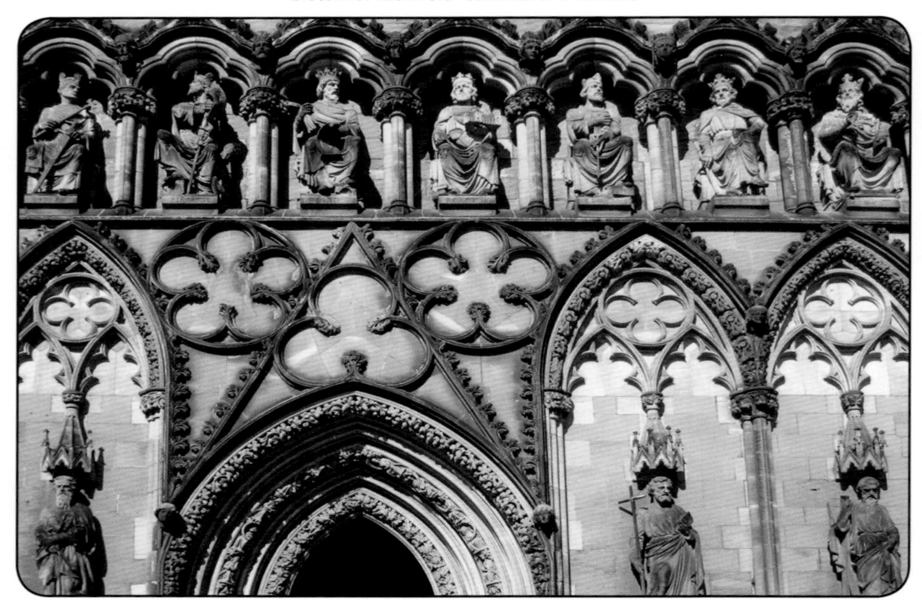

Rose Window templates, full-size

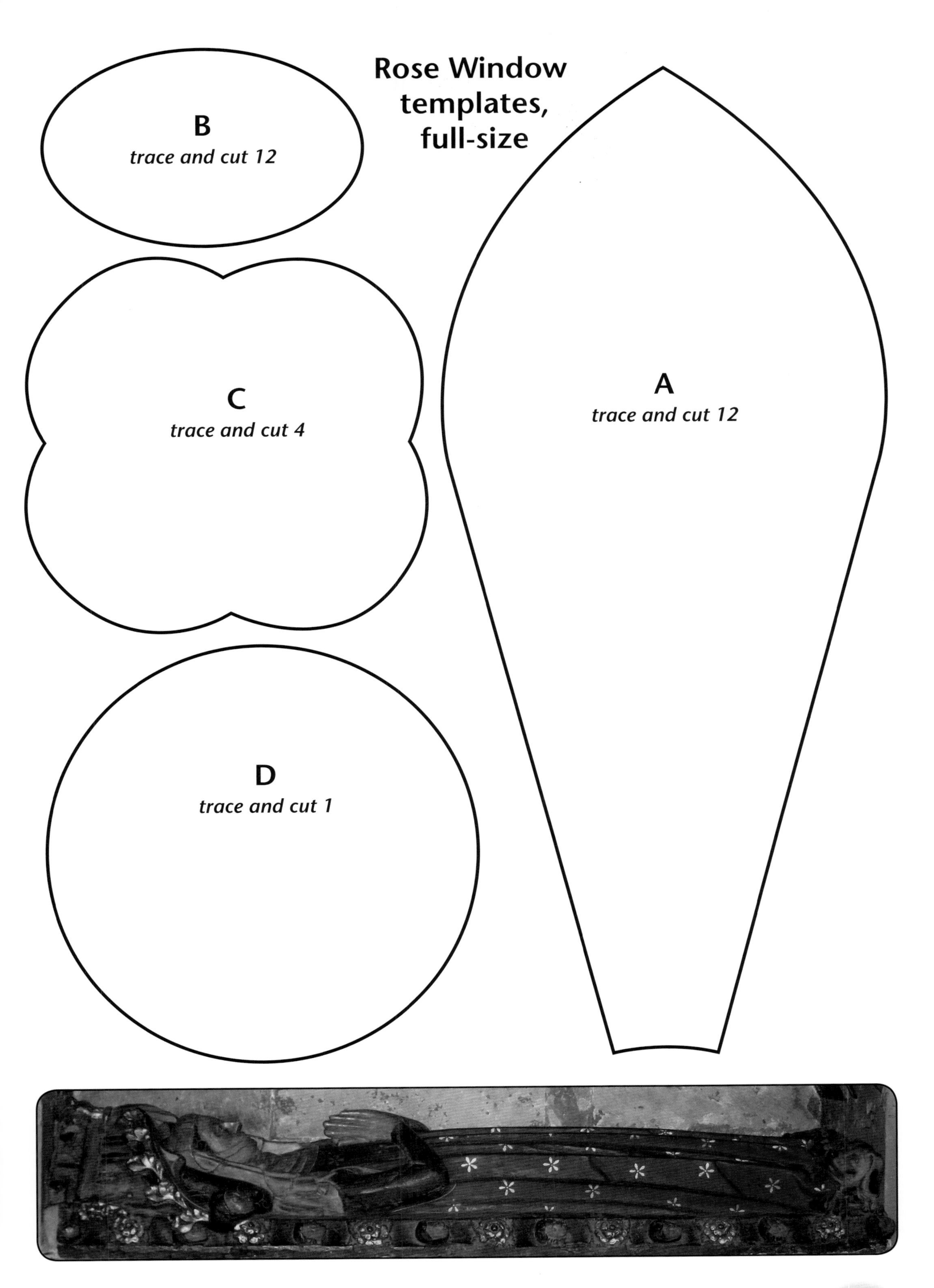

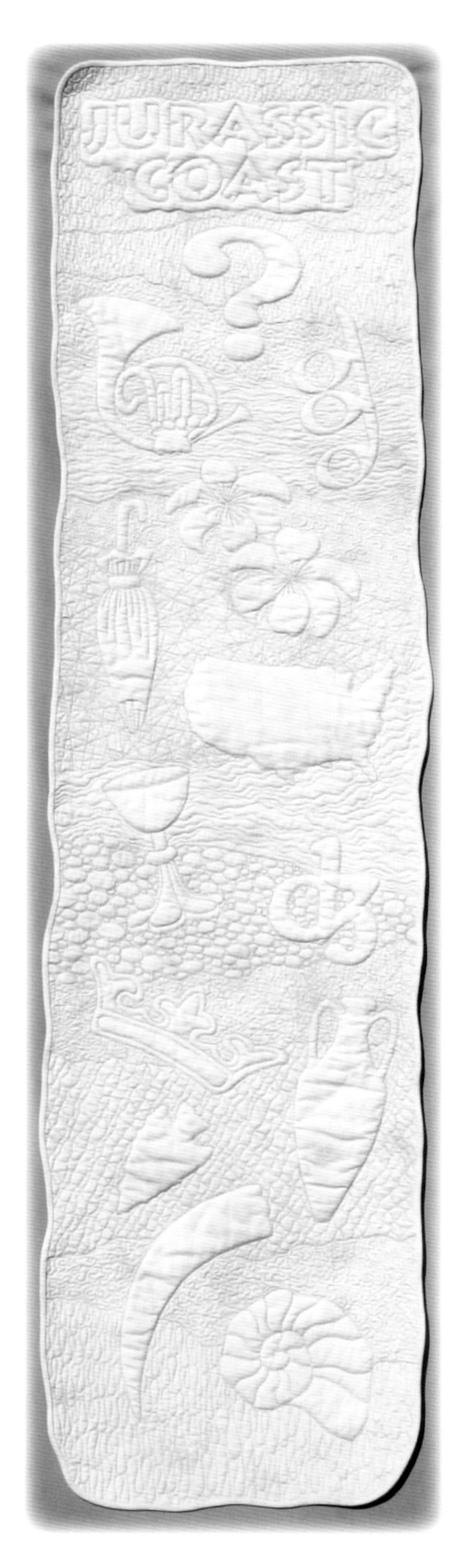

Jurassic Coast

Archaeological strata can reveal more than we suspect …

Of course the story of the British Isles begins much further back than even our earliest ancestors: all over the islands, geological traces can be found of our ancient history. For such a small area geographically, we have a very rich and varied geological heritage. Tectonic plates have shifted and clashed, volcanoes have erupted and spat out new mountain ranges, sea levels have risen and fallen, depositing various materials on top of the bedrock, and temperatures have peaked and crashed, producing everything from heatwaves to glaciers (sounds like a typical year's weather – see p12!)

The oldest rocks in Britain are found mainly in north-west Scotland and the Channel Islands; the youngest bedrock is in south-east England. Each rock layer tells its own chapter of the earth's biography, and where the land-mass has tipped, or been eroded, we can often view several of these layers together. For many amateur geologists, of course, the great prizes are fossils, and the most famous fossil-hunting-ground is the Jurassic Coast. This spectacular site covers almost 100 miles of the Dorset and East Devon coast, and the rocks on view span the Triassic, Jurassic and Cretaceous periods – 185 million years.

The region has become a popular destination for fossil-hunters; Lyme Regis was made particularly famous by resident Mary Anning who, when she was just 12, discovered the first complete ichthyosaur skeleton. We once joined a keen friend, Mark, for a day's fossil-stalking at Lyme. Guided by his knowledge, we found various small fossils on the beach, but the big prize came as we explored a new road development. Almost immediately we came across an enormous ammonite (the snail-shaped ones), which Mark generously let us keep. For many years we used it to hold down our notes for the milkman, until the perhaps inevitable day when someone nicked it. We were a bit sad, but philosophical. We were a lot sadder when, years later, I saw an ammonite a fraction the size of ours being valued at £250 on the ***Antiques Road Show*** …

I must just reproduce here a sentence I found on a geology website, because it makes me smile every time I read it: 'This was followed by the Ipswichian Stage, during which hippopotamus are known to have lived as far north as Leeds.' Who'd have guessed it?

A few years ago there was a large landslip near Lyme, and the authorities appealed to people not to come fossil-hunting on the unstable ground. They also pointed out that people were far more likely to find old fridges or bits of cars than significant fossils. This idea stayed in my mind and eventually became this quilt: I started thinking about other things that people have lost at different stages of history, and which might have become fossilised in different layers of the rock. From the earliest (oldest) layers upwards, they are:

- A classic ammonite (and also a nod in the direction of the Fossil family from Noel Streatfield's book ***Ballet Shoes***).

- Mammoth tusk; woolly mammoths may have been alive in Britain as recently as 14,000 years ago. I wonder if any of **them** lived in Leeds?
- Our human ancestors have arrived, and begun the habit of mislaying things; here a hunter has lost his arrowhead.
- The Romans have invaded, and left their amphoras everywhere just as they did at home in Italy.
- The crown is part of King John's Treasure; in 1216, John seemingly lost his crown jewels in The Wash (the estuary on the east coast of England, not the laundry). As he was the arch-villain in the Robin Hood stories, it probably served him right.
- Texts written in Old English are almost incomprehensible to us, as they use many characters that don't appear in our modern alphabet; this is one of them, which represented the sound 'j.'
- the Holy Grail – it must be lost, as everyone's always looking for it.
- Lord Frederick North has the dubious distinction of being known as 'the Prime Minister who lost America,' because he led Britain through the American War of Independence.
- Umbrella: because there's always at least one umbrella in any Lost Property office. The modern (steel-ribbed) umbrella was invented by Briton Samuel Fox in 1852. Sarah Gamp, a nurse in Dickens' ***Martin Chuzzlewit,*** is invariably shown sporting an umbrella, and so is Mary Poppins. And one of my personal heroes, geographer Nick Crane, always carries an umbrella as rain protection/parasol/depth-tester/dog-fender-offer etc.
- Two flowers, to represent two other lost things: the Lost Gardens of Heligan (now happily rediscovered); and the French Lieutenant's Woman's virginity (lost in Lyme Regis, as it happens ...)
- ***The Lost Chord***, a song composed by Arthur Sullivan in 1877.
- The French horn lost by Flanders and Swann
- Finally, the Higgs Boson, which remains elusive and camera-shy no matter how hard they look for it.

Inside information

To discover more about the Jurassic Coast, visit www.jurassiccoast.com. The official website of the Lost Gardens of Heligan can be found at www.heligan.com.

If politics is more your thing, Peter Whiteley has written a book called ***Lord North: the Prime Minister who Lost America****. By way of contrast,* ***What Was Lost*** *is the title of a novel by Catherine O'Flynn which is a wonderful depiction of the soullessness of the modern shopping centre and the society that has bred it.*

Materials

This is a wholecloth quilt, using only one background piece of very pale marbled cotton fabric; I used the same pastel multicoloured thread for all the quilting. For the lettering at the top of the design, I used a similar typeface to the one used for the *Jurassic Park* films – just to strengthen the palaeontological connection!

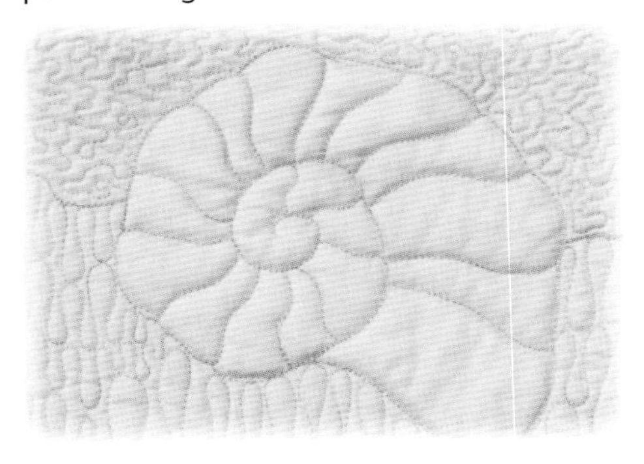

Techniques

Before I layered the quilt, I cut an extra silhouette of all the motifs from wadding, and glued these lightly behind the matching shapes: this made each motif stand out in extra relief from the quilting around it. I divided the background roughly into strips of different depths, to represent geological strata, and decorated each one in a different pattern of free machine-quilting – a good challenge for my free quilting skills!

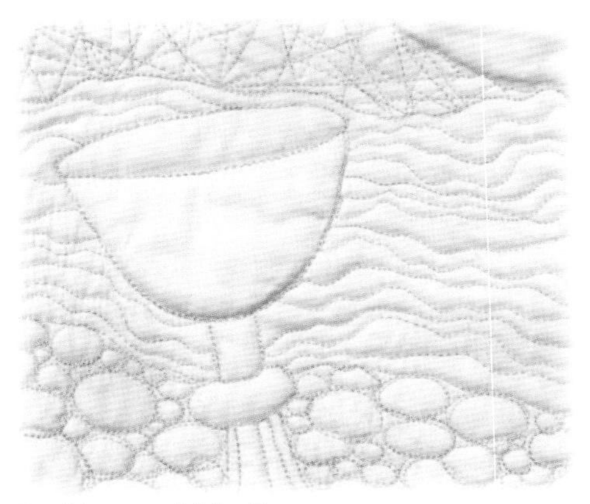

Backing and binding

The back of the quilt is another piece of the pale marbled fabric used for the front. I cut the edges of the quilt into a random wavy shape, to echo the irregular lines of the strata, and bound them with a very narrow double-fold bias strip of the same fabric.

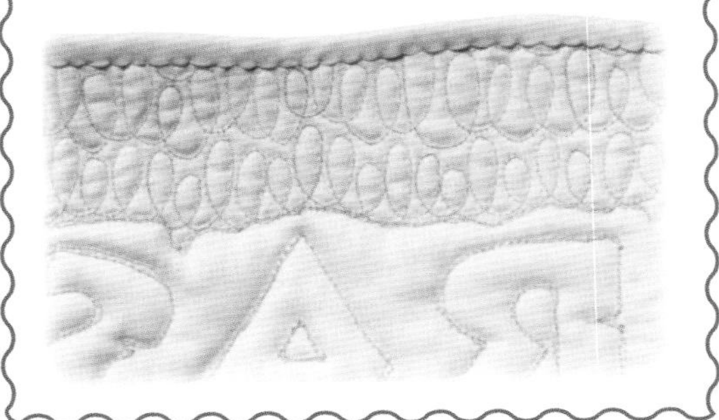

PROJECT
Fossil Picture

Three cute curly ammonites decorate this wall-hanging. I've created mine in a multicoloured batik, layered up with exotic fabrics underneath, then machine-quilted with a toning multicoloured thread. The layering allows you to cut back through the different fabrics to reveal the ones underneath – a textile equivalent of excavating geological layers! I used three different-coloured selections of exotic fabrics, each set complementing the colours in the top fabric of that particular shell, but if you prefer you can use the same selection for each ammonite.

finished size: 26 x 12in (65 x 30cm)

You will need:

- 26 x 12in piece of background fabric (I used a pale marbled cotton)
- 26 x 12in piece of flat wadding
- 26 x 12in piece of backing fabric (I used another piece of the marbled cotton)
- three 10 x 9in (25 x 23cm) patches of top fabric, one for each shell (I used multicoloured cotton batik)
- three sets of sheer or semi-sheer fabric patches, one set for each shell; each patch should measure 10 x 9in (25 x 23cm). You need 3-4 different fabrics for each set.
- three 10 x 9in (25 x 23cm) patches of gold fabric (this creates the base of each set of cut-back fabrics)
- machine-quilting thread to tone or contrast with your top fabric
- 2½yd (just over 2m) binding strip; I used the multicoloured batik fabric, and cut my strip 2in wide to give a ½in-wide finished binding
- soft pencil
- small, sharp-pointed scissors
- tracing/greaseproof paper or A4 piece of template plastic, or a photocopy of the template
- extra fabric strip for making a casing, or ribbon/tape for making hanging loops

Instructions

1 Trace the fossil template (page 86) onto paper or template plastic, or use a full-size photocopy. Lay one top fabric patch (the equivalent of my green batik) right side up over the template, so that there's an even border of fabric all the way around the design, and trace the lines in pencil (**a**). (If you can't easily see through the fabric, use a light-box or tape the design to a window.) Trace the design onto the other two patches of top fabric in the same way, reversing the template for the centre ammonite if you wish.

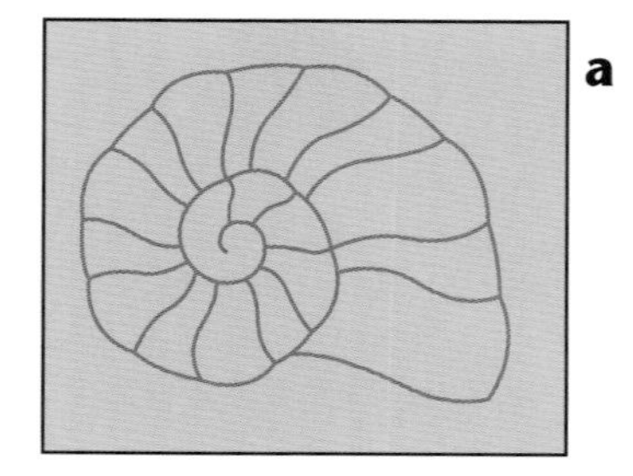
a

2 Lay one piece of gold fabric on a flat surface, right side up, and cover it with your first collection of sheer/semi-sheer fabrics (**b**); finish with one of the marked shell shapes, right side up (**c**), and pin the layers together. Prepare the other two shell designs in the same way.

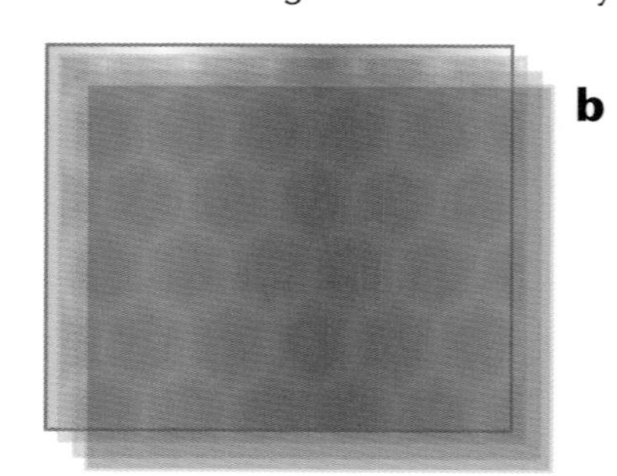
b

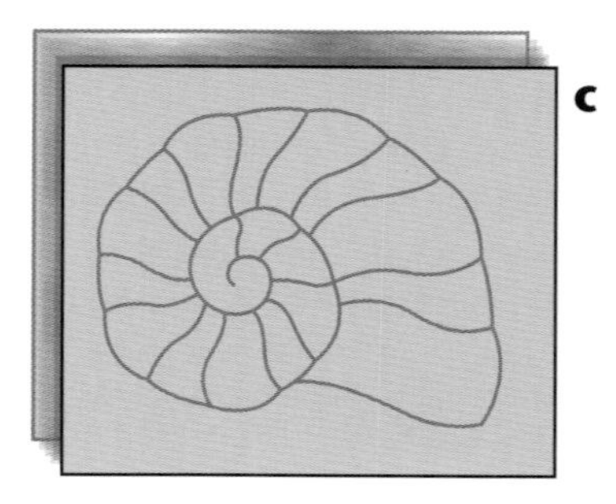
c

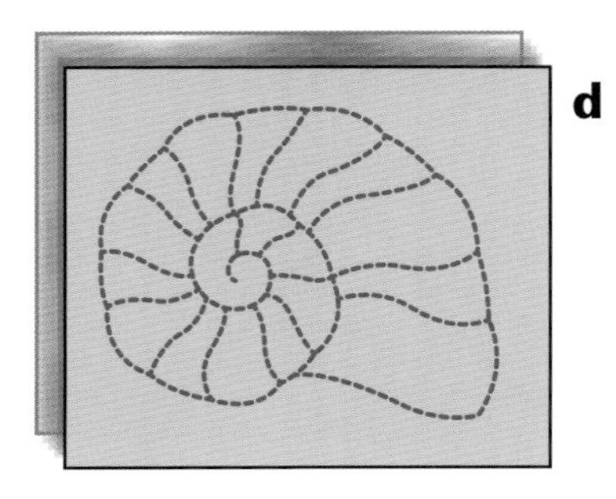

3 Using free machine stitching, quilt around the pencil lines (**d**); don't try and follow them too closely – part of the appeal of this design is a casual effect on the stitched lines. Keep the stitched line going around the drawn line; you don't need to stop and start – it's fine if different parts of the line are stitched several times.

4 Using the small, sharp scissors, and making sure that you're only cutting the top layer of fabric, cut a random line inside each of the large swirls of the shell shape, cutting roughly ¼in inside the stitching (**e**).

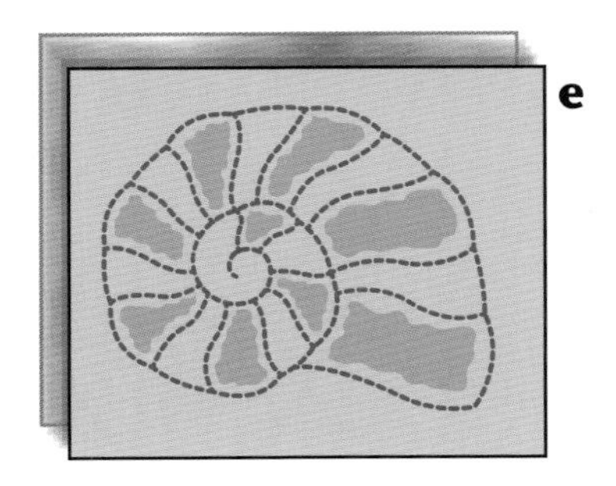

Now cut each of the underneath layers of fabric in the same way (**f**), each time cutting a little inside your previous line; you can cut right down to the gold base fabric if you like, or leave it shining through the final sheer/semi-sheer layer.

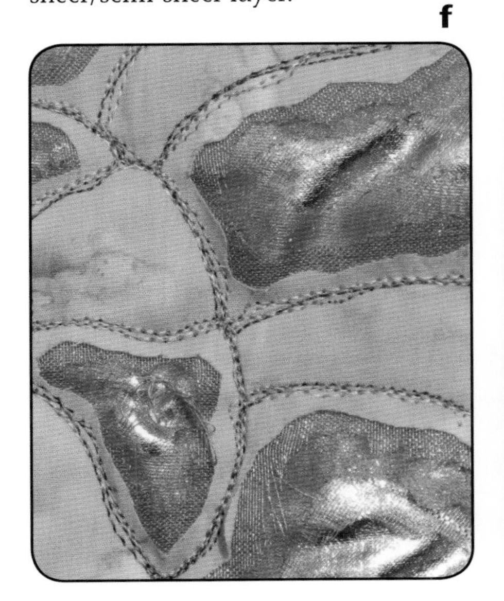

TIP

If you have a soldering iron, you can use this to trim the exotic fabrics; use a pin to hold each layer slightly away from the layers underneath, then run the tip of the soldering iron around the line you want to cut.

5 On the back of each shape, trim the gold and sheer/semi-sheer fabrics back to just outside the stitched shell shape (**g**); then, working on the front of the shape, trim the top fabric randomly about ½in outside the stitched line (**h**).

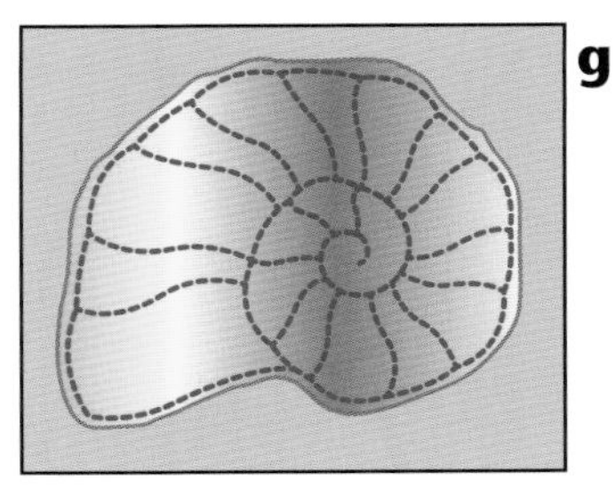

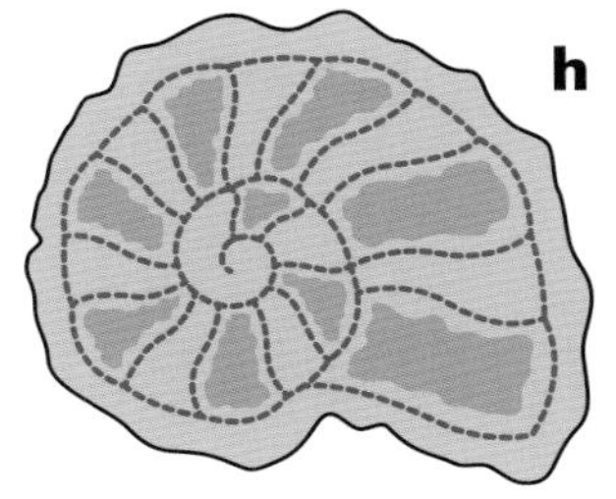

6 Lay the backing fabric right side down on a flat surface, and cover with the wadding; finish with the background fabric piece, right side up. Use your favourite method to secure the layers (see p136). Position the three shell shapes, right side up, on the background (**i**). Now work another line of free machine quilting all around the lines of each ammonite shape to secure it and quilt it.

Horsetails, one of our most ancient plants

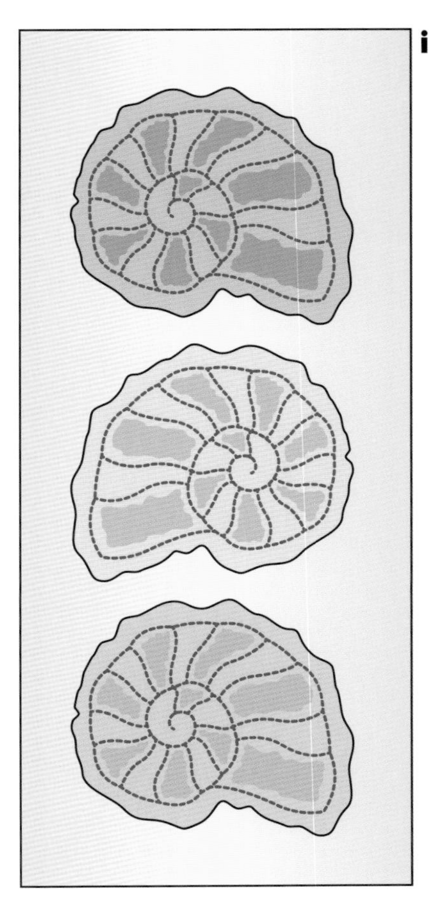

7 Follow the instructions on page 136 to attach the binding, then add a hidden casing on the back of the work, or hanging loops of ribbon or tape.

VARIATION

You can use the same method to make as many or as few ammonite shapes as you like. Try stitching a larger wall-hanging with 9 or 12 shells in a square, or enlarge the design and create one really exotic shell, perhaps adding hand embroidery and beads.

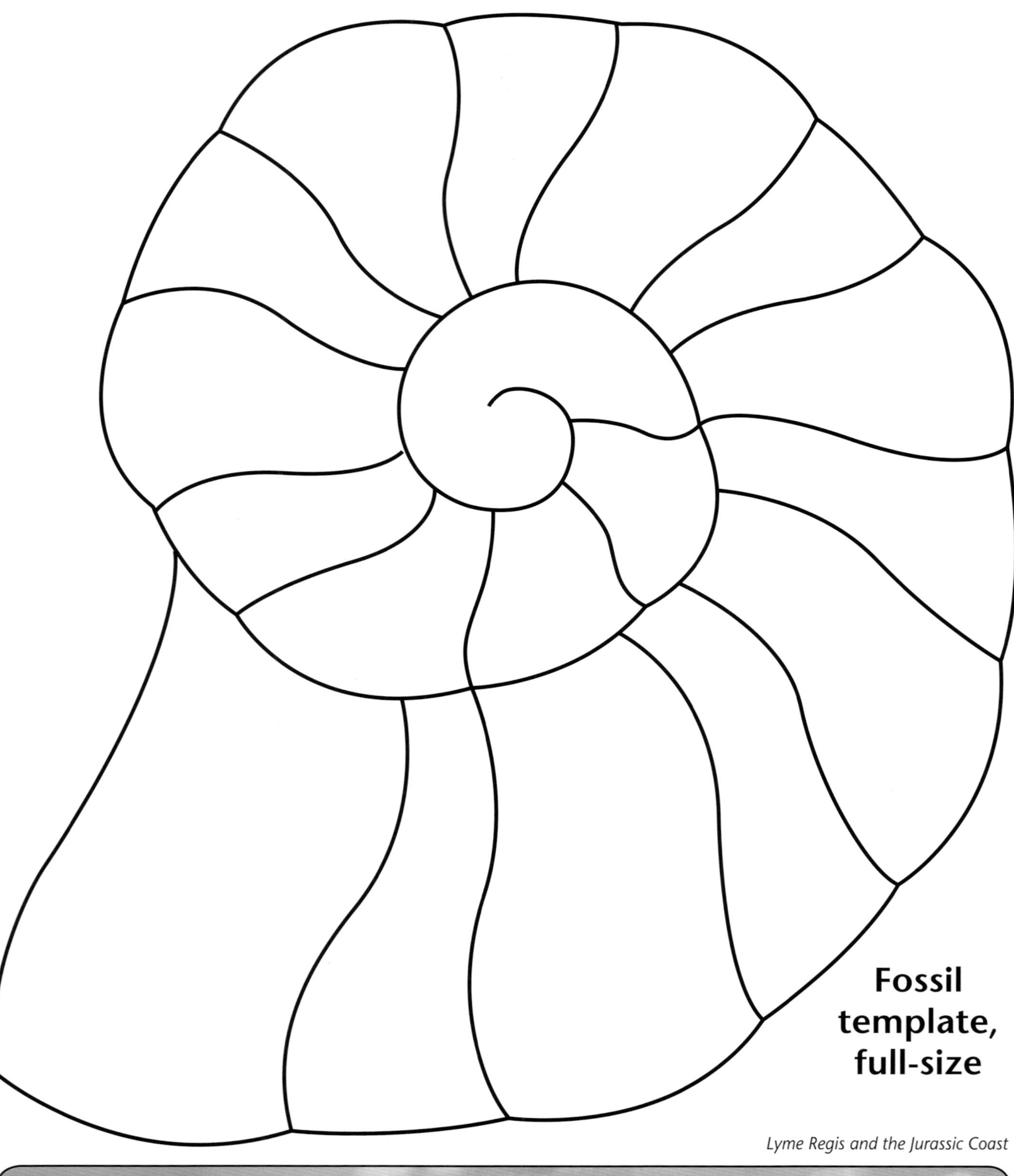

Fossil template, full-size

Lyme Regis and the Jurassic Coast

Chalk and Cheese

Remember the talk about EEC butter mountains? Well, here's a cheese mountain – complete with appropriate mountaineer!

Cheese-eating is one of my great talents (others include sunbathing and sleeping ...), so very early in the planning stages of these quilts I decided to do one devoted to British cheeses. As well as being the home of Cheddar, we are of course also the home of Stilton, and some of our other home-grown cheeses have wonderful names: Stinking Bishop, Yarg, Sussex Slipcote, The Lord of the Hundreds, Bouncing Berry, Harlech, Connage Crowdie, Perl Lâs Blue, Cashel Blue, Grimbister, Red Dragon, Rhayder Speckled, Gubbeen, Tintern, Pantysgawn (honestly!), Mynachlog-ddu Old Contemptible, Channel Island Blue etc.

Quite a few years ago there were rumours of literal mountains of food (particularly butter) and 'lakes' of milk or wine, bought up by the European Union to ensure that farmers weren't left with unsold stock. These came into our minds the first time we visited Cheddar, where we took a rather infantile delight in the names Cheddar Mines ('didn't realise they had to quarry it'), Cheddar Reservoir ('that must be for melted cheese') and so on. So why not a Cheese Mountain, for the really intrepid explorer, the truly dedicated turophile? (Yes, that really **is** the word for a lover of cheese ...)

I was also intending to do a quilt called ***Chalk***, featuring famous landmarks such as the White Cliffs of Dover (immortalised by Vera Lynn), the Needles on the Isle of Wight, and the chalk carvings that are scattered like confetti across the south of England. Many of these figures are horses, a craft known as leucippotomy, but there are other motifs too. These include the Long Man of Wilmington (*below*) and the chalk cross war memorial in East Sussex, the Cerne Abbas Giant in Dorset, and the regimental badges in Wiltshire. The Osmington white horse in Dorset is shown carrying King George III, and the chalk crown in Wye, Kent, commemorates the coronation of Edward VII. Although we like to believe that all these carvings are ancient, only the strangely-shaped Uffington White Horse (sometimes considered to be a rabbit, or a dog!) is truly old, dating back around three thousand years. In contrast, there is a very beautiful modern white horse on Cheriton Hill in Folkestone, which was made in 2003; this one was not actually carved, but created from slabs of limestone.

Some of these figures just seem to lend themselves to spoofing. In 2004, pro-hunt campaigners added a huntsmen and hounds to a couple of the white horses. A few years later the figure of Homer Simpson holding a doughnut was painted next to the Cerne Abbas giant; presumably he was just about to play hoopla. (The paint used was biodegradable, so that it would wash away in the next rain-shower.) A couple of years ago the Sussex Food and Drink awards used an image of the Long Man of Wilmington holding a knife and fork, and while I was working on this book a betting firm added a jockey to the Uffington white horse.

While I was mulling over the two ideas, one of our strange British sayings came into my brain: *as different as chalk and cheese*. I then began thinking of other eccentric phrases that relate specifically to either chalk or cheese, and so this hybrid quilt was born. On each layer of the mountain I've embroidered an idiomatic saying; from the top downwards they are:

- **big cheese** (the most important person; this saying had a revival when the game ***Trivial Pursuit*** came out, as the winner becomes the Big Cheese).
- **say cheese**: the constant cry of the photographer
- **chalk dust!*!** I know it was said by an American, but he said it on English soil! The most famous words of the legendary John McEnroe, whose antics on court amused and enraged opponents and crowds alike.
- **cheesy grins**; falsely exaggerated smiles
- **cheesed off ...** meaning fed up, irritated or disgusted
- **chalk-white** – pretty self-explanatory
- **so, hard cheese!** A slightly insulting version of 'bad luck'; perhaps the closest equivalent would be 'you'll just have to lump it!'
- **cheeseparing**; miserly, penny-pinching
- **walk your chalk!** This phrase dates back to the time when bailiffs would come to evict someone, and would mark the door of the house with chalk. The original version was: 'Walk: you're chalked.'
- **at the real chalk face** originally related to the work of schoolteaching
- **bread and cheese**; relating to income, this phrase traditionally meant 'enough to eat, at least simply.'
- **not by a long chalk** = nowhere near! This relates to pub life, where the score of games such as skittles would be drawn up in chalk (something that's still true of darts).
- **not quite the cheese?** An obsolete phrase which meant 'not quite the thing,' used of someone who was considered a bit off-colour or of dubious origins; presumably the opposite of The Big Cheese.
- **like chalk and cheese** – two things that might look similar outwardly, but are actually very different.
- **chalk it up to experience**; the same as 'put it down to experience.'

A miniature mountaineer is planting his flag at the top of the edifice; the flag also acts as a modesty panel for the lewd Cerne Abbas Giant behind (who is clutching a cheese sandwich). At the top is the Cherrill White Horse, and under the giant is a chalk carving that the mountaineer has created to celebrate his exploits. And at the bottom I've included another use of chalk; the line drawn around the body in a murder. This is a reference to our wonderful history of crime writers (from Agatha Christie to Ian Rankin), as well as to the contribution of British scientists to crime detection, particularly the use of fingerprinting. The traffic sign relates to our road-signing system, which is admired around the world; this one means *Danger: Falling Cheese*.

Inside information

*The I Love Cheese website (www.ilovecheese.co.uk/) is a turophile's dream, and has a section on British cheeses; the Cheese Enforcement Agency (www.jasperfforde.com/specops/cheeseindex.html) is a great site devoted to 'dangerous' cheeses. Useful books include **The Great British Cheese Book**, by Patrick Rance, and the more recent **Great British Cheeses** by Jenny Linford.*

For inside information on leucippotomy, have a look at www.wiltshirewhitehorses.org.uk/, which also covers white horses in other parts of the country and other parts of the world. The website www.fovantbadges.com/index.htm is the official website for the regimental badge carvings.

Materials

The cheese mountain is built from creamy-yellow cotton fabrics that give the impression of different cheeses: many of them are marbled or hand-painted, and some feature small prints. The green background fabric has a soft nap which vaguely resembles grass. I used cord and firm interfacing for the flag, and cotton fabrics for the mouse, the chalk figures and the road sign.

Techniques

The mountain, mountaineer, rocks and road sign are created in machine appliqué, and the 'chalk' figures are fused on with bonding web. I made the flag in simple machine cutwork, and couched the cord down with machine zigzag. The sayings are embroidered by hand, using backstitch in coton perlé; I chose a simple letterform so that the words have a hand-drawn feel. The background is machine-quilted in random wavy lines; beads for the mouse's eye and the top of the flag complete the design.

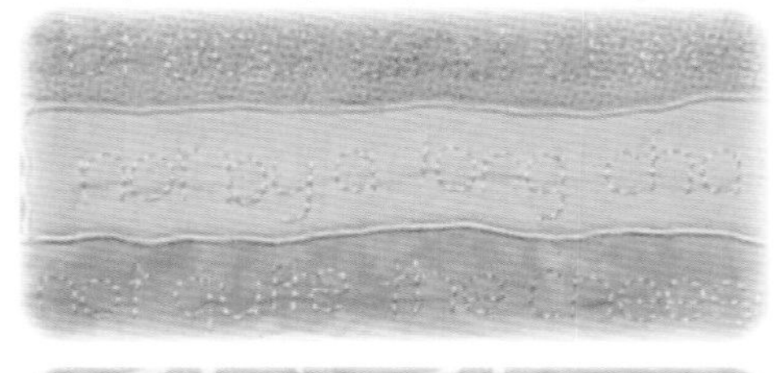

Backing and binding

I couldn't have found a more appropriate backing fabric than this print! The binding is a long strip pieced from the 'cheese' fabrics.

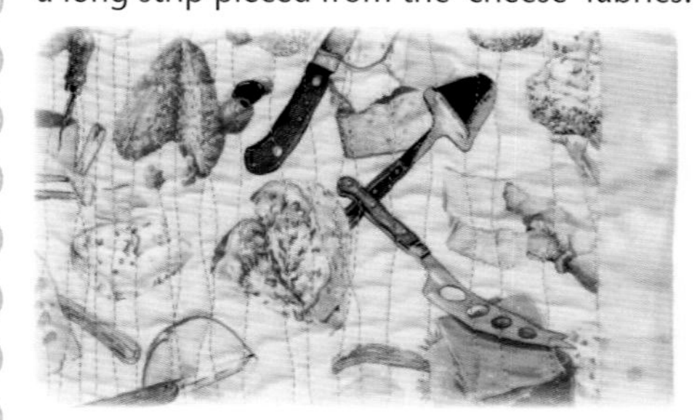

PROJECT

Meece

Like the mountaineer on page 87, these three (not-blind) mice are definitely out to find the cheese. You can create the mice in virtually any print or plain fabric, but each one will look specially handsome if his nose and ear linings contrast with the main body fabric. If you're stitching the mice for small children, it might be better to embroider the eyes on instead of using beads; we wouldn't want small fingers to unpick the buttons and stuff them up small noses or down small throats ...

finished size: each mouse is roughly 8in (20cm) long excluding tail ...

For each mouse, you will need:

- two 11 x 4in (28 x 10cm) pieces of print cotton fabric for the body
- one 12 x 7in (30 x 18cm) piece of contrast cotton fabric for the nose, base and ear linings
- polyester stuffing
- 8in (20cm) cord for the tail
- two small beads or buttons for the eyes (or embroider them on)
- thick embroidery thread for the whiskers (I used soft cotton), plus a large, sharp needle
- sewing thread to match your fabrics and buttons
- pencil, paper scissors

Instructions

1 Trace templates A-D onto paper, or use photocopies, and cut them out (**a**). Put the two pieces of body fabric right sides together, and pin on templates A and B; cut round the shapes to give you two body sides and two ears (**b**).

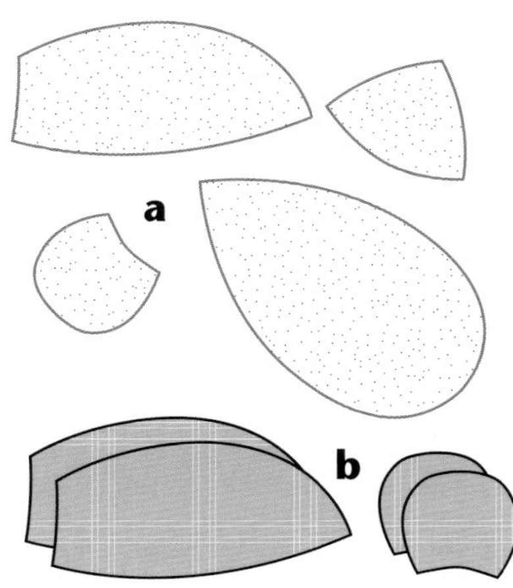

2 Pin template C onto the contrast fabric and cut out one shape (**c**); from the remaining contrast fabric, cut two ear shapes (using template B again), and one nose patch (**d**), using template D.

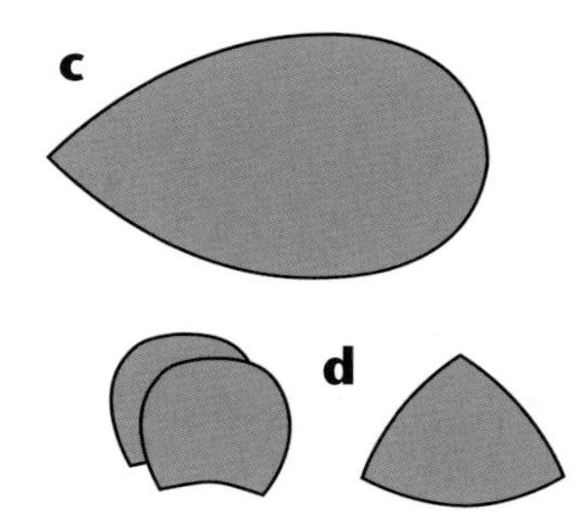

3 Use ¼in seams throughout. Lay the two side pieces right sides together, and stitch the centre back seam (**e**). Pin each print ear patch right sides together with a contrast patch, and stitch round the large curve (**f**); turn the shapes out to produce two ears (**g**).

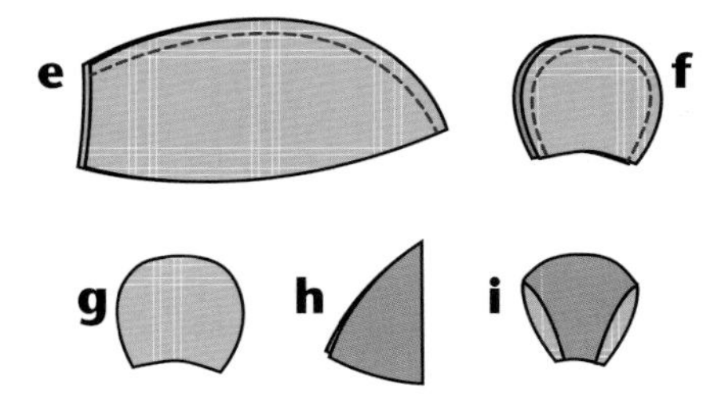

4 Fold the nose patch in half, and finger-press the fold to mark the centre (**h**). Fold the edges of each ear inwards slightly (**i**), then pin the ears in place on the right side of the nose piece as shown, easing the curves together so that they fit (**j**); make sure that the ears are spaced evenly each side of the centre fold, and that the contrast side is against the nose patch. Use a machine zigzag to tack the ears to the nose patch, stitching slightly inside the seam allowance (**k**).

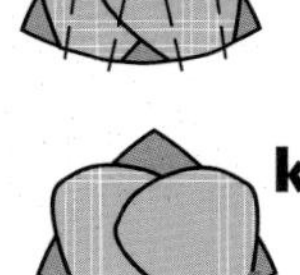

TIP

Note that the folded edges of the ears are underneath when you stitch the ears onto the nose patch.

5 Pin the nose patch to the body piece, right sides together, easing the curves so that they match snugly; stitch the seam (**l**).

6 Make a knot near one end of the tail cord. Position the other end of the cord at the centre back of the base, and zigzag into place as you did for the ears (**m**); you can see that the knotted end of the tail lies along the length of the base at this stage.

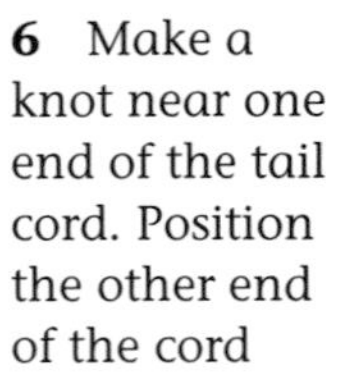

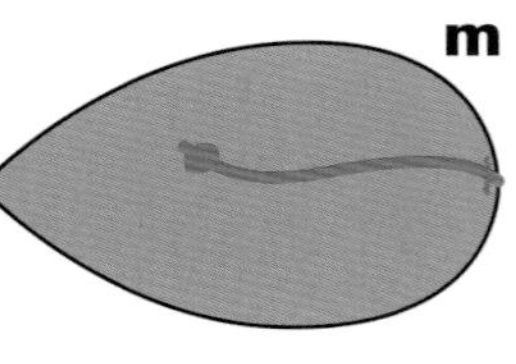

7 Pin the body section onto the base around the edges, right sides together (**n**); make sure that the ears are tucked out of the way of the seam line. Stitch the seam, leaving a gap of about 3in (8cm) along one side for turning (**o**). Turn the shape out, and stuff it fairly firmly with the stuffing; ladder-stitch the opening closed.

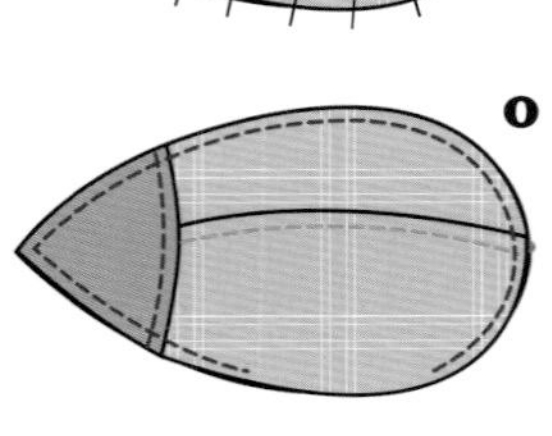

8 Make the whiskers by threading the cotton into a large, sharp needle and pulling it through the nose section from one side to the other; make a knot at each side of the face, pulling the thread quite tightly (**p**). Once all the whiskers are in place, trim them to an even length on each side.

9 Stitch the eyes on firmly, and hide the cheese ...

VARIATION

You can easily make these mice larger or smaller; simply enlarge or reduce all the templates by the same percentage. You could make a whole family – Mum, Dad and several smaller kids! (Don't forget that your fabric requirements will change if you alter the size.)

Above: two different aspects of Cheddar Gorge;
This photo: the chalk Needles on the Isle of Wight

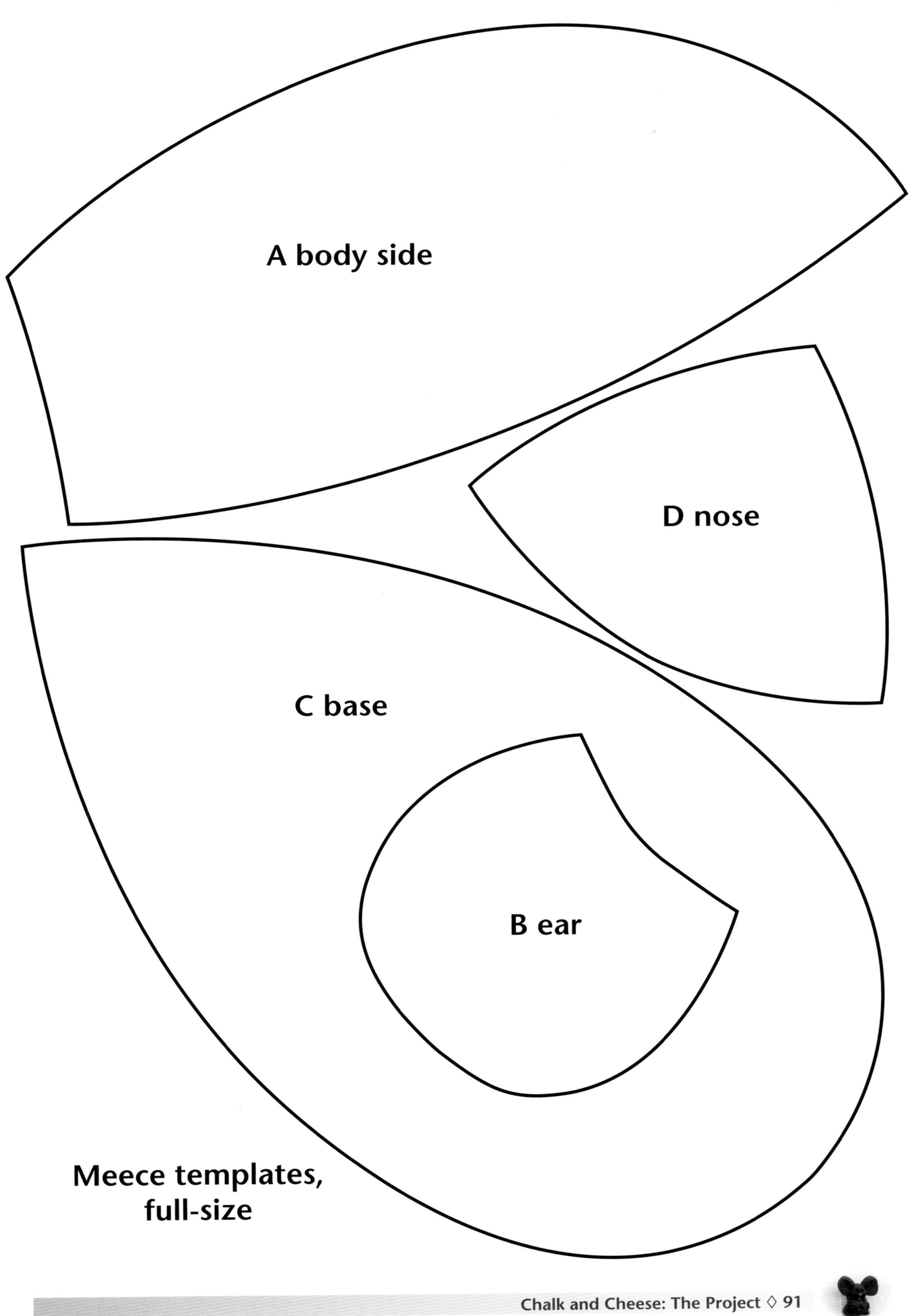
A body side
D nose
C base
B ear
Meece templates, full-size

Cuppa?

Every Briton knows that any crisis can be minimised with a nice cup of tea.

As I planned the quilts for this book, I had great fun asking people what I ought to include: the results were very revealing! One of the answers that came up again and again was: tea. The British are famous (notorious?) for believing that a nice cup of tea solves almost everything – and even if the problem isn't solved, well: we'll all feel better for a cuppa, won't we? From war breaking out to a broken fingernail, the response is the same: I'll put the kettle on.

This isn't just moonshine, either. Tea leaves contain antioxidants and other substances which improve our physical or mental wellbeing. Green tea consumption in particular tends to produce a lower risk of stroke, many different kinds of cancer, and osteoporosis. Add the natural 'high' that the caffeine in black tea provides, plus the sucrose rush you get from adding sugar, and it's not surprising that things look better after a good cuppa … Of course these days you can buy herbal and fruit teas, but why accept substitutes when you can have a dose of the real thing?

Surprisingly, all types of 'real' tea are made from the same plant: the leaves of *Camellia sinensis*. The different types (eg black, green, white, oolong etc) depend on how the leaves are dried and oxidised. The dried leaves can be flavoured to produce particular blends; two of the best-known are Earl Grey (flavoured with bergamot), and jasmine tea, often drunk with Chinese food. The tea plant grows best in tropical and subtropical climates, but (perhaps courtesy of global warming – see p13) the temperate climate of Britain has also recently spawned some tea plantations. The popularity of Alexander McCall Smith's ***No1 Ladies' Detective Agency*** books, starring the traditionally-built Mma Precious Ramotswe, has increased the consumption of redbush or rooibis tea; this is made from *Aspalathus linearis*, a relative of our broom plant.

Inevitably, there are nursery-rhymes about tea (***Polly Put the Kettle On*** etc): the lyrics are devastatingly banal, but as with most nursery rhymes, they are often considered to have subliminal political meanings. Other popular songs about the beverage include ***'Right,' said Fred***; ***Everything Stops for Tea***; ***Tea for Two***; and the classic ***I Like a Nice Cup of Tea***. A cuppa also makes a guest appearance in Ralph McTell's signature song ***Streets of London***. Tea dances were all the rage from Victorian times onwards, and can still be found in a few rarified places in Britain; they were a development of the afternoon tea ritual, enlivening it with live music, dancing – and, if you were lucky, booze.

The Mad Hatter's Tea Party, immortalised in Tenniel's illustrations for ***Alice in Wonderland***, celebrates another teatime nursery rhyme:

The Queen of Hearts made some tarts
all on a summer's day;
the knave of hearts, he stole the tarts,
and took them clean away.

Gail at primary school being the Queen of Hearts, making tarts

Tea parties are a British institution, and I doubt if there's another part of the world with quite so many traditional teatime foods. Just some of these include Bakewell Tart (or Bakewell Pudding – they're different); sandwiches of cucumber, egg-and-cress or smoked salmon; jam tarts; fruit cake; teacakes; Victoria sponge; sausage rolls; fairy cakes; lardy cake; Chelsea buns; battenburg; crumpets; cinnamon toast. And no visit to the west country is complete without a Cornish or Devon cream tea (the proper ones use clotted cream on the scones). Patum Peperium, or Gentleman's Relish, is a very salty fish paste created in 1828 by John Osborn, used for the traditional teatime treat anchovy toast. 'High tea' is a hybrid meal, eaten in the early evening, which typically begins with a hot savoury dish followed by teatime-style cakes and buns.

Although tea is generally considered to have arrived on these shores in the 17th century, I have my doubts. How could the people of Britain possibly have survived, let alone thrived, through their turbulent history without their favourite tipple? How could we have developed our traditional stiff upper lip in the face of trials, if we didn't have a cuppa to cure the vapours? So, I'm sure that tea must have been around since our ancestors first covered themselves in woad; the first meaningful communication between our male and female forebears was probably a grunt that signified 'Put a brew on, luv.' What on earth were the neolithic Beaker People making beakers for if it wasn't to hold a cuppa? And there's no need to look further to interpret those strange ancient carved cup-and-ring designs: they're obviously inspired by the ring-marks made by damp teacups on a flat surface.

So that's the theory behind my quilt, which is a brief history of the role of tea in British life. At the top a neolithic beaker rests on a background cup-and-ring design: the runic inscriptions, which have baffled historians for centuries, are obviously all versions of *'I like a nice cup of tea in the morning.'* Next comes a 17th century cup and saucer; by this time the habit is well ingrained in the British psyche – *'just to start the day, you see.'* A cup inspired by potter Clarice Cliff continues the tea ceremony: *'at half past eleven, well my idea of heaven …'*; and the answer, of course, *'is a nice cup of tea.'* The final legend appears under a 60s-style mug, in an appropriate typeface.

Inside information

To discover more about tea in Britain, visit the Tea Council's website (www.tea.co.uk/). Tregothnan Estate (tregothnan.co.uk/), is the only current producer of English-grown tea (the plantations are in Cornwall and Kent); The Redbush Tea Company (www.redbushtea.com/) distributes rooibis tea in the UK.

If you'd like to know more about Clarice Cliff's work, visit www.claricecliff.co.uk/.

Materials

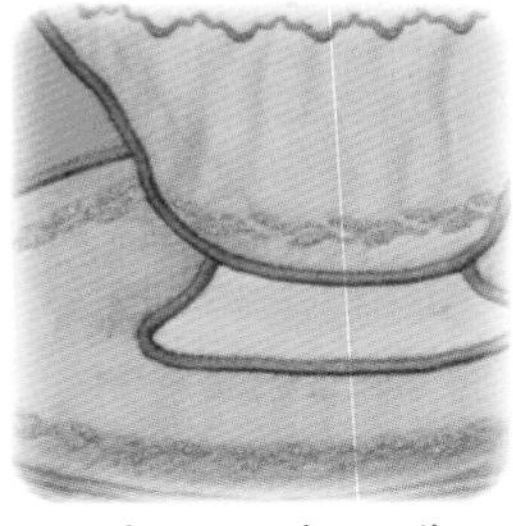

Apart from the hessian square behind the beaker, all the other fabrics in this quilt are cotton. I found a print featuring all kinds of bizarre 19th century teapot designs, each one based on the shape of a different fruit or vegetable, and used these for the little square appliquéd panels; they also inspired the palette of colours used across the quilt. Fabric paint and embroidery thread were used to add extra details.

Techniques

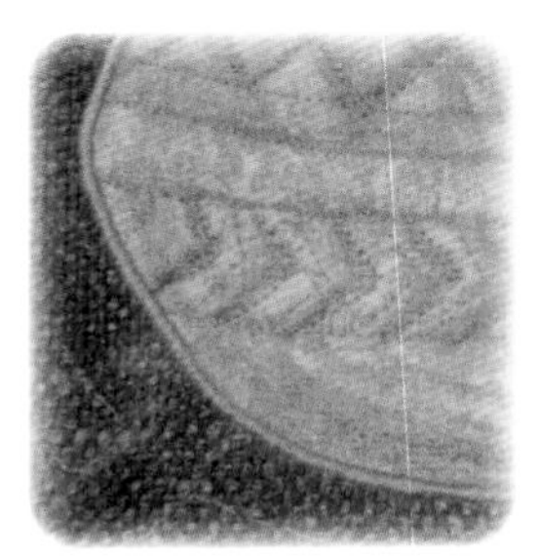

Most parts of the design, including the little squares, are built up using appliqué patches edged in machine satin stitch. On the hessian I appliquéd inside the edge of the square then frayed the edges back to the stitching; a line of large running stitches looks suitably primitive as an embellishment, and the legend is embroidered by hand. The other letters, and the cup-and-ring shadow behind the beaker, are created in fabric paint. I also used fabric paint to shade the details on the beaker itself, which were then machine-quilted to provide texture.

Backing and binding

To make this quilt a slightly different shape, I cut the edges to echo the angles of the main squares. The backing is the same 'tealeaf-print' fabric as the quilt background, and the multicoloured fabric I used for the binding picks up all the main purple and orange shades of the design.

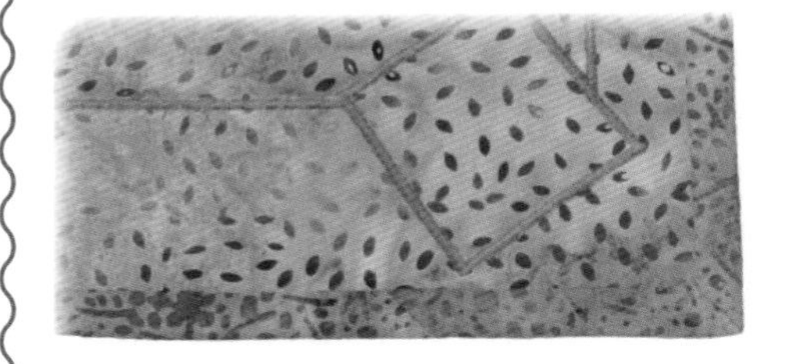

PROJECT

Teatime Table-Mats

Simple Japanese folded patchwork is used to create these pretty mats (how appropriate, when the famous Tea Ceremony is so important in Japan!) I've used Fast2Fuse™ to stiffen the mats, but any firm double-sided fusible interfacing will do; this extra layer will also help to protect your table-top from heat. Pick a fabric with a striking motif (the teapot fabric I used was just perfect), then quilt round the motif by machine, or choose a strong print fabric and quilt along the main lines of the design.

finished size: 7½in (19cm) diameter

For each mat, you will need:

- 8in (20cm) square of cotton fabric with an attractive print (if you want to feature a particular motif, make sure that it's right in the centre of your square)
- 8in (20cm) square of double-sided interfacing
- 10in (25cm) square of backing/binding fabric
- machine-quilting thread
- thread to match the backing/binding fabric

You will also need:

- ruler, short quilt rule, and pencil
- 8in square of template plastic
- non-stick ironing sheet

Instructions

1 Use the ruler and pencil to trace the hexagon template (p95) onto template plastic, and cut out the shape along the pencil lines. This transparent template will allow you to see the exact patch of fabric you will be cutting, so that you can centre any decorative motif right in the middle of the mat (what the Americans delightfully call 'fussy cutting').

2 Position the template on the *right* side of the motif fabric; once you're happy with the positioning, draw round the template with pencil (**a**).

a

b

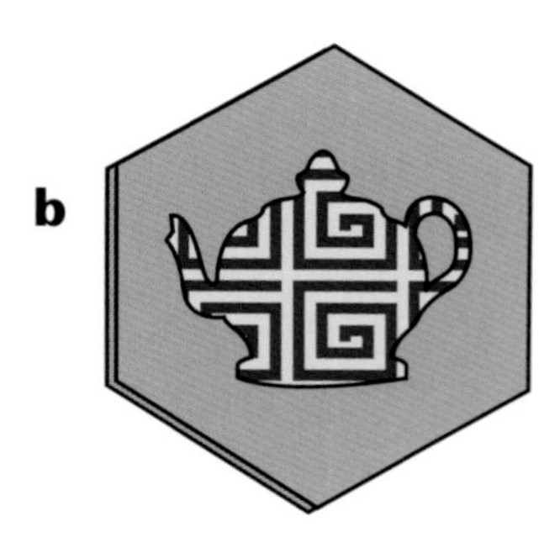

3 Lay the marked fabric square on top of the square of interfacing, right side up, and use a warm iron to fuse the two layers together; cut out the hexagon shape along the marked line (**b**).

TIP

To prevent the underneath of the interfacing fusing to the ironing board, use a non-stick pressing sheet or a piece of greaseproof paper between the interfacing and the ironing board.

4 Lay the square of backing/binding fabric right side down on a flat surface, and position the hexagon shape, right side up, in the centre; fuse the layers together. Now use your quilt rule and pencil to draw an extra outline 1¼in beyond each edge of the hexagon (**c**); cut out this shape along the marked line (**d**).

c

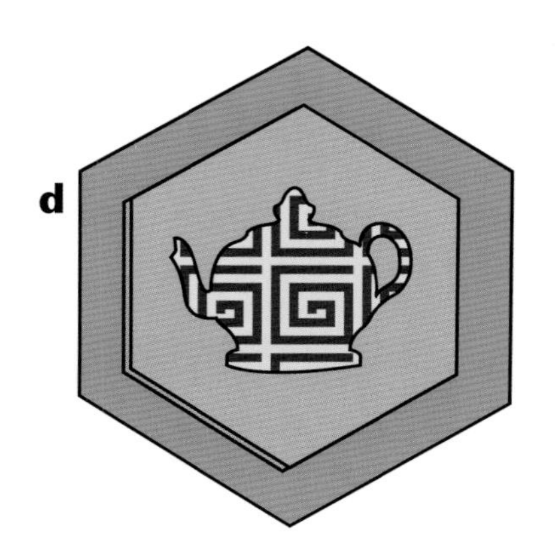

5 Working on each edge of the backing fabric in turn, work a double fold to the front of the work (**e**) and pin. Each edge will create a nice angled corner fold on top of the previous edge (**f**); when you fold the final edge, ensure that it tucks under the first edge at the corner. Stitch the folded edge down using a line of either hand or machine stitching; this can be plain or decorative. I used a small wavy stitch in a toning colour.

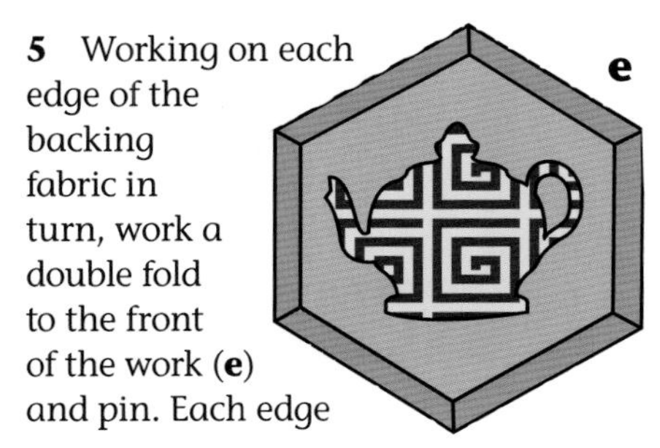

6 Quilt the mat by machine as you wish – you can follow the lines of your print fabric, or simply stitch an overall design across the mat. Or, if the shape of your motif is quite simple, you could work blanket-stitch or other decorative stitch by machine all around the edges of the shape to create the impression of appliqué.

VARIATION

For a more contemporary feel to your table-mats, use fabrics printed with bright cake motifs or large splashy blossoms. If you can't find a fabric that features isolated motifs, you could fussy-cut individual motifs out of a print fabric and fuse them onto a plain background with bonding web.

Teatime Table-Mat template, full-size

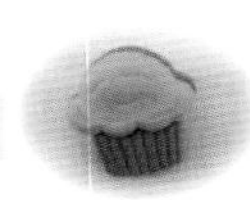

A Christmas Carol

The Victorians virtually invented our festive Christmas – and no-one did it better than Dickens!

When we think of a traditional British Christmas, dozens of visions dance in our heads. Cards, trees, baubles; sideboards groaning with rich food including a plum pudding; carol-singers huddled under a street-lamp, singing in front of a snow-covered village church. Many of these images have their roots in Victorian times. The Victorians were great sentimentalists, loving songs, paintings and stories that brought a little tear to the eye: if they could feature an heroic struggle, and ideally a ragged orphan or two, so much the better. The paintings of John Everett Millais embodied this approach. Having turned his back on his Pre-Raphaelite roots, Millais earned vast sums for sugary paintings depicting cute children; the most famous was ***Bubbles***, which was used for many years to advertise Pears Soap. To the Victorians, both childhood and motherhood were virtually cults, and what could be a better celebration of the two than Christmas?

CHARLES DICKENS

Although trees had long been used to celebrate midwinter festivals, it was Victoria's consort Prince Albert who began the real vogue for Christmas trees, when he brought one over from Germany to decorate Windsor Castle. Presumably inspired by this trend, Woolworth's began selling the first manufactured Christmas tree ornaments in the 1880s. A typical Victorian Christmas illustration shows a vast decorated tree: next to the tree is The Mother, the symbol of everything that's safe, tender, nurturing. Often she'll be cradling a baby in her arms, or lifting a toddler to put the angel at the top of the tree. The Mother will be surrounded by numerous children, and perhaps a few men or household servants, all adoring her – spot the almost religious imagery. Sometimes in the background, or outside the border, there will be an image of a 'ragged' child, or a Boer War soldier at the battlefront. This was the other side of Victorian sentimentality; the upper classes, en masse, were beginning to realise that social injustice was something that they needed to be concerned about – and, ideally, do something about. Philanthropy as a mass movement was emerging.

The time was ripe for a writer who would explore all of these themes, and feed the Victorians with exciting writing that showed life in all its complexity. Step up, Charles Dickens. His own childhood couldn't have provided better literary material, as the Dickens family went from plenty to poverty then back again within a few years. At one stage his father was imprisoned in the Marshalsea, a debtors' prison immortalised later in ***Little Dorrit***. Charles lodged with a family friend, and for a year worked ten-hour days in a boot-blacking factory. Not surprisingly, he never forgot this insight into the harsh lives of the poor, and all his novels include depictions of people living in poverty alongside those who live in plenty.

And Dickens also created some of the best-known depictions of Christmas. In ***Great Expectations***, the pie that Pip raids for escaped convict Magwitch has been baked for the Gargerys' cheerless Christmas celebrations. In ***The Cricket on the Hearth,*** the heart of miser Tackleton is softened by the Yuletide season. Most famous of all are the different celebrations Scrooge witnesses in ***A Christmas Carol***: what could be more

Old mills like this one are now highly-desirable flats!

festive than the Fezziwigs' Christmas Ball – and what could be more tear-jerking than dead Tiny Tim's crutch, resting against the chimney-piece?!

Dickens was a man of contradictions. His novels are sentimental to the point of being schmaltzy, but he was deeply embarrassed by any real-life show of affection. He was part of the upper class, while at the same time pricking their bubbles of hypocrisy, greed and narrow-mindedness. His 'good' women are all depicted as child-women, even reflected in their names (Little Dorrit, Little Nell); others are naive fools, and many more are harridans. Lots of his male figures, too, are grotesques or caricatures, which is part of their appeal; his novels contain nearly 1,000 characters, many of them highly memorable. But Dickens did open the eyes of the Victorians to many social injustices, just as the great philanthropists such as William Wilberforce and Elizabeth Fry did before him. His crossing-sweepers, orphans, debtors, factory workers and poor widows inspired people to get involved as never before in 'public works,' and the Victorians built schools, almshouses, orphanages, churches, public baths, museums and libraries in their thousands.

It seemed only right to represent Dickens by a Christmas scene. The main part of the design is adapted from a print by Randolph Caldecott, a very popular Victorian illustrator; the typical Dickensian child-women, and the slightly caricatured men, are all wrapped up for winter and singing their hearts out in church. I've added holly and Christmas roses, and some contemporary music for my favourite carol, ***It Came Upon the Midnight Clear***. The words are in a wood-effect typeface – very popular on Victorian Christmas cards and sheet music.

Inside information

You can visit the Charles Dickens Museum housed in Dickens' own London dwelling: www.dickensmuseum.com/. An intriguing website devoted to the author is charlesdickenspage.com/; it's run by David Perdue, an American Dickens fan. Here you can find a wealth of information about Dickens, as well as links to things such as a list of over 200 films that have been made from his novels.

The Caldecott illustration was reproduced in the Dover book ***An Old-Fashioned Christmas in Illustration and Decoration.***

Materials

This is in effect a wholecloth quilt, painted onto a single piece of white cotton; the only embellishments are a few snowflake buttons at the top of the design.

Techniques

After I'd assembled all the different parts of the design, I traced it onto the cotton fabric ready for painting. I began with the coloured areas, watering the fabric paint down with neutral medium where I wanted pale shades, then allowed these to dry before I set them with a hot iron. I then added all the black lines, using a fabric pen so that I could control the details. The whole design is free machine-quilted in black along the main outlines.

Backing and binding

A green-and-gold starry print for the binding continues the Christmas theme. The backing of the quilt is plain white fabric, which shows off the quilting as though it's a line illustration.

PROJECT

Angels from the Realms of Glory

These pretty angels are bringing the Christmas message of joy to the world. I've used a slight variation on the traditional seasonal colourscheme of red, green and gold; I've gone for grey-greens and pinky-reds, set off by glints of silver. If you're using the border, cut the background and border fabrics to the exact sizes I've mentioned so that the maths works for the piecing: to keep things easy, I've kept these measurements in imperial.

finished size: 58 x 41in (148 x 104cm)

You will need:

- cotton fabric for the background, 40½ x 24½in (I used a pale grey-green and silver print)
- cotton fabrics for the angel motifs: I've put the colours I used in brackets
  - 15in (38cm) square for the hair (white-and-silver print)
  - 15in (38cm) square for the wings (slightly glittery white)
  - 18in (45cm) square for the dresses and sleeves (grey-green print)
  - 10in (25cm) square for the dress borders (pale grey-green print)
  - 12 x 10in (30 x 25cm) for the underskirts (green-and-pink print)
  - 10 x 6in (25 x 15cm) for the faces, hands and feet (pale pink)
  - 10in (25cm) square for the hearts (pink print)
- large reel of machine embroidery or machine quilting thread for attaching the motifs; you can pick a colour that either blends in with your fabric or contrasts with them
- 2½in fabric strips for the border; you will need a total length of 28-30yd (25-28m) to give you plenty of choice when you're joining patches
- buttons in assorted sizes for quilting and embellishing the border
- four small round beads for the angels' eyes
- pack of small round white pearl beads for the haloes (or you could embroider these)
- thread for piecing, and to match the buttons and beads
- 45in x 18in (115 x 45cm) double-sided bonding web (this is 18in wide on the roll, so buy it by the metre rather than in a pack)
- two A4 pieces of template plastic
- pencil, paper scissors
- flat wadding, 60 x 43in (152 x 110cm)
- backing fabric, 60 x 43in (152 x 110cm)
- long quilt rule, rotary cutter and board
- fabric for the binding, 12in (30cm) x the width of the fabric
- extra fabric for a hanging sleeve, or ribbon or tape for hanging loops

Instructions

1 Use pencil to trace all the templates (A-J) onto the template plastic; draw in the arrows, too. Cut all the templates out along the marked lines (**a**).

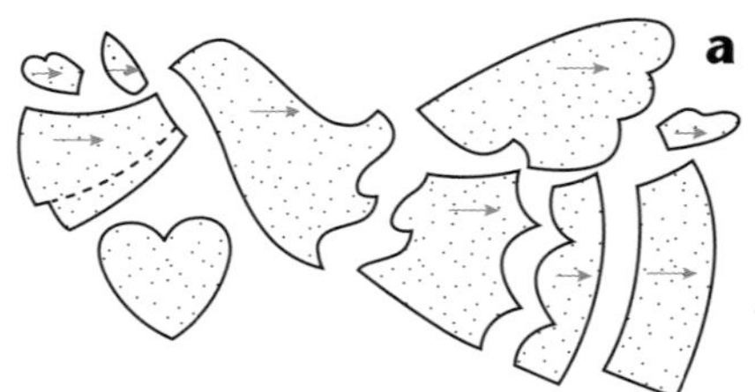

2 On the paper side of the bonding web, draw round the hair shape twice and draw in the arrows (**b**); then flip the template over the other way and trace round it twice, again adding the arrows (**c**). Cut these shapes out as a group, cutting roughly outside the marked lines (**d**). Do the same with all the other templates (**e**).

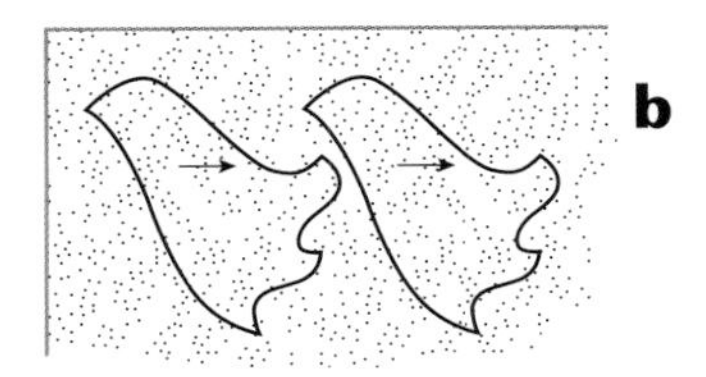

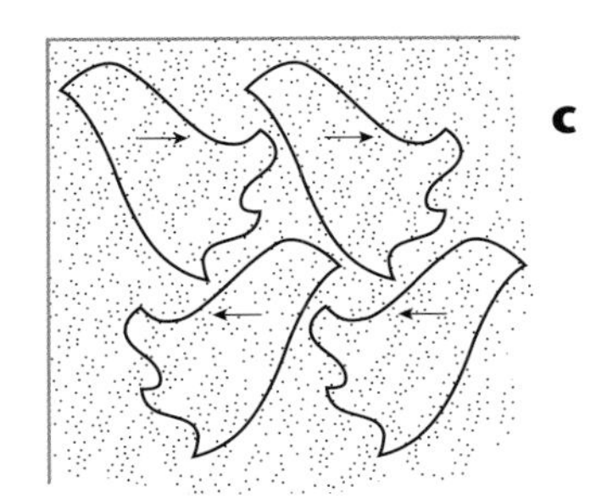

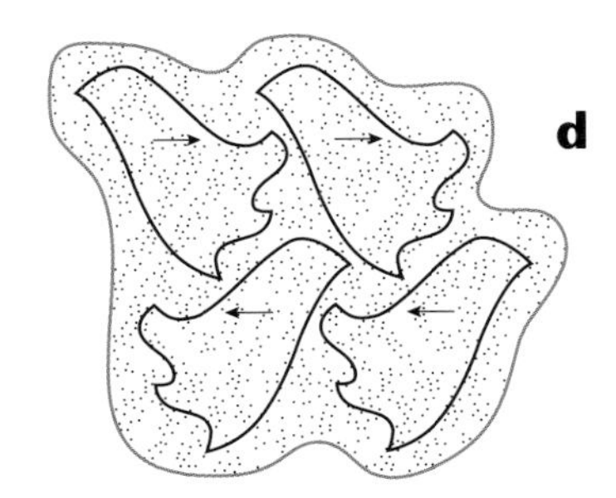

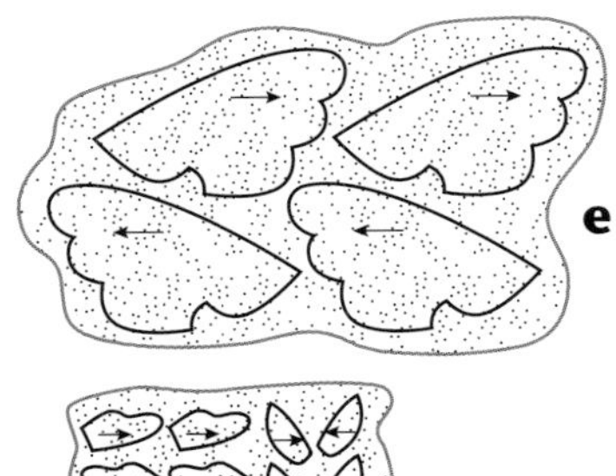

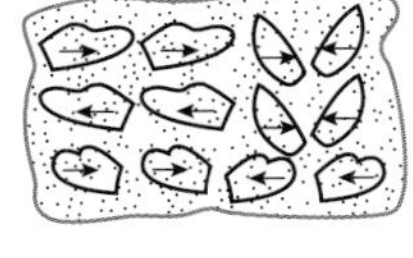

TIP

All the shapes for the hands, faces and feet can be grouped, as they'll be cut from the same fabric, and the same is true of the sleeve and main dress pieces. Note that you don't need to turn the heart template over, as it's symmetrical.

3 Fuse each bonding web patch onto the wrong side of the relevant fabric, and cut the shapes out along the marked lines (**f**).

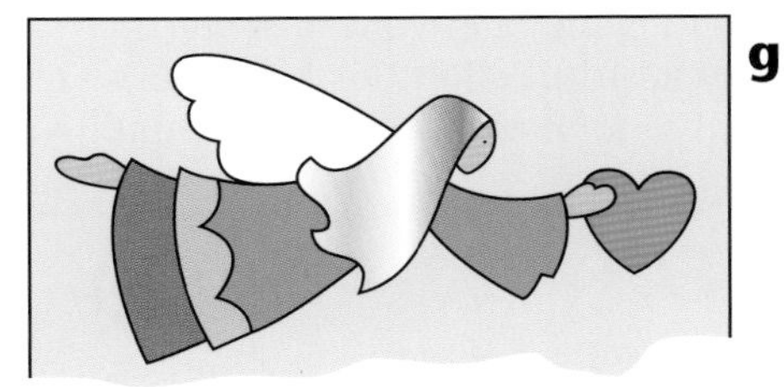

4 Press the background fabric and lay it on a flat surface. Lay the shapes out roughly in position, to create four angel designs (**g**). The arrows will help you to see which shapes go together; when the paper sides of the patches are towards you, all the arrows pointing in one direction form the angels facing left, and the others form the angels facing right.

5 Working on one angel at a time, peel the papers off and lay the patches in position (don't pin them at this stage, in case you have to adjust the positions when the other angels are in place). Once all the angels are laid out, check that they are evenly spaced, and that there's a more-or-less even border all the way around the edge of the design; keep at least ½in (1.5cm) in from the raw edges of the background fabric (**h**). Once you're happy, pin the patches in place, then fuse them in position (again, work on one angel at a time).

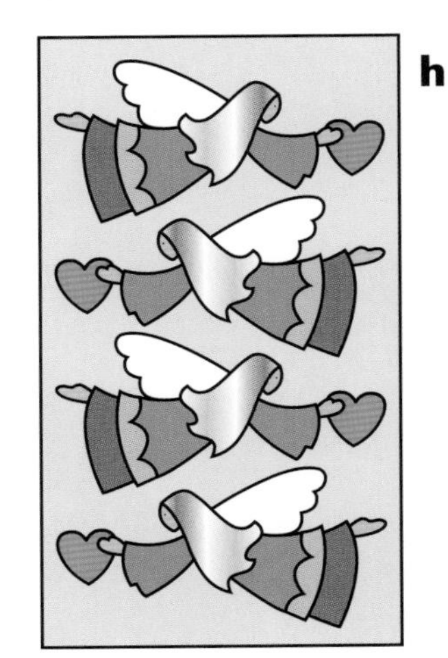

6 Using ¼in seams throughout, join the strips in groups of four; join them fairly randomly, but make sure that each group has a good mixture of colours and tones (**i**).

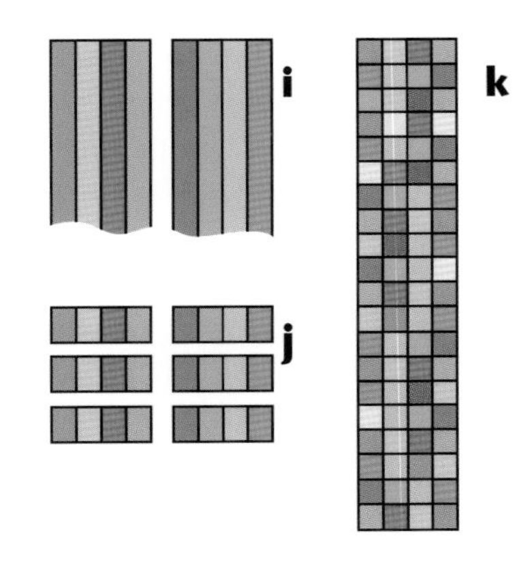

7 Press all the seams in one direction, then sub-cut these units into 2½in strips (**j**). Join these into four groups of 20 units (**k**), matching the seams at the corners (you don't need to be too fussy – the buttons will hide any little inaccuracies!)

8 Add two of these units to the sides of the quilt (**l**), then the others to the top and bottom (**m**), again matching the seams.

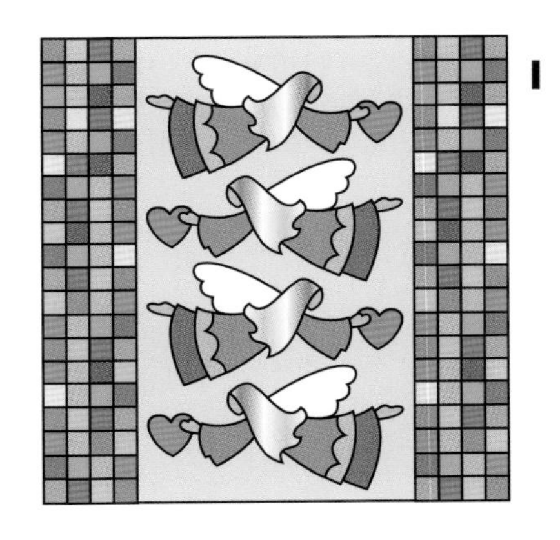

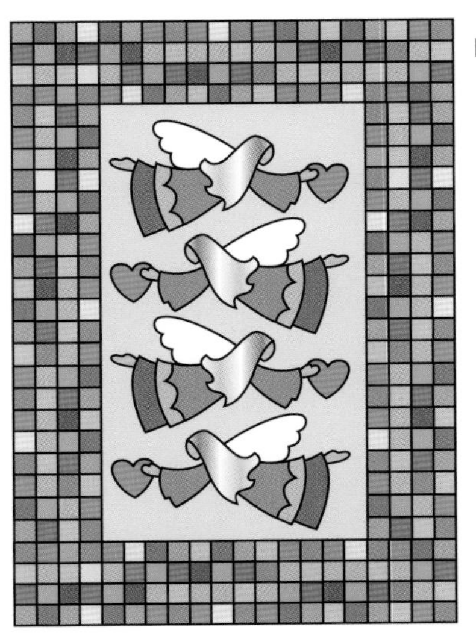

9 Lay the backing fabric, right side down, on a flat surface and cover with the wadding. Position the quilt top on the wadding, so that there is an even border of wadding all the way around. Use your preferred method (see p136) for securing the layers.

10 Use a decorative machine stitch round the edge of each appliqué patch; I used a machine blanket stitch in black (**n**). To ensure that the

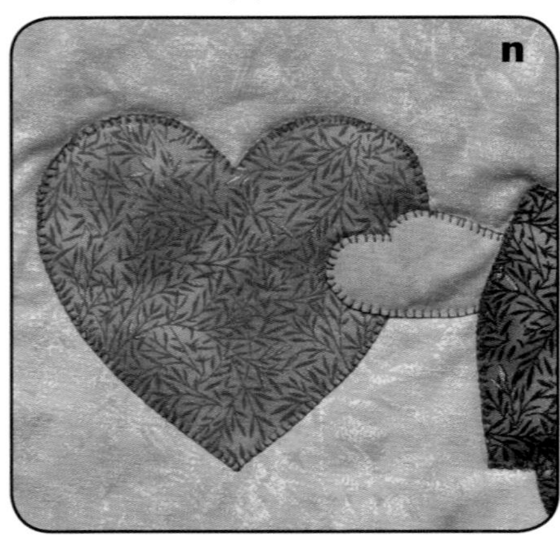

ends of all the stitching lines are sealed under later lines, stitch the patches on each angel in this order:

- heart, face, wing, foot, lower sleeve and top of dress border (**o**)
- hand, underskirt (**p**)
- top sleeve, dress (**q**)
- finally, the hair (**r**); begin the line of stitching at the top of the face.

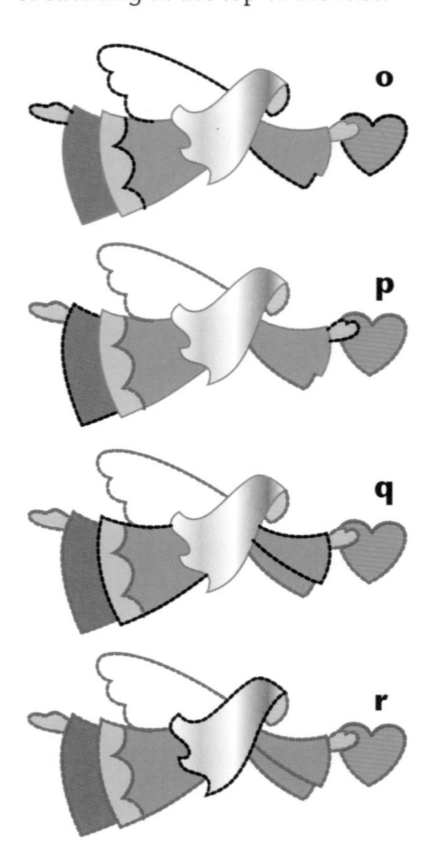

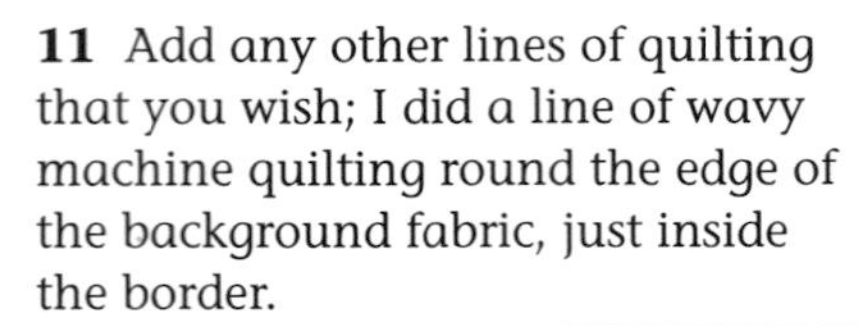

11 Add any other lines of quilting that you wish; I did a line of wavy machine quilting round the edge of the background fabric, just inside the border.

12 Trim the edges of the quilt to ½in beyond the raw edges of the pieced border (**s**). From the binding fabric, cut five strips 2¼in wide x the width of the fabric, and join these with diagonal seams to create one long strip. Follow the instructions on p136 to bind the edges of the quilt.

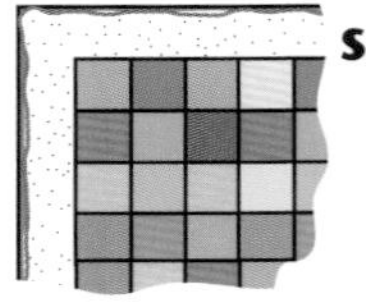

TIP

To create a nice wide binding, line up the raw edges of the binding with the raw edges of the border (not the wadding) as shown (**t**). When you come to the folds for the

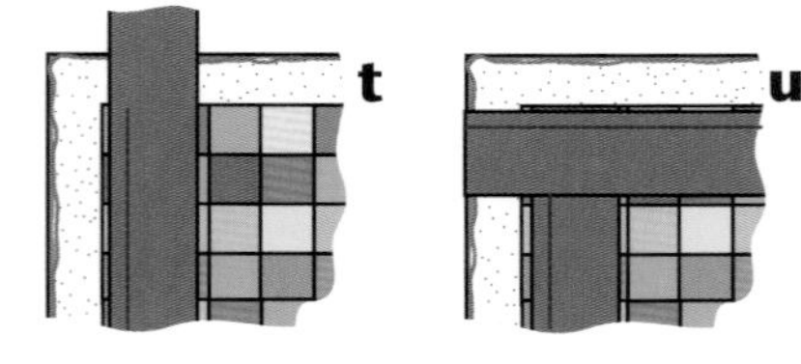

corner mitres, make sure that the folds (and your stitching) go right out to the edges of the wadding (**u**), not just to the edges of the pieced fabric.

13 Stitch on the beads for the angels' eyes, and add either beads or embroidery to create the haloes (**v**). Decorate the border with buttons, stitching them on at random intervals and mixing up the colours and sizes. Add a hidden casing on the back of the quilt, or hanging loops of ribbon or tape.

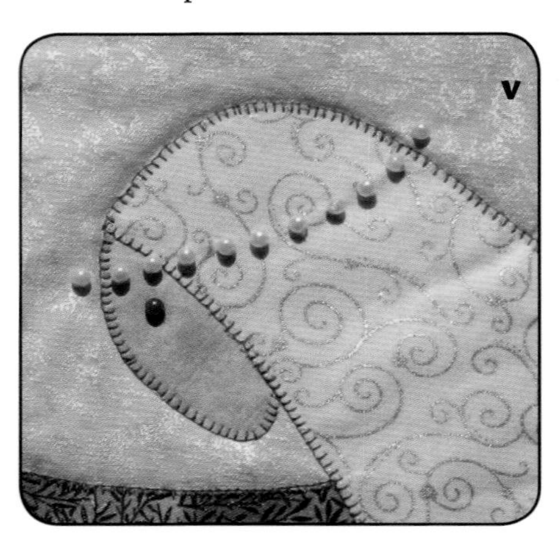

VARIATION

If you want to keep the hanging simpler, omit the border; this will produce a hanging measuring 40 x 24in (102 x 61cm) – or you could add a narrow, plain border. If you're lacking in wall space, just make one angel and surround her with a decorative print or pieced border.

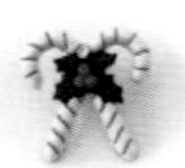

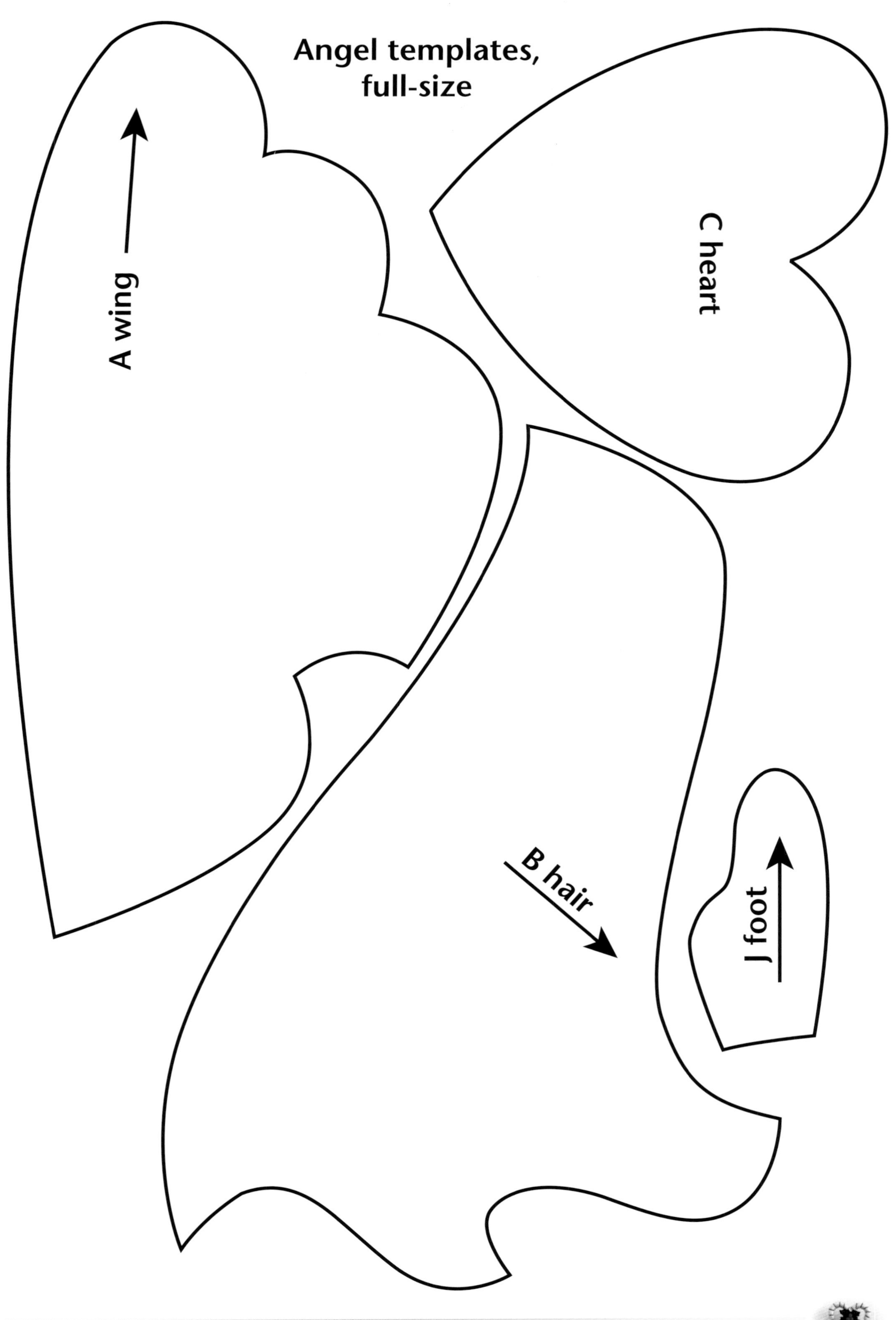
Angel templates, full-size
A wing
C heart
B hair
J foot

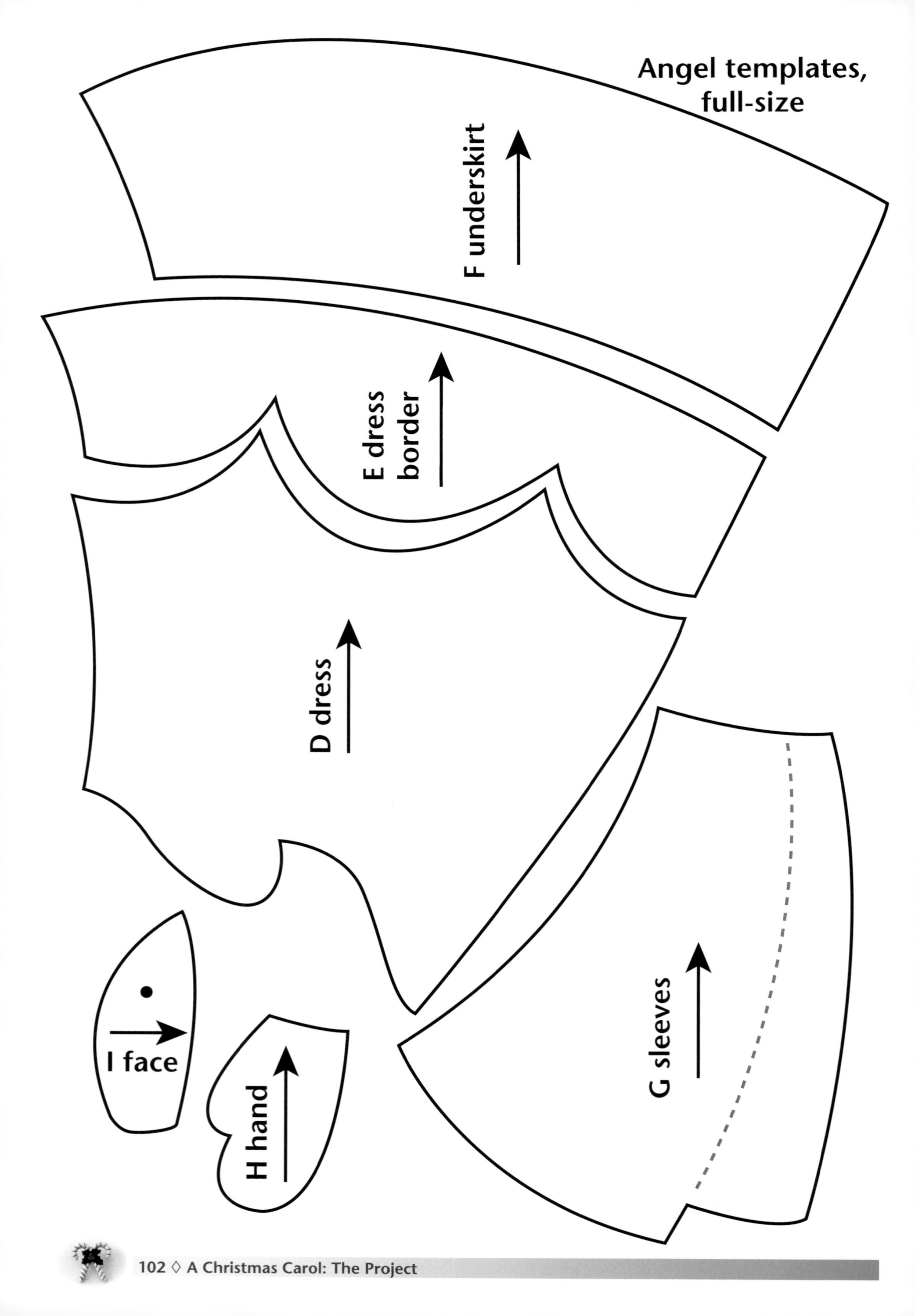
Angel templates, full-size
F underskirt
E dress border
D dress
G sleeves
I face
H hand

Wales

A classic Welsh red-and-white quilt is not quite what it seems ...

Wales: the land of the dragon and St David. Leeks and daffodils. Dylan Thomas and Richard Burton. Welsh cakes and castles. Owain Glyndŵr and Aneurin Bevan. Charlotte Church and Katherine Jenkins. Male voice choirs and eisteddfodds. As the old saying goes: everyone sings in Wales – and I certainly have noticed that Welsh people have the most enviable ability to sing instinctively in harmony. The country's male voice choirs are known the world over; these grew out of the nonconformist ('chapel') congregations, and originally consisted almost entirely of working-class men, many of them miners (see below).

The Big Pit pit head at Blaenavon

As well as music (and, of course, Welsh), another language that is spoken fluently in Wales is rugby. In some regions the sport is almost akin to a religion, and Wales has produced many great players. Castles are another features of Welsh life; it's hard to go more than a few miles without bumping into one. At least 400 are known of, and more than 100 are still standing – either restored, or as significant ruins. It's almost iniquitous to single individual ones out, but particularly spectacular are Caerphilly, Beaumaris, Raglan, Caernarfon, Harlech, Pembroke, White Castle and Manorbier.

Wales is also famous for two totally different types of mining. Welsh gold, which was known to the Romans, is some of the finest in the land – although known sources are almost exhausted. It's traditionally used for royal wedding bands, including the one put on Katherine Middleton's finger by Prince William in 2011. The other yield from the mountains, of course, is 'black gold': coal. It's impossible to think of Wales without thinking of mining, and impossible to visit the country without seeing visual reminders of the industry; coal mined in Wales fuelled the Industrial Revolution, both literally and metaphorically. Many thousands of Welsh men and boys worked down the pits. Accidents and explosions were common; sadly, while I was still working on this quilt, the latest Welsh mining disaster claimed four lives. A ballad called ***The Gresford Disaster*** tells the story of an explosion in the Gresford Colliery near Wrexham in 1934, which killed 266 people. A hymn tune called ***Gresford*** has become known as The Miners' Hymn, and is played at the annual Durham Miners' Gala.

And yet, mining is a part of Welsh life that is now almost confined to the history books; only a few small mines are still producing. Big Pit in Blaenavon, once the employer of 1,300 miners, is now the home of the

National Coal Museum; it's possible to visit the underground workings, travelling in the same cages that took the miners underground. Stilgoe and Skellern's ***By God, We're Good Now*** is a poignant song about a male voice choir; the choir is improving because its members are unemployed miners, who have nothing else to do but practise.

There was a wealth of history, culture, art and music in Wales to draw on for inspiration for my quilt. Lovespoon carving is not exclusively a Welsh craft, but the Welsh ones are most famous. Each lovespoon is carved from a single piece of wood; this makes the complex designs (such as cages containing wooden balls, and chains with individual links) particularly impressive. A young man would traditionally carve a spoon for a young woman who had taken his fancy; if she accepted the spoon, that would show that the interest was reciprocated – the origin of our term 'spooning.'

The language of lovespoons is quite intriguing: each motif has a different meaning. Here are some of them:

- heart: *love* (of course)
- double spoon: *togetherness*
- knot: *eternity*
- bell: *wedding*
- dragon: *protection* (the Welsh emblem)
- key or keyhole: *home* and *security,* and the concept of *locking my heart up safely*
- wheel: *work* or *provision;* also, a symbol of *steering life's path together*

Wales also has its own rich heritage of quilt designs; as in other parts of Britain, these were often created by tracing round everyday items such as cups, saucers, plates, flat-irons etc. The paisley motif, sometimes known as the Welsh Pear, appears often, and Welsh quilters also frequently included heart motifs (considered unlucky elsewhere, unless the quilt was for an engagement, wedding or anniversary). Many traditional Welsh quilts are pieced using a mixture of red and white fabrics, while others are exquisitely-stitched wholecloth designs.

I decided to piece my quilt in the classic red-and-white colourscheme, and to quilt the whole design by hand in the Welsh tradition. The top and bottom squares feature a feathered heart motif, and lovespoons decorate the sashing bands – apart from the one that says Cymru (the Welsh name for Wales). To honour the mining industry, I made the central motif of my quilt a stitched depiction of a pit-head. I wanted to encapsulate the idea that one of the dirtiest, most physically difficult jobs in the world has become a part of history, cleaned up and sanitised – an image stitched into pristine white fabric. Finally, the small corner squares are embellished with a musical motif: a Welsh harp.

Inside information

Making Welsh Quilts *by Mary Jenkins and Clare Claridge includes a library of Welsh quilting patterns. Antique Welsh quilts can be seen at the Welsh Quilt Museum in Lampeter (www.welshquilts.com/), and also at the Minerva Centre (www.minervacentre.co.uk/).*

Mumbles (wonderful name) on the Gower Peninsula has a shop devoted to lovespoons carved by different artists: www.thelovespooongallery.com. If you'd like a flavour of male voice choirs, www.treorchymalechoir.org/home/listen.htm gives you the chance to listen to many recordings.

The National Botanic Garden in Carmarthenshire (www.gardenofwales.org.uk) boasts the largest single-span greenhouse in the world, and the Theatr Botanica (a 360° cinema); www.castlewales.com/ details the location of all the known castles in the country.

Materials

To maintain the classic appearance of the quilt, I used plain red and white cotton fabrics for the basic piecing. The lovespoons and lettering are quilted in red on red, and the pit-head in white on white; the harps are stitched in red to produce a little bit of contrast against the white backgrounds.

Techniques

The main design is created with simple machine patchwork; I used foundation-piecing to ensure that I got good sharp points on the border triangles! All the motifs are hand-quilted, and the pit-head motif is thrown into relief with thousands (and we're talking *thousands*) of tiny seeding stitches ...

Backing and binding

The heart theme is reflected in two different red-and-white heart prints, one for the backing and one for the binding.

PROJECT

Feathered Heart Quilt

Welsh wholecloth quilts are famous for their beautiful motifs, often including hearts, and I've incorporated two traditional Welsh motifs into this quilt. The top is created using simple piecing, then each block is quilted with a classic feathered heart; the sashing strips are decorated with lovespoons – another lovely Welsh tradition! I've quilted my designs using traditional hand quilting, but if you want to speed up the quilting process you could use big-stitch quilting in coton à broder, or even quilt the motifs by machine. I made my quilt using a multicoloured batik for the blocks and corner squares, set off by cream sashing strips and a mid-aquamarine binding, but of course you could create yours in the traditional red-and-white colourscheme of the main quilt, or in any other colourway you fancy.

finished size: approx 36in (90cm) square

You will need:

- four 13in (33cm) squares of cotton fabric for the heart blocks
- nine 4in (10cm) squares for the cornerpieces
- twelve 13 x 4in (33 x 10cm) strips of contrast fabric for the sashing (these can all be cut from half a metre of fabric)
- 38in (1m) square of flat wadding
- 38in (1m) square of cotton backing fabric
- 4½yd (4.25m) binding strip in a contrasting or toning colour; the width depends on the width you'd like the finished binding to be, and whether you prefer to use a double or single binding strip
- quilt-marking method that will show up on your chosen fabrics (remember that you will be marking the squares, the cornerpieces and the sashing, so you might need more than one marking tool if the colours are very different)
- sewing thread to suit your fabric choices
- your choice of hand-quilting or machine-quilting thread
- tracing/greaseproof paper, pencil, fine black felt pen
- quilt rule

Instructions

1 Use quarter-inch seams throughout. Each main row of the quilt is created by joining two large squares and three sashing strips as shown (**a**); make two rows like this. The sashing rows are made by joining two sashing strips and three small corner squares as shown (**b**); make three sashing rows. Press all the seams towards the darker fabric.

2 Join the main rows and the sashing rows as shown (**c**) to create the quilt top; press the seams towards the darker fabric.

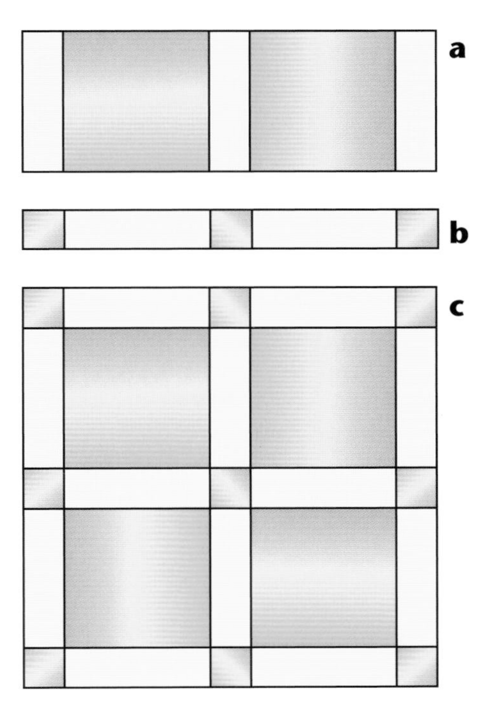

3 Fold one piece of tracing/ greaseproof paper in half, and fingerpress the crease; unfold. Lay the paper over the heart template (template A) so that the fold aligns with the dotted line on the template, and trace all the lines (**d**). Turn the paper over and lay it over the heart template again, tracing the lines again to complete the template (**e**). On one side of the paper, go over the lines with felt pen to strengthen them. Now trace the lovespoon template (template B) onto tracing/greaseproof paper (**f**).

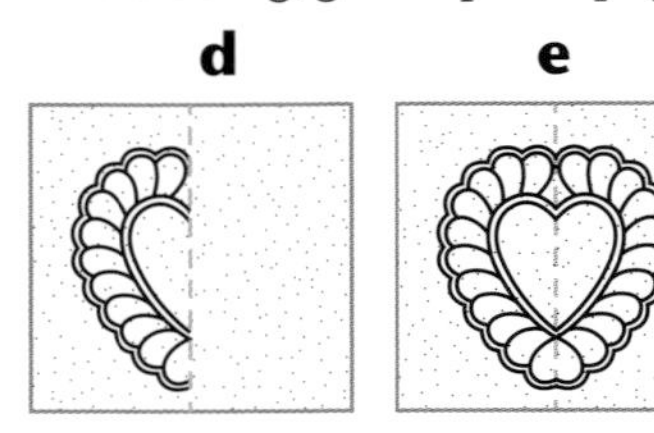

4 Use your preferred method to trace the heart template onto each large square of the quilt top, making sure that the design is centred on each square (**g**). Next, trace the lovespoon template onto each sashing strip (**h**) – on the outside (raw) edges of the quilt top, remember to allow for the ¼in seam allowance that will disappear under the binding when you are positioning the lovespoons.

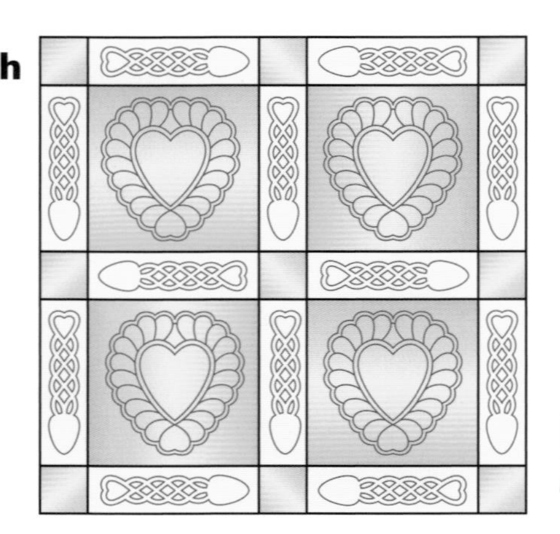

TIP

When you're marking the lovespoon motifs, keep checking the diagram to see how each one is orientated.

5 If you wish, add a chequer-board background behind the heart designs. Begin by laying the quilt rule diagonally across one square, and draw the line in from corner to corner wherever it goes over the background fabric (**i**). Then use the quilt rule to measure out and draw lines at 1in intervals across the square (**j**). Do the same across each square in the other direction (**k**).

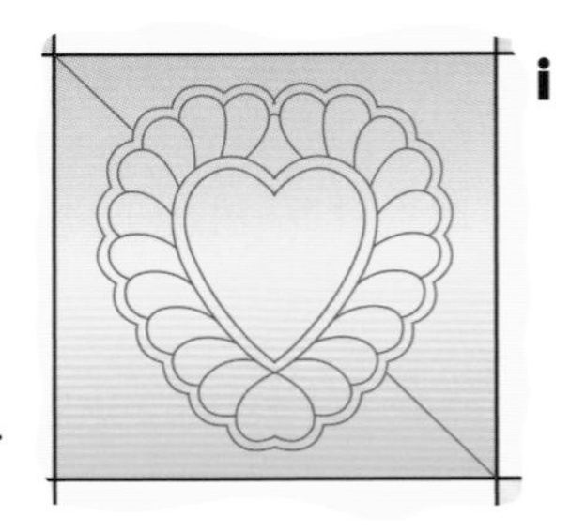

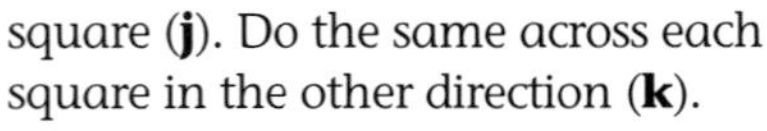

6 Layer the quilt with the backing and wadding, securing the layers as you wish (see p136), and use your chosen stitching method to quilt all the lines. Whether you're quilting by hand or machine, work your way outwards from the centre of the quilt. I also quilted ¼in inside each of the sashing strips and small squares.

7 If necessary, remove any marking lines. Follow the instructions on p136 to bind the edges of the quilt.

VARIATION

If you prefer to make a smaller quilt, you can just use one heart block surrounded by sashing. This creates a design about 20in (50cm) square, which would be an ideal size for a cushion-cover or bag front, or a special small wall-hanging to celebrate a wedding or anniversary.

Top: Fortified gate across the river at Monmouth; Below: Welsh slates; Bottom: waterfall feeding Lake Vyrnwy

Feathered Heart templates, full-size

Oak

Our reverence for the mighty oak, the king of British trees, goes back to ancient times.

Richard Perry's Freedom Tree *in St Helier, Jersey*

As well as our flowers providing many Christian names (see p24), our shrubs and trees also provide a fertile hunting-ground for monikers: Ash, Hazel, Ivy, Holly, Hazel, Laurel, Aspen, Willow, May. A trawl through the local phone directory yields several of the above also used as surnames, as well as Alder, Bay, Beech, Birch, Box, Elms, Hawthorne and Redwood. Not to mention Furze, Greenwood, Sylvester, Wood and Woodman. But if you really want to evoke the idea of the quintessential solid, reliable British man, you can't do better than give him the name Oak. Think of Gabriel Oak in Hardy's ***Far From the Madding Crowd***: the salt of the earth, the honest farm-worker, but with just a touch of the angels in his first name. The Irish names Derry and Dara also relate to oak: the place-name Kildare literally means 'church of oak.'

The classic British oak (*Quercus robur*) is native to our islands, and in many ways has become symbolic of the land. Along with the oakleaf and acorn, it's a kind of shorthand for everything British, particularly its countryside: both the National Trust (see p108) and The Woodland Trust use the oakleaf as part of their logo. In Gainsborough's painting ***Mr and Mrs Andrews***, the quintessential landed gentry couple are standing under an oak. Various folk songs include references to the tree: '*Oh the oak and the ash, and the bonny ivy-tree*' etc.

Some of this association is because of the importance of oak in our history. It was used for centuries in ship-building, and the official march of the Royal Navy is called ***Heart of Oak***. The wood was widely used for building (think of all our half-timbered houses, see p116), and is still popular for furniture. Oak makes good firewood, and along with other trees the smaller branches and twigs were turned into charcoal; oak bark was used for tanning leather, and also as a brown dye, and oak gall for many years was the main constituent of black ink. Oaks support more types of invertebrate than any other British tree (and no doubt, late on a Saturday night, quite a few inebriates as well …) And acorns (as any reader of A A Milne knows) are the favourite food of pigs; if you live in the New Forest, you have an ancient right known as 'pannage' or 'common of mast,'

which allows you to graze your pigs in the Forest for a couple of months each autumn. The pigs are fattened up nicely for the winter, and the ground is cleared of acorns, which are poisonous to the region's ponies.

The oak has a long association with folklore, too. Because the tree often seems to attract lightning bolts (producing so-called 'blasted oaks'), it's sometimes associated with the god of thunder. Various traditional saws, or sayings, mention oak:

If the oak before the ash,
then we'll only have a splash;
if the ash before the oak,
then we'll surely have a soak.

– only one of many sayings which try unsuccessfully to predict the maverick British weather (see p12!)

And there are even royal connections with the beloved oak. The round table which hangs in Winchester Cathedral, and which purports to be King Arthur's original (I'm saying nothing), is made of English oak. According to tradition Charles II hid from the Roundhead forces in an oak tree at Boscobel; any inn called The Royal Oak will usually include a face, a crown, or some other royal symbol alongside the tree on its pub sign – sometimes obvious, sometimes hidden. The oak leaf is also the symbol of the Royal Clan Stewart. Particular oaks often have specific stories attached to them: the ancient Gog and Magog oaks in Somerset are the remnants of an oak-lined avenue which was said to lead to Glastonbury, and the Major Oak in Sherwood Forest is supposed to be the meeting-place of Robin Hood and his Merry Men; certainly the hollow in its trunk is large enough to hold a good dozen people.

The Romans wore crowns of oak leaves during their triumphs, or victory parades. And, of course, the Romans couldn't resist coming to our islands (must have been attracted by the weather); the Roman conquest of Britain began in around AD43, and they didn't go home until 410. When they returned to warmer climes, they left a legacy of disconcertingly straight roads, as opposed to the traditional winding thoroughfares following the routes of rivers and valleys, and astonishingly solid buildings. Roman ruins can be seen in hundreds of places; some of the best-known are the remains of Hadrian's Wall and the Antonine Wall, Caerleon in Wales, and Fishbourne Roman Palace.

My quilt combines the themes of the mighty oak and the mighty Romans. I've taken the quotation '*Tall oaks from little acorns grow,*' from ***Lines Written for a School Declamation*** by 18th century poet David Everett. Because the Romans were famous for their beautiful mosaics, I've created the lettering from a mosaic of fused fabric in shades of green, tan and brown, and set the quotation on two large oak-leaves decorated with acorns. The letterforms are, of course, Roman capitals, inspired by the ones used in Roman inscriptions.

Inside information

The Woodland Trust (www.woodlandtrust.org.uk/) is particularly involved in woodland conservation; some of their subsidiary websites include www.british-trees.com/, www.ancienttreehunt.org.uk/, and VisitWoods.org.uk.

www.mightyoakbrewing.co.uk/ is one of our many small private breweries, producing award-winning beers and ciders. For more on the Roman invasion, www.roman-britain.org/describes itself as 'the No1 website for all things Romano-British,' and includes information on Roman sites, calendar etc.

Materials

All the fabrics on this quilt are cotton; for the lettering I picked various marbled, batik and leafy prints to echo the idea of foliage. I've used bonding web for the fusing, and the tops of the acorn cups are decorated with a velvet braid in the form of oak leaf motifs.

Techniques

The lettering is created in fused mosaic. I backed my chosen prints with bonding web, then cut them into random snippets; on the large leaf shapes I drew out the letterforms in chalk, then filled each letter with mosaic patches. Once I was happy with the positioning and the flow of colours, I fused all the pieces in position and then added lines of machine quilting to keep them in place. The textures on the acorns are also created with machine quilting, using decorative stitches on the acorns and a grid of straight stitching on the acorn cups.

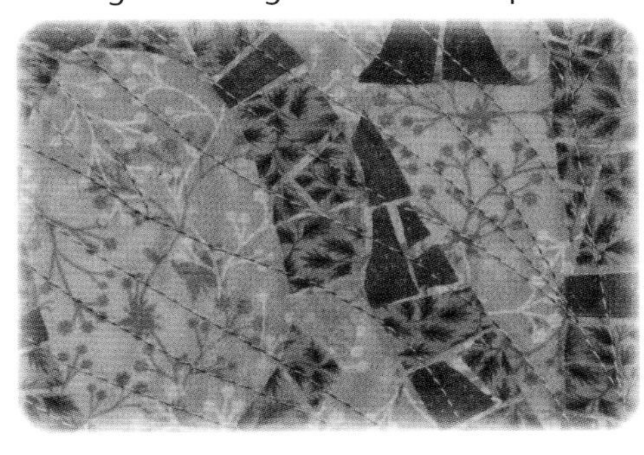

Backing and binding

A pretty green-and-tan oak leaf print beautifully complements both the colours and subject-matter of the quilt front. To edge the shapes, I used bias strips folded double to create a very narrow binding.

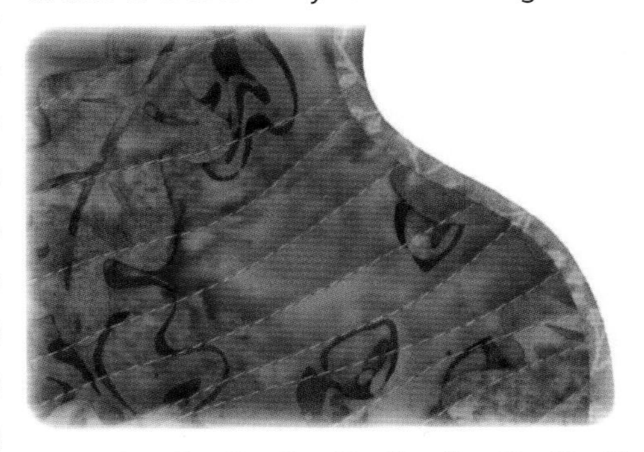

PROJECT

Roman Oaks

The Roman influence and the oak leaf motif come together perfectly in this lap quilt. The basic design is often called Amish Stripes, but is also known as Roman Stripes; it's a very easy design to piece, made even easier if you use strips from a Jelly-Roll™ pack. I've used autumnal colours (from a Moda pack called Summer's End), to pick up the leaf theme; the oak leaf motif itself is stitched into each triangle using big-stitch quilting in coton à broder.

finished size: approx 52 x 65in (132 x 166cm)

You will need:

- 25 strips of cotton fabric in toning colours, each 2½in wide by the width of the fabric (at least 42in/107cm)
- five 20in (51cm) squares of contrast fabric for the plain triangles (these can be all the same fabric, or a mixture)
- wadding roughly 54 x 67in (roughly 138 x 170cm)
- backing fabric roughly 54 x 67in (roughly 138 x 170cm)
- template plastic 11 x 6in (28 x 15cm)
- pencil, paper scissors, chalk marker
- quilt-marking tool of your choice
- sewing thread to tone with your fabrics
- rotary cutter, quilt rule and cutting board
- your choice of hand or machine quilting threads
- fabric for binding, 12 in (30cm) x the width of the fabric (if you prefer to do a double binding, double this amount)

Instructions

1 Use ¼in seams throughout. Divide the strips into five groups of five, so that you have a good mixture of tones and prints within each group. Join each set of five strips as shown (**a**), staggering each new strip you add by a scant 2in.

2 Press the seams all in the same direction. Using the quilt rule, chalk marker and board, mark the pieced strips at a 45° angle, first one way (**b**) and then the other (**c**) to create large triangles; each pieced strip should give you four triangles with a long edge of 20in (51cm). If your triangles need to be a bit smaller, it doesn't matter; just make them all the same size. Once you're happy with the marked lines, use the rotary cutter, rule and board to cut the triangles (**d**).

Above: Part of the Roman defensive wall of Portchester Castle in Sussex

3 Cut each square of contrast fabric across one diagonal and then the other to produce triangles (**e**); if necessary, cut these down to the same size as your pieced triangles.

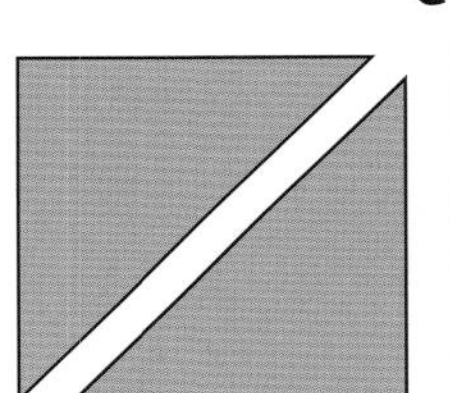

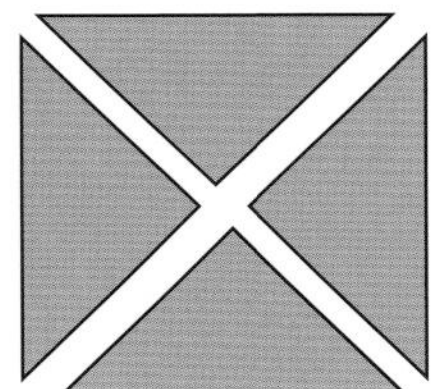

TIP

By creating the triangles this way, you ensure that the straight grain of the fabric is on the long edge of each patch; this makes it easier when you're joining them to the pieced triangles, as the edges of both fabrics will be on the straight grain.

4 Join the plain and pieced triangles in pairs (**f**) to give you 20 squares.

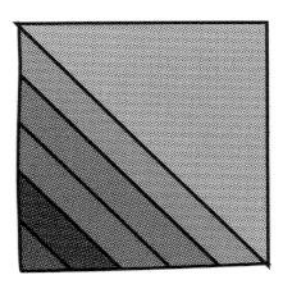

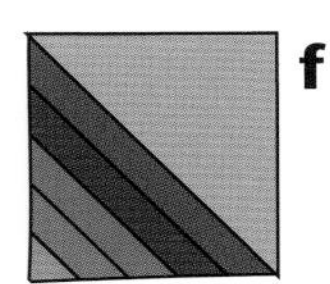

Press the seam on each square in the same direction as the piecing. Trim the squares slightly to ensure that they are even and straight, making sure that the central seam forms the exact diagonal of each square; each square will now measure roughly 13½in (roughly 35cm) on each side.

5 Lay the squares out in a 4 x 5 design as shown (**g**); if you've used different fabrics for the contrast patches, make sure that you have a good distribution of tones and shades across the layout. Once you're happy, join the squares into rows (**h**), and then join the rows to complete the quilt top (**i**).

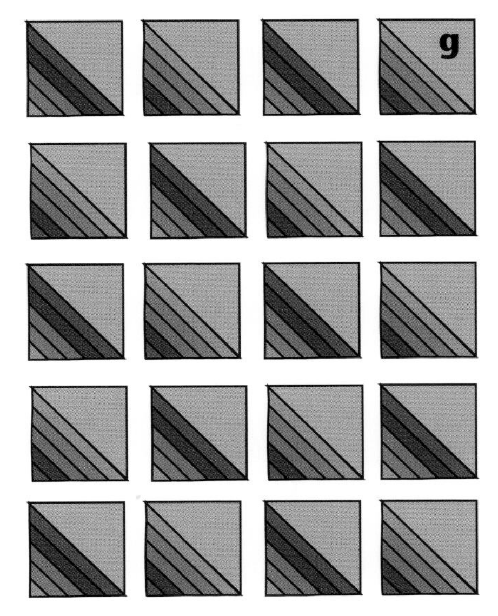

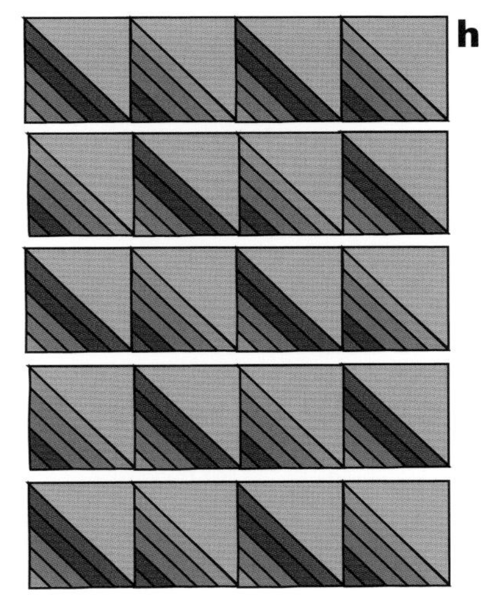

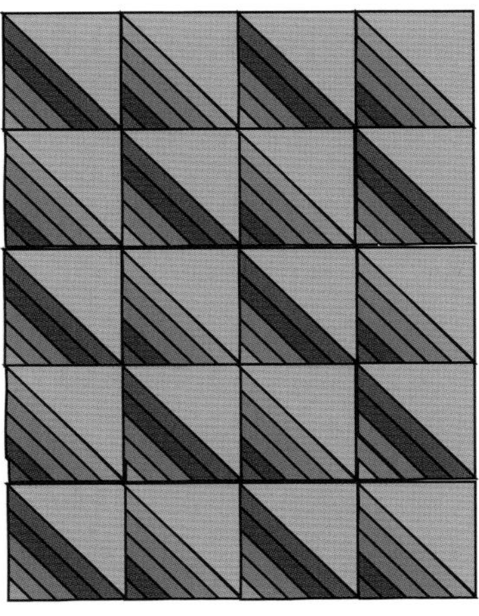

6 Trace the oak leaf template onto the template plastic and cut it out along the marked line (**j**). Use this to mark an oak leaf motif into each plain triangle (**k**), then turn the template through 180° and mark all the pieced triangles as shown (**l**).

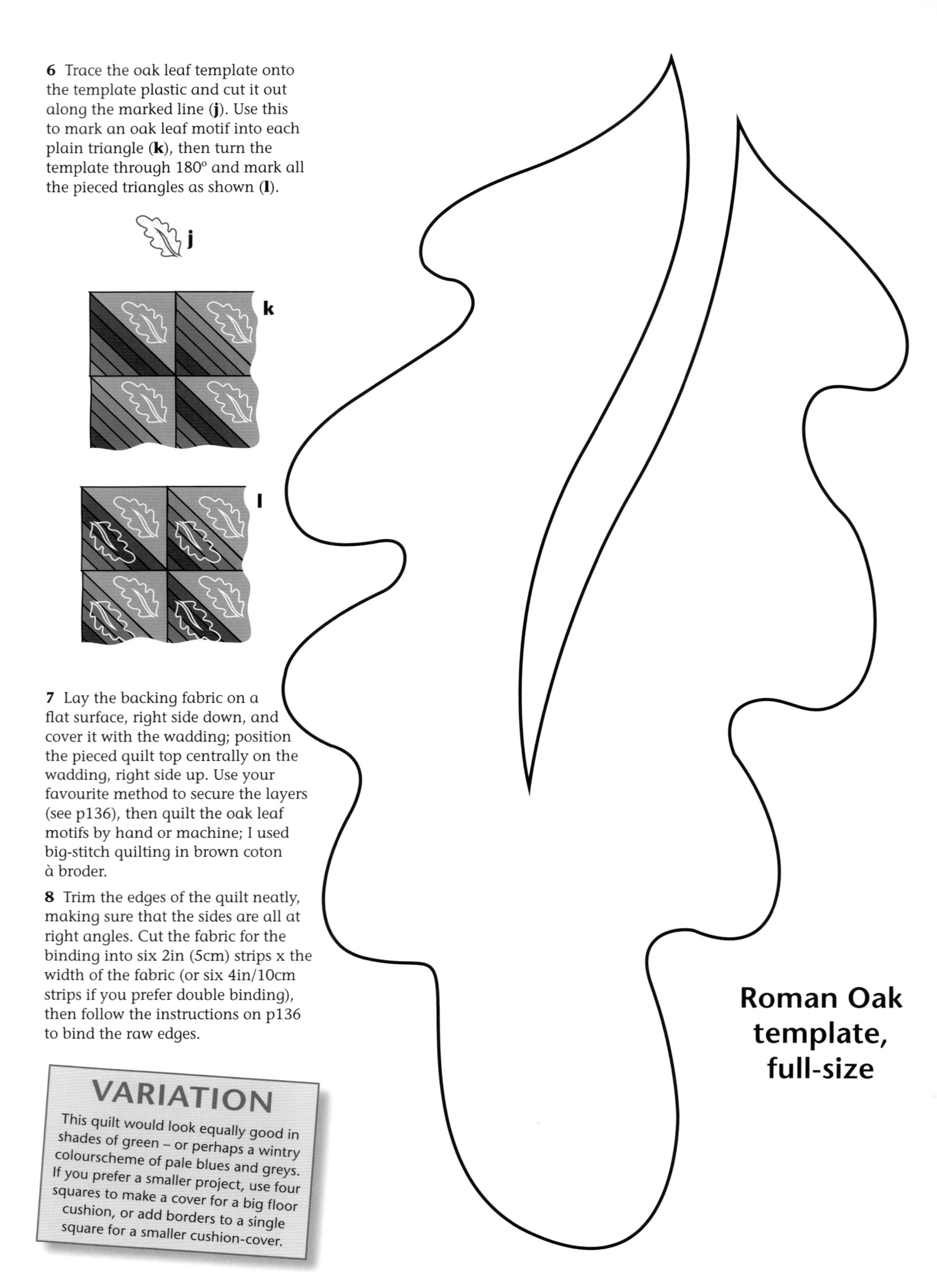

7 Lay the backing fabric on a flat surface, right side down, and cover it with the wadding; position the pieced quilt top centrally on the wadding, right side up. Use your favourite method to secure the layers (see p136), then quilt the oak leaf motifs by hand or machine; I used big-stitch quilting in brown coton à broder.

8 Trim the edges of the quilt neatly, making sure that the sides are all at right angles. Cut the fabric for the binding into six 2in (5cm) strips x the width of the fabric (or six 4in/10cm strips if you prefer double binding), then follow the instructions on p136 to bind the raw edges.

VARIATION

This quilt would look equally good in shades of green – or perhaps a wintry colourscheme of pale blues and greys. If you prefer a smaller project, use four squares to make a cover for a big floor cushion, or add borders to a single square for a smaller cushion-cover.

Roman Oak template, full-size

Dream

Under the strange light of a midsummer moon, it's easy to feel we can peep into the fairy world ...

If you asked anyone in the world to name the most famous writer in the English language, virtually everyone would come up with the same answer: Shakespeare. William Shakespeare, also known as The Bard of Avon or just The Bard, was born in 1564, in the place that has become irrevocably associated with his name: Stratford-upon-Avon. The large house where he was born still exists (below), right in the centre of the town; it was built by his father John between 1556 and 1575 (obviously builders were just as slow in those days). For about ten years Shakespeare lived and worked in London, but returned to Stratford to retire; he died there in 1616.

During his 52 years, he wrote numerous plays and poems; although there has been endless speculation about whether he actually wrote everything attributed to him, if he wrote even a fraction of it he was phenomenally talented. Shakespeare was single-handedly responsible for introducing an astonishing number of neologisms (new words), figures of speech and quotable phrases into our language: here are just

a few of them. Parting is such sweet sorrow; all that glisters is not gold; out, damned spot; if music be the food of love, play on; there's method in my madness; Romeo, Romeo, wherefore art thou Romeo?; dancing attendance; pound of flesh; bated breath; this sceptred isle; to sleep, perchance to dream; is this a dagger that I see before me?; alas, poor Yorick; it's all Greek to me; short shrift; green-eyed jealousy; knitting your brows; foul play (and fair play); the truth will out.

Shakespeare seemed to deserve his own quilt, but I found it difficult to narrow down which part of his vast work to use for inspiration. After a while I hit on the idea of using ***A Midsummer Night's Dream*** to combine the work of The Bard with another aspect of British life and folklore: the Little People. This is a generic name for all kinds of small mythical beings: fairies, goblins, gnomes, elves, sprites, brownies, leprechauns (see p6) etc. Many different parts of the British Isles have

their own local Little People; for instance, the Green Children of Woolpit is a 12th century legend about two green-skinned children, a brother and sister, who appeared in the village and would only eat green beans. The knacker, knocker, bwca (Welsh) or bucca (Cornish) was a small sprite who lived in a mine; if you treated these sprites well, they'd show you where the tin (or other booty) was. Cornish miners would often leave them the tail ends of their pasties, as a kind of votive offering.

Some of these beings are particularly associated with the sea; the Blue Men of Minch inhabit the stretch of water around Lewis, the Shiant Islands and Long Island in Scotland. Selkies (or silkies, or selchies) are seals in human form, which appear in stories from northern Scotland, Ireland and up to Iceland. Kelpies are mythical water-horses that live in Scotland's rivers and seas. Like Shakespeare, the Little People have also contributed several words to our language: *fay* (related to the word fairy), *elfin*, and the wonderful word *eldritch*, used to describe something that seems to come from another realm.

Fairy folk appear in the art and literature of all ages; Spenser wrote ***The Faerie Queene*** as long ago as the 1590s. Fairies became an obsession for the Victorians, and the strange paintings of paranoid schizophrenic Richard Dadd were very popular. The modern image of fairies, as small feminine beings with butterfly wings, comes largely from the Victorian Cottingley Fairy Photographs, supposedly taken by young cousins Elsie Wright and Frances Griffiths in 1917. Much later in their lives the girls, now old women, admitted that most of the photographs were faked, but rather confusingly insisted that **one** of them was genuine. In the early years of the 20th century J M Barrie's ***Peter Pan*** was published, complete with Tinker Bell (or Tinkerbell), and a little later Cicely Mary Barker's ***Flower Fairy*** books came out to great acclaim.

In my quilt, Titania (Shakespeare's Queen of the Fairies) has emerged under the light of the moon; assorted flowers and leaves create her kingdom. To produce a dreamlike effect, the whole piece is made in sheer fabrics and skeleton leaves; if you hold the quilt up against the light, you can see all the motifs but also see right through the layers. The lion's pawprint is a reference both to the lion that the Players in ***Midsummer Night's Dream*** think might be prowling around, and to Aslan in CS Lewis' ***Narnia*** books.

Inside information

If you'd like to know more about The Bard, try www.shakespeare-online.com/, which offers a wealth of information on topics related to the man and his work. If you'd like access to any of Shakespeare's texts, they can be found on shakespeare.mit.edu/.

Several years ago we first discovered the wonderful Reduced Shakespeare Company (www.reducedshakespeare.com/). Although they're Americans, they perform a show consisting of the entire works of Shakespeare, and another show on the great works of English literature. (A word of warning: if you go to one of their performances, don't sit near the front …!)

Quilters might like to know of the Flower Fairy fabrics, produced by Michael Miller Fabrics from Cicely Mary Barker's illustrations.

Materials

The entire quilt is constructed from different sheer fabrics and coloured skeleton leaves, plus various embroidery threads.

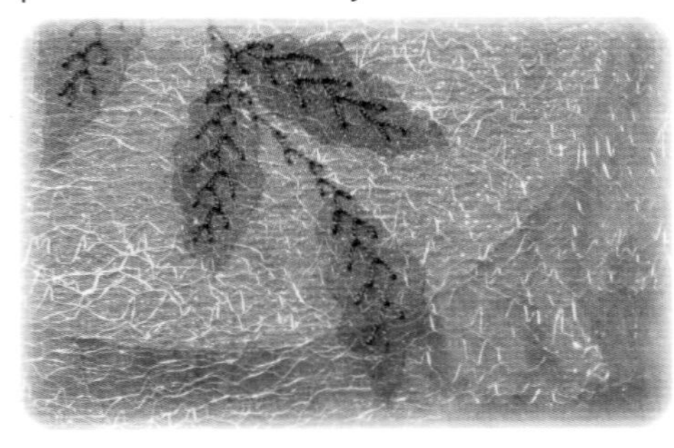

Techniques

I used a soldering iron to cut various motifs out of different sheer fabrics – the flowers, leaves, moon, letters, and different sections of Titania etc. I then trapped these motifs at different levels between full-size layers of sheer fabric, along with lots of skeleton leaves, and stitched round them by hand. All the quilting and embroidery is done by hand.

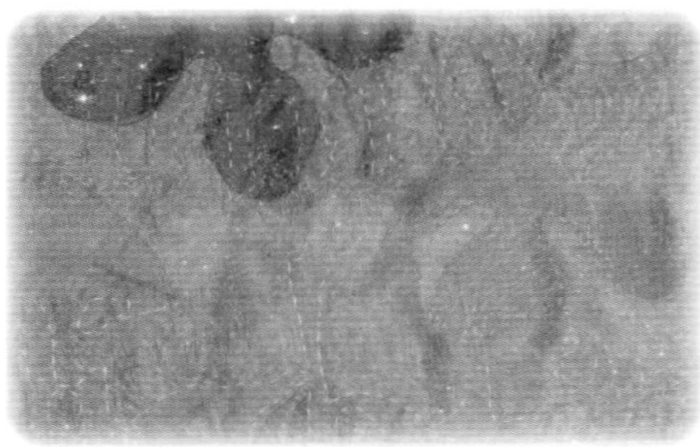

Backing and binding

The backing is simply the final layer of sheer fabric. Once the design was completely stitched, I sculpted the outside of the quilt by running the tip of the soldering iron along a shaped ruler; this also sealed the sheer edges together so that they won't fray.

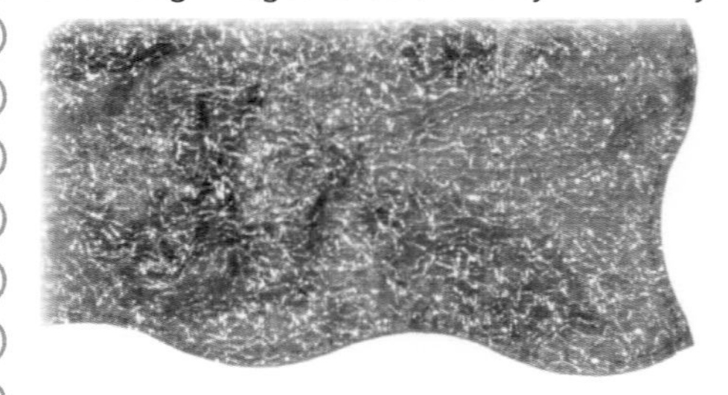

PROJECT

Tudor Cottage

This is your chance to stitch your own traditional half-timbered cottage from the time of the Bard. If you like you can decorate it with lace and quilting to create the impression of pargeting, or you can add your own details to personalise the house – perhaps roses round the door, or a friendly cat at a window? As Shakespeare lived under the Tudor dynasty (which lasted from Henry VII's accession in 1485 to Elizabeth I's death in 1603, see p39), I've put Tudor roses in the corners.

finished size: 20 x 18in (51 x 46cm)

You will need:

- pale green cotton fabric for the background
- two pieces of flat wadding: one piece 20 x 18in (51 x 46cm), one piece 16 x 11in (41 x 28cm)
- backing fabric 22 x 20in (56 x 51cm)
- cotton fabrics for the house:
  13 x 11in (35 x 30cm) white or cream for the house itself (I used a white-on-white print)
- – 14 x 4in (36 x 10cm) tan print for the thatched roofs (main roof and door)
- – two 3in (8cm) red print squares for the curtains
- – 3 x 3½in (8 x 10cm) wood print or coloured print for the door
- three 3in (8cm) squares of black net or mesh fabric for the windows
- cotton print fabric for the borders:
- – two 3 x 14in (8 x 36cm) strips
- – two 3 x 12in (8 x 31cm) strips
  (if the print is strongly directional, bear this in mind as you cut the borders)
- four 4½in (12cm) squares of pale yellow cotton fabric for the corner squares
- soft pencil
- for the tudor rose cornerpieces (optional):
- – 9in (23cm) square of green cotton fabric
- – 8in (20cm) square of red cotton fabric
- – 5in (13cm) square of white cotton fabric
- – 2in (5cm) square of yellow cotton fabric
- – squares of bonding web the same size as the fabric pieces above
- – four 4½in squares of tearaway foundation fabric (or cartridge paper)
- – black machine sewing or embroidery thread for the satin stitch
- 6yd (6m) black fusible bias binding, ¼in (6mm) wide
- sewing thread for doing the appliqué, and to match your bias binding

Instructions

1 Use a photocopier to enlarge the cottage template (A) on p119 by 141% (A4 to A3). Press the fabric for the building and lay it right side up over the full-size design, so that there's a margin of fabric all the way around, and pin the layers together; use a soft pencil to draw in all the lines. Use your pencil to shade in the window areas as shown (**a**) – this will remind you exactly where the window shapes begin and end. Unpin.

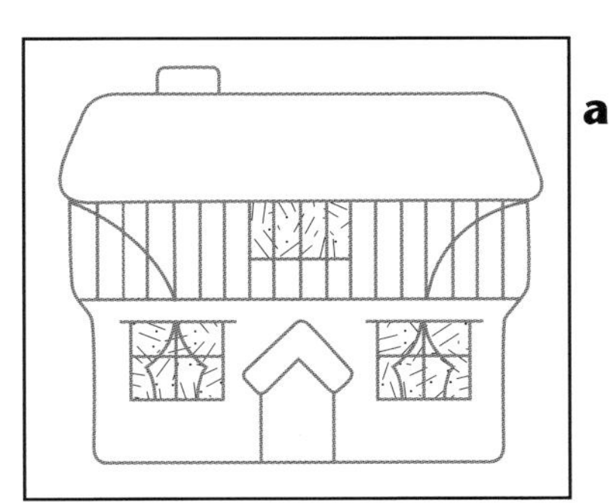
a

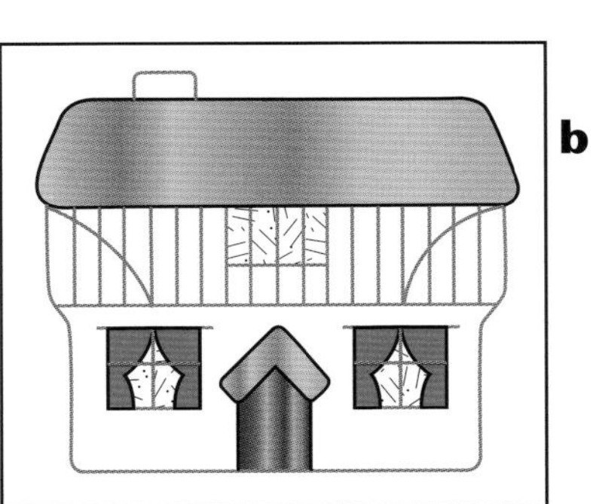
b

2 Follow the instructions on page 135, for reverse appliqué from the front, to add the curtain shapes, the roof and thatch over the door, and the door shape itself. Using pencil, re-draw the window lines that go across the curtain shapes (**b**).

3 Lay the patches of black net over the window shapes on the right side of the work, making sure that they fully cover the window areas, then stitch around the outside of the window rectangles using the small zigzag (**c**).

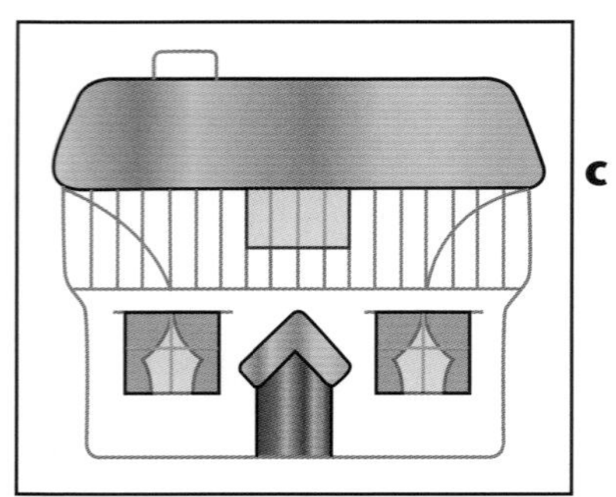

c

TIP

As the net has a very open texture, you might find it useful to stitch around the net patches twice – this will help to ensure that the raw edges of the net can't creep out from under the binding at a later stage.

4 Lay the smaller piece of wadding on a flat surface. Position the design on top, right side up, and pin the layers together. If you'd like to add any lines of quilting or lines of white lace to represent pargeting, now is the time to do it – or you can quilt by hand, or add beads or ornaments, when the house design is complete.

5 Now it's time to add the bias binding! Follow the sequence of diagrams (**d**) to add the lines of binding in turn; fuse in place the lines of binding shown as thick black lines on the first diagram, then stitch these before you go on to the next diagram, and so on (see p135 for tips on using and stitching fusible binding). At step **d3**, begin and end the line of bias binding at the top inner corner of the door thatch; cut the final end of binding ¼in longer than the line, and fold the raw end under itself to neaten the ends.

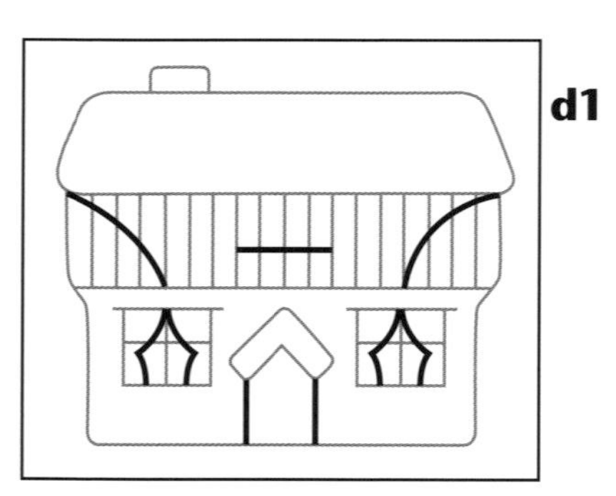

d1

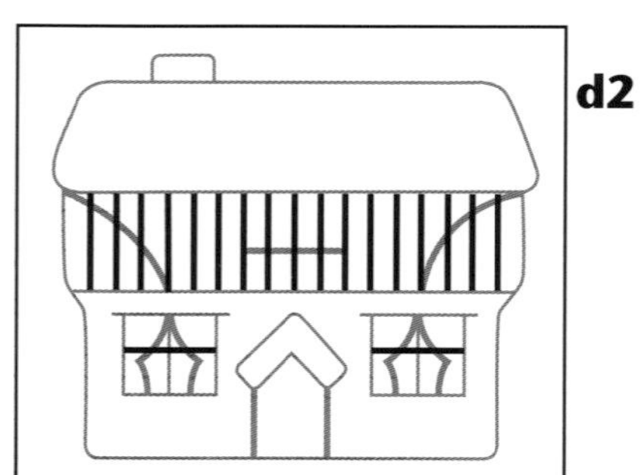

d2

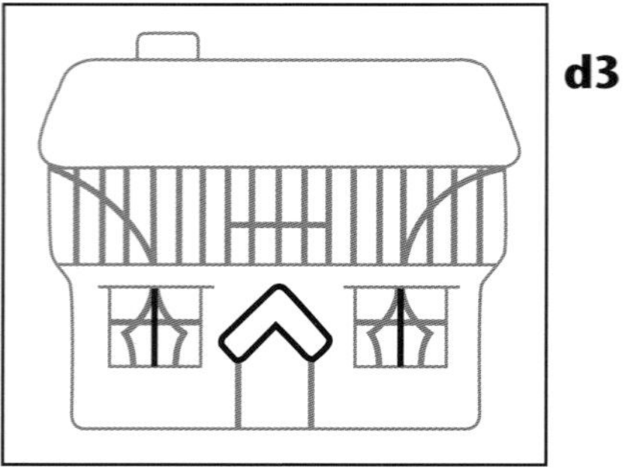

d3

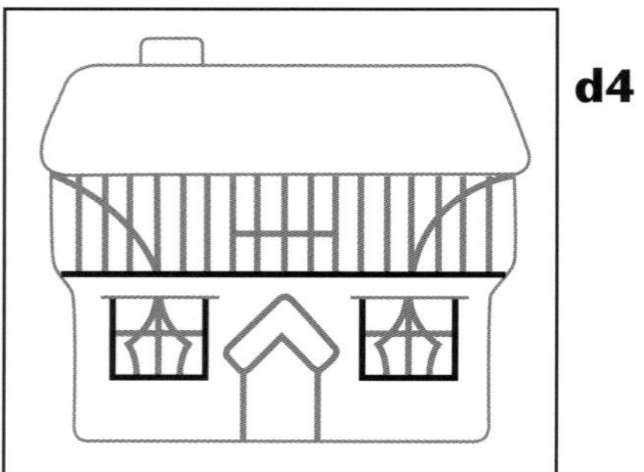

d4

d5

For the main horizontal line across the centre of the house at step **d4**, you could use black braid rather than bias binding to suggest the thick carved beams that are often used on half-timbered houses (**e**).

e

6 When you've completed all the lines on the diagrams, you'll notice that there are still some design lines that haven't been covered with binding. This is because you'll add those to finish off the building once it's been positioned on the background. First of all, work a line of small zigzag (around 2 length and width) all round the outline of the design, then trim the fabric and wadding close to this line around your design (**f**).

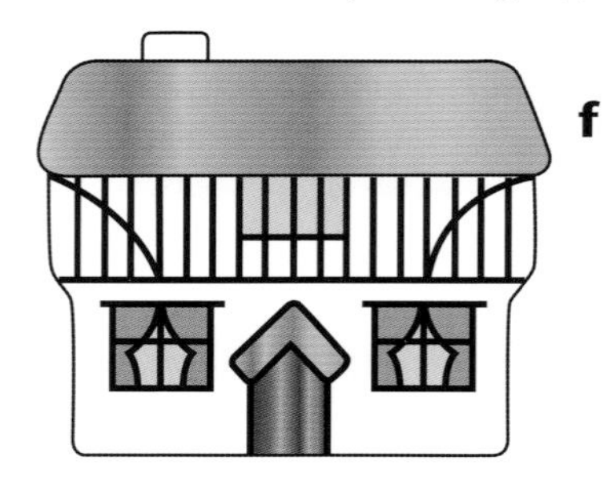

f

7 If you'd like to add the Tudor roses to the corner patches, follow the sequence below (**g**); if you prefer to leave your corner squares plain, move on to step 8.

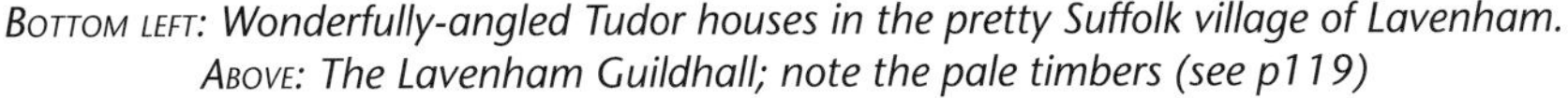

Bottom left: Wonderfully-angled Tudor houses in the pretty Suffolk village of Lavenham.
Above: The Lavenham Guildhall; note the pale timbers *(see p119)*

- On the paper side of the bonding web, trace each of the Tudor Rose shapes (templates B-E) four times. Cut each group of shapes out roughly (**g1**), then fuse each group onto the back of the relevant fabric; cut out along the marked lines (**g2**).
- Peel the papers off all the shapes, and fuse the green leaf shapes onto the centre of each corner square (**g3**).
- Position the red rose shapes on top, so that the green leaf-tips show between the petals, and fuse (**g4**).
- Add the white rose shapes so that the white petals lie on the joins between the red petals, and fuse (**g5**).
- Now fuse the yellow centres (**g6**).
- Thread your machine with black thread and set it to a medium satin stitch (about 2.5–3 width; see what works best on your machine). Put a piece of tearaway foundation fabric (or plain cartridge paper) behind each square, and work satin stitch around the edges of the leaf-tips, followed by the red petals (**g7**).

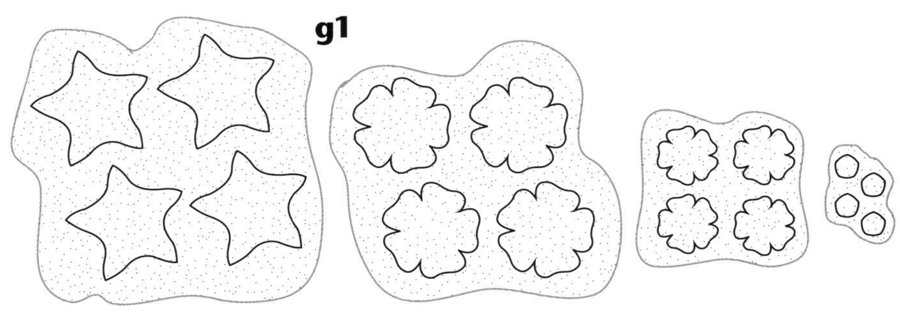

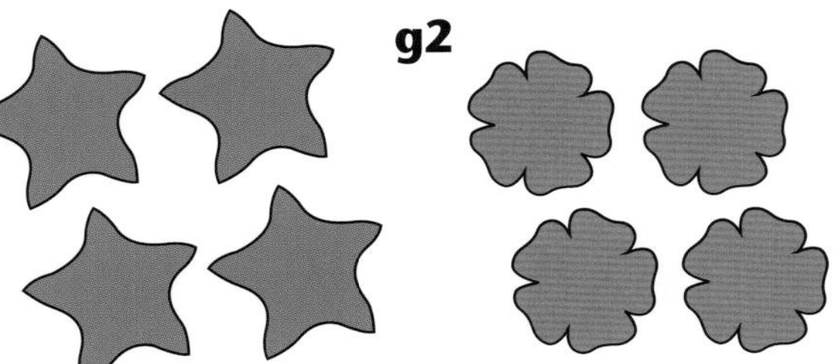

- Now edge the white petals (adding lines out from the centre as shown), and then the yellow centres (**g8**).
- Tear the foundation fabric/paper away from behind each design; you're now ready to move on to step 8.

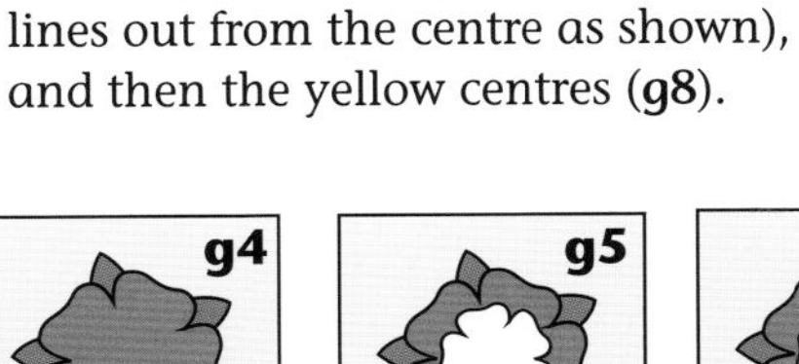

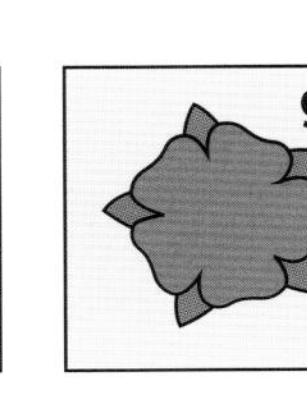

8 Lay the background fabric right side up on a flat surface, and position the border strips along the edges so that their corners just touch, aligning the raw edges with the edges of the background piece (**h**); use a medium zigzag to secure the inner edge of each border strip.

9 Position the plain or decorated corner squares so that the raw edges align with the edges of the background piece (**i**); secure the two inner edges of each square with a medium zigzag.

10 Lay the larger piece of wadding on a flat surface and cover it with the background fabric, right side up, matching the raw edges; pin the house in position (**j**), then go round the edge

of the shape with another line of zigzag to secure it in place. Now add the final lines of bias binding in sequence as shown (**k**); at step **k2**, begin and end the line of binding at the bottom corner of the chimney, so that the join is as unnoticeable as possible.

11 Press the backing/binding fabric and lay it right side down on a flat surface; position the design on top, right side up, so that there's an even border of fabric all the way around. Fold the backing over to the front of

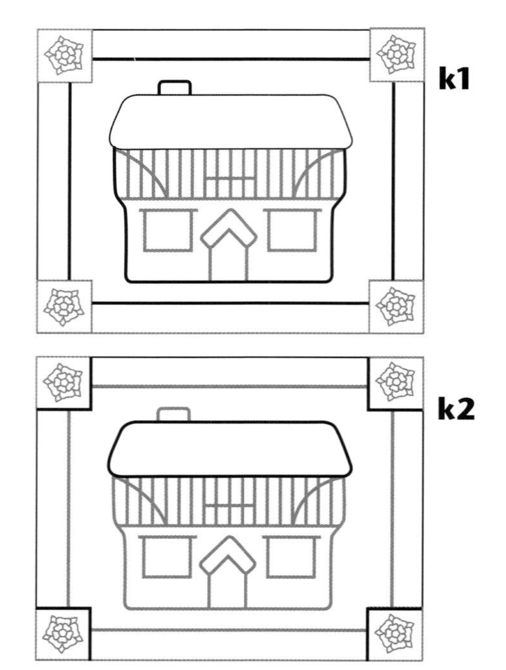

the design in a small double fold, and stitch the fold by hand or machine (**l**). Add any extra quilting you wish to your background, plus any extra embellishments on the house, then add a hidden casing on the back, or hanging loops of ribbon or tape, to hang your design.

Tudor Rose templates, full-size

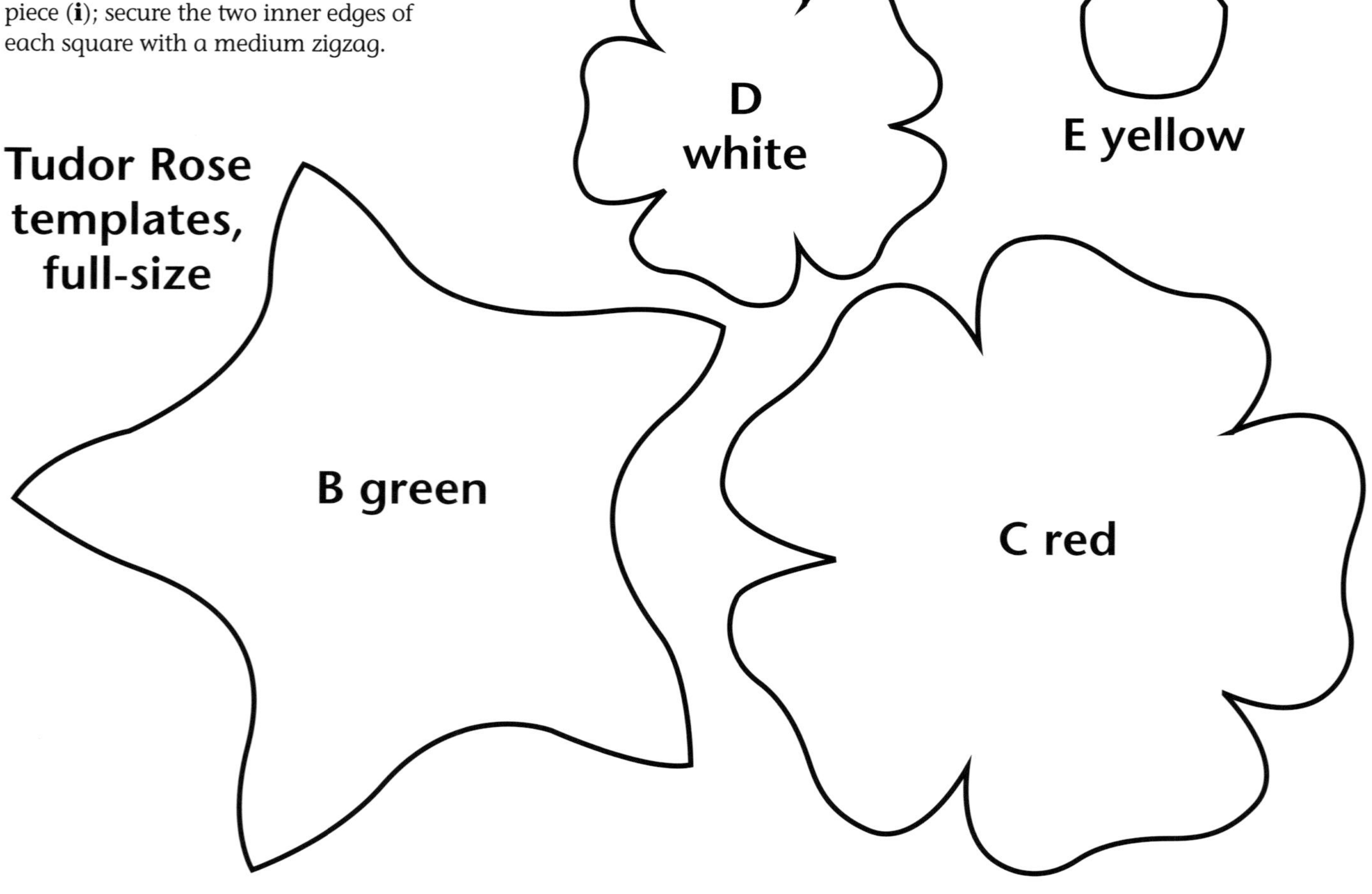

VARIATION

Many Tudor houses originally had plain wood beams; it was only in Victorian times that the passion for painting them black took over! To create this more authentic effect, use the marbled brown fusible bias binding for the half-timbering, perhaps with a dark brown thread to outline the Tudor rose motifs.

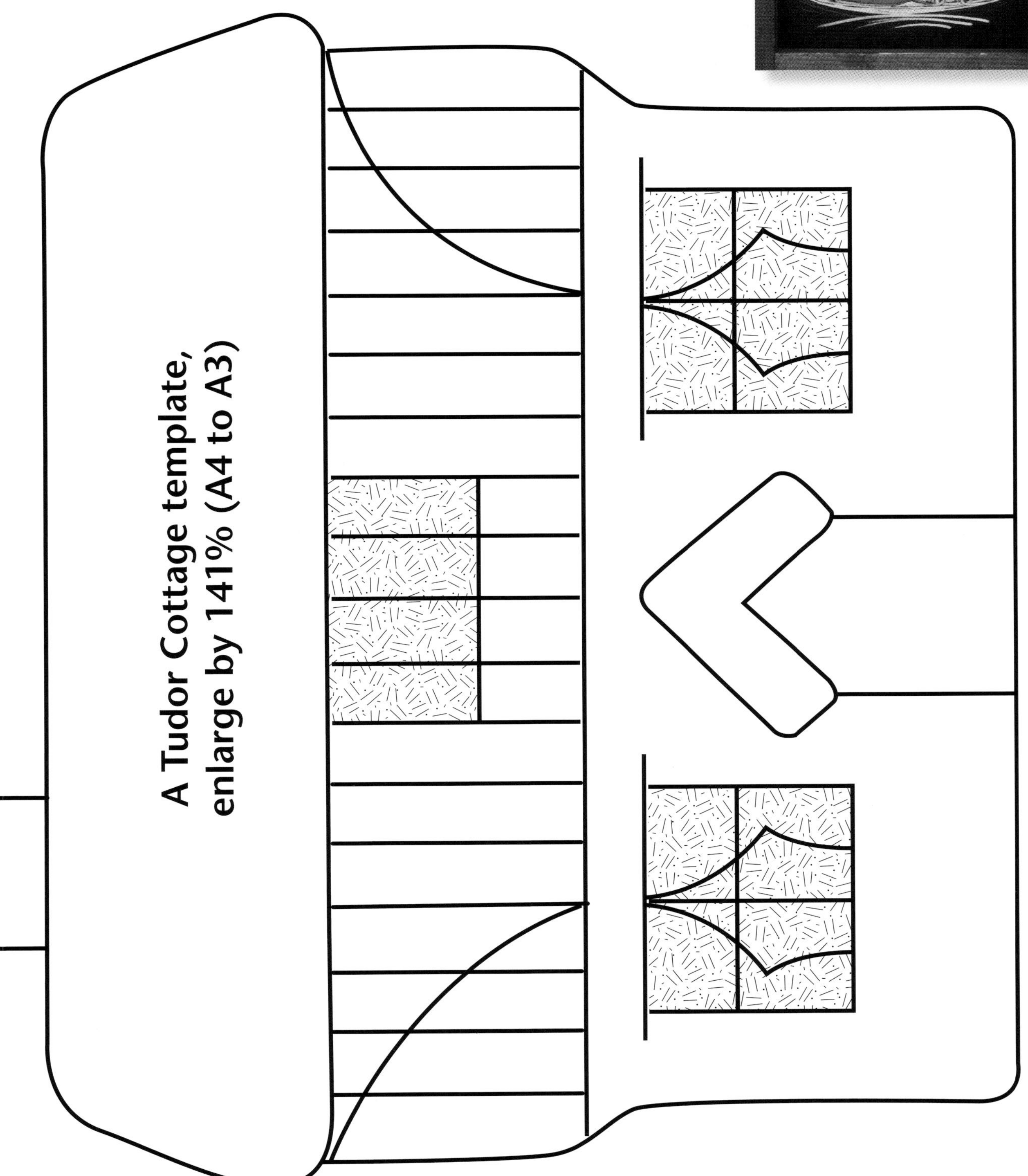

Seaside

It's true: we really do love to be beside the seaside!

Two sandcastles – by two very different architects!

The 1930s were the heyday of the British seaside holiday; by the end of the decade, around 15 million people annually were heading for our coastal resorts. Piers and botanic gardens had been built in their dozens at the end of the 19th century, and these created attractive places for the upper-class visitors to promenade, but between the wars members of the lower and middle classes also began to realise that they could spend a day or two at the seaside. This was aided and abetted by affordable rail travel, and special offers on day returns – the roots of our 'awaydays'! Councils spent thousands improving the seafront facilities, adding pavilions, theatres, music-halls, fairgrounds, cafes etc so that the new visitors had something to do when they arrived. In 1939 Billy Butlin built the first of the holiday camps that still bear his name; his aim was to provide affordable accommodation for ordinary working-class people.

Many of the elements of the classic seaside holiday were established around this time: swimming, for instance. Fashions were becoming simpler for both men and women, so suddenly it was acceptable to wear a swimsuit (or 'bathing suit') that allowed you actually to swim, as opposed to just standing in the water. This tied in with the inter-war vogue for fitness generally, and for pastimes such as hiking, cycling, rambling, tennis etc. A rash of lidos – open-air swimming pools – were built around our coasts to provide safe swimming facilities.

So it was becoming OK for people to show large amounts of bare skin, and they wanted that skin to be brown. The vogue for suntans was led by the upper classes. Previously, women protected their skin from the sun with parasols: a fair skin signalled that you didn't have to do manual labour outside. In the 1930s, though, the rich were heading to exotic resorts abroad, so to sport a tan suddenly became a sign that you could afford to travel. People down the social scale imitated the fashion, but their tans had to be homegrown. And so began the trend that continues every sunny weekend in Britain: the sight of beaches ten-deep in white bodies slowly turning puce.

In 1894, the Royal Mail brought in a law that allowed postcards to be sent through the post. The first picture postcards featured scenes and famous landmarks, just as they do now, but a whole subculture of slightly risqué seaside postcards also grew up. When you were having a day or weekend by the sea, sending comic postcards, complete with *double-entendres,* was all part of the fun. (If you look at the postcards available at modern-day seaside resorts, not much has changed!) The king of the saucy postcard was artist Donald McGill, and I've imitated one of his illustrations in my postcard at the top. I have slightly edited the design, though: in the original a seaside jobsworth is saying 'Oi, missus; move over and let the tide come in!'

Popular songs about the seaside include ***Didn't We Have a Lovely Time*** (*the day we went to Bangor*), and the music-hall song I've used on the quilt: ***Oh We Do Like to be Beside the Seaside***. These songs conjure up images of cheery working people crammed into charabancs, clutching their bags stuffed with hard-boiled eggs and paper packages of sandwiches, singing on their way to a day of freedom.

Beach huts are a peculiarly British custom; they are little wooden huts, which can be used for a little privacy while changing into your swimsuit, and shelter from the inevitable inclement weather. Some sophisticated beach huts have electricity and running water, but to stop the huts from becoming alternative housing it's generally illegal to stay in them overnight. On some shores all the beach huts have to be painted a uniform white, or blue, but other resorts are more imaginative. Southwold's beach huts are particularly famous; they are painted in all kinds of bright colours, and change hands for enormous sums. If you're determined to buy one, be prepared to spend at least £50,000 for something with a footprint of about 7 square feet …

I've included a couple of bright beach huts in my quilt, alongside some of the other items associated with a sunny day on the beach: ice-creams and lollies, brightly-coloured windmills, and sticks of rock full of every E-number known to mankind. Seaside culture isn't famous for its subtlety, so I've used plenty of bright cheery colours and prints. The gingham and ricrac also add a wonderfully retro feel.

Inside information

You can explore the seaside of the past at www.seasidehistory.co.uk/; www.piers.org.uk/pierpages/NPSOlinks.html will tell you all about piers. Various sites are devoted to reminiscences of stays at Butlins holiday camps; explore www.butlinsmemories.com/, and www.bygonebutlins.com/.

The wonderful sandcastle at the top of page 120 was made on Jersey by Simon Smith the Sandwizard (www.flickr.com/photos/sandwizardsimon/)

Materials

The design is built up from cotton fabrics, plus additional gingham bias binding, ricrac, cord, and assorted beads and charms for embellishment. The windmills and postcard are stiffened with fusible interfacing, and I used fabric paint for details on the postcard design.

Techniques

The windmills began as squares of fabric fused onto interfacing, then slit diagonally; I sealed the edges with machine satin stitch, then folded the corners in. The letters are all fused in place, then edged with satin stitch, and I've used machine appliqué for the ice-creams and lollies. The postcard combines fabric paint, appliqué and free machining.

The beach huts are stitched in invisible machine appliqué – also used to stitch down the strips of bias binding. The beach itself is decorated with free machine quilting, machine appliqué of the rocks, plus beads and scraps of net.

Backing and binding

A cheery fairground print creates the back of the quilt, and I've chosen a spotty print in sea colours for the binding; I cut the binding on the bias, so that I could ease it round the shape I'd sculpted round the sea at the bottom of the quilt.

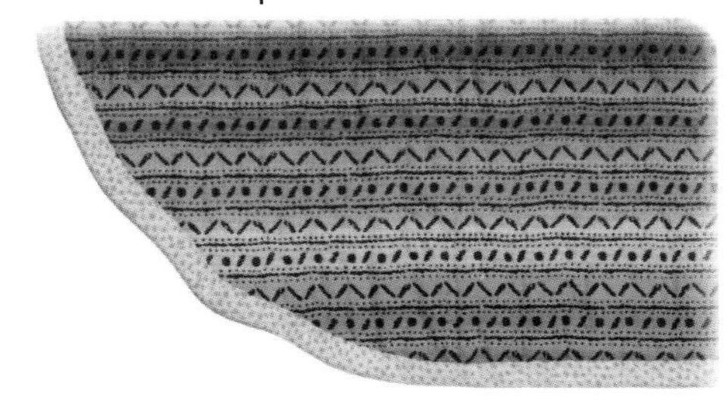

PROJECT

Starfish Pinwheels

Celebrate the British seaside with this eyecatching starfish quilt. The design is put together with a simple mixture of rough-edge appliqué and easy piecing, so even though the quilt looks quite sophisticated, it's suitable even for beginners. The final design can be quilted by hand or machine. If you don't want to make a full-size quilt, just make four blocks and join them into a cushion-cover, small hanging or bag front – or edge them individually as pretty table-mats.

finished size: 34in (98cm) square

You will need:

- sixteen 8½in squares of background fabric (I used lots of different purples and mauves); these can either be all different, or four squares in each of four fabrics.
- sixteen 8in (20cm) squares of starfish fabric (I used lots of different sandy yellow and ochre colours); again, these can either be all different, or four squares in each of four fabrics.
- four border strips, each 30 x 3½in (76 x 9cm)
- four 3½in (9cm) corner squares
- 36in (90cm) square of flat wadding
- 36in (90cm) square of backing fabric
- soft pencil (eg 2B)
- template plastic, minimum of 7in (18cm) square, and paper scissors
- pinking shears
- ruler
- rotary cutter, board and quilt rule
- sewing threads to match the starfish fabrics and the background squares
- quilting threads of your choice
- 3yd (3m) strip of binding fabric; I cut mine 2½in (6.5cm) wide, but if you like a double binding you will need it twice this width.

Instructions

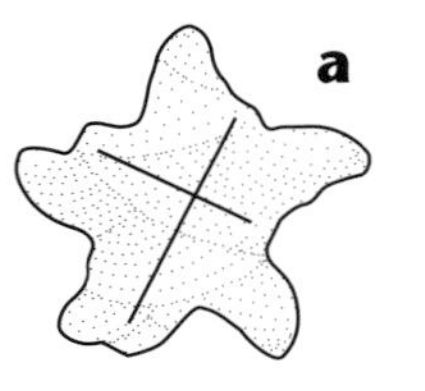

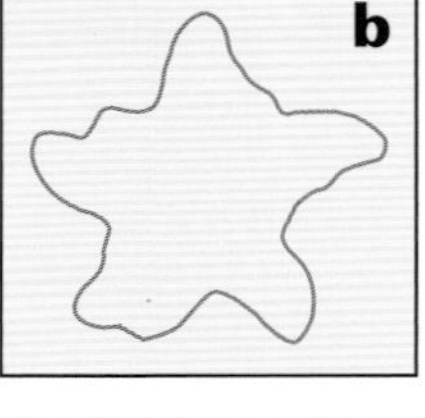

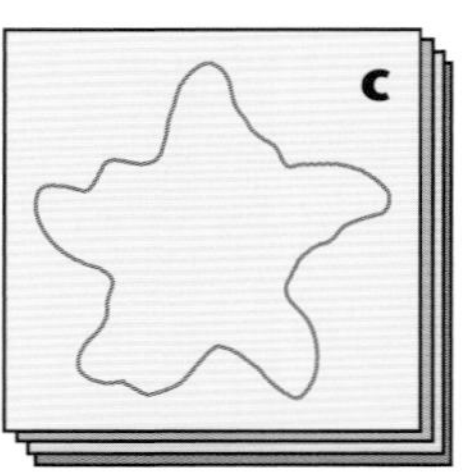

1 Trace the starfish template (p124) onto the template plastic, and cut it out along the marked lines; where the cross is marked in the centre, cut a cross-shaped slit (**a**), so that you can draw through it with a pencil. Don't worry that the starfish looks a rather strange shape; all will become clear as the design progresses!

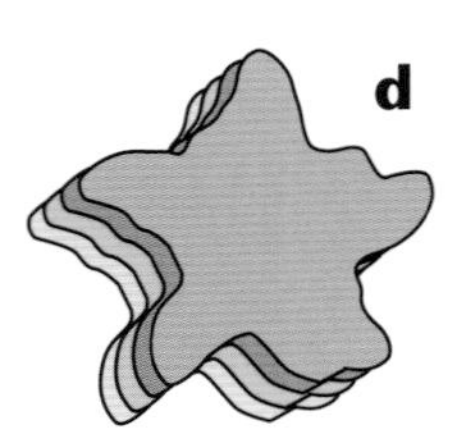

2 Make four piles of your starfish patches, with each fabric **right side down**. Take the top four patches, and trace round the outline of the starfish template on the **wrong side** of each patch (**b**) – you don't need to trace through the central cross shape at this stage. Replace these on the tops of the piles, and pin each pile of four patches together (**c**); now cut round the starfish shape with pinking shears (**d**). Each pile will produce four starfish motifs.

TIP

The pinking shears create zigzag edges on the motifs, which helps to stop them from fraying.

3 On the **right side** of each starfish patch, lay the template over the shape and use pencil to draw in the central cross shape (**e**).

4 On the **right side** of each background square, measure 2½in along the edge of the patch from each corner, and mark the position with pencil (**f**).

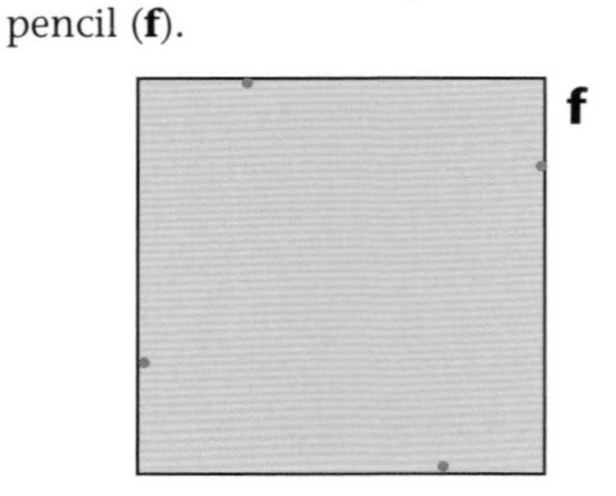

Use a pencil and ruler to join these points across the square (**g**).

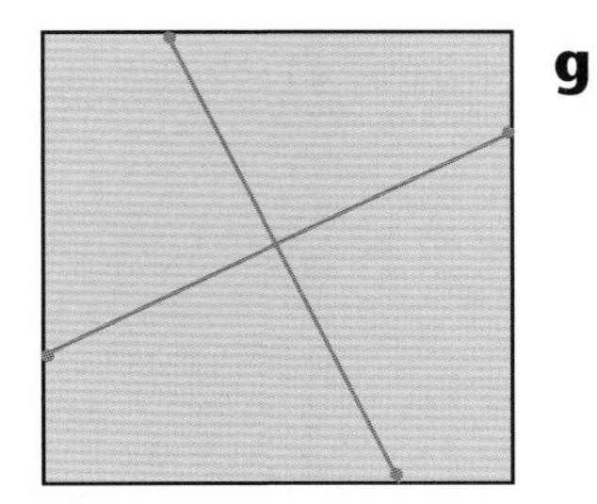

5 Lay out all the background squares and 'audition' the starfish patches against them so that you have a good mixture of tones and patterns. Once you're happy, pin the starfish motifs onto the squares, matching the central cross with the lines you've drawn onto the background (**h**).

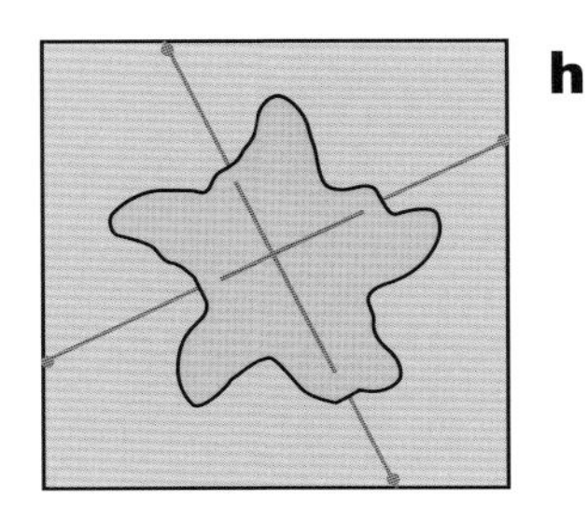

6 Use a small zigzag stitch just inside the raw edge of each starfish motif to appliqué the patches onto the background squares; zigzag, as shown in the detail of the finished quilt (**i**), looks prettier than straight stitch, and also disguises any slight unevenness in the stitching.

7 Press the appliquéd squares, then pile them up in sets of four, right side up; as you put them into piles, check that the top of each starfish motif (marked on the template with a blob) is at the top of each square. Use the rotary cutter, board and ruler to cut each pile into four along the marked lines (**j**); as you work your way through each set of squares, make four stacks of patches – top left, top right, bottom left and bottom right (**k**).

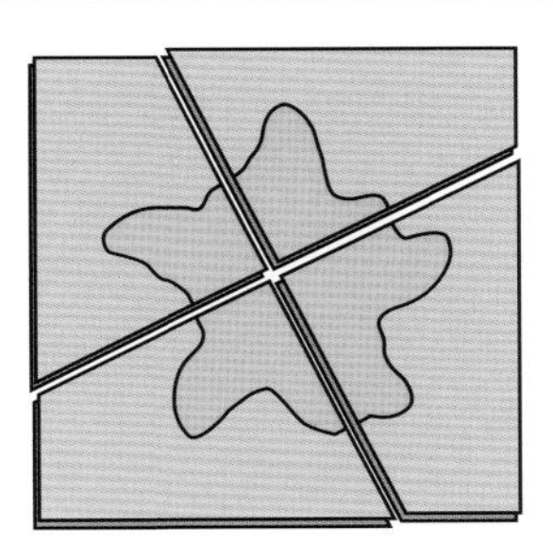

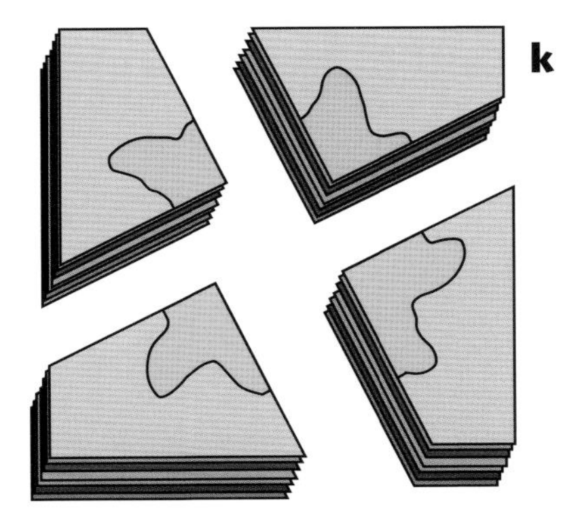

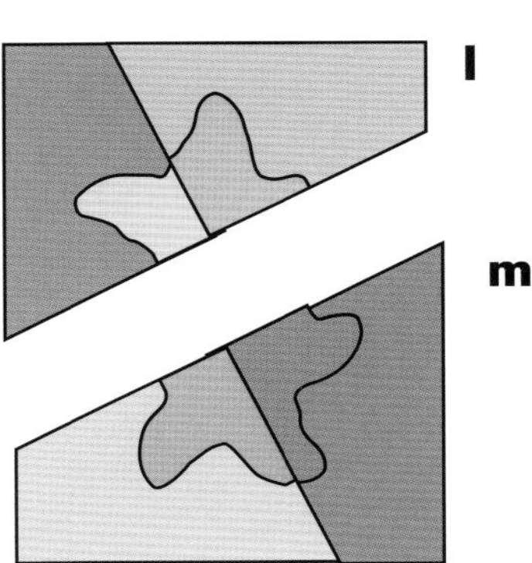

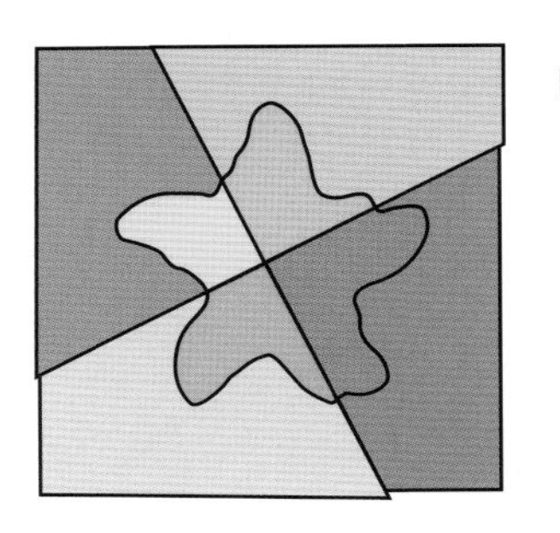

8 Pin the top left and top right patches together in pairs, mixing them up so that each pair has a good contrast of background and starfish fabrics; stitch these pairs using ¼in seams (**l**) and press the seams to one side. You will have sixteen of these top units. Now join the bottom left and bottom right patches in the same way (**m**), to create sixteen bottom units. Join the tops and bottoms, again mixing up the tones and fabrics, to give you sixteen pieced starfish blocks (**n**); match the seams at the centre of the block. Press these new seams open to reduce the bulk – and don't worry that there are kinks at the edges of the squares.

9 Use the rotary cutter, board and ruler to trim each unit to an accurate 7½in square. Lay the squares out in an attractive design; don't worry

about keep the starfish the same way up – turning some of the squares round will give you more opportunities to mix up the colours and tones. Once you're happy with the arrangement, join the squares in rows and then join the rows to create the centre of the quilt top (**o**).

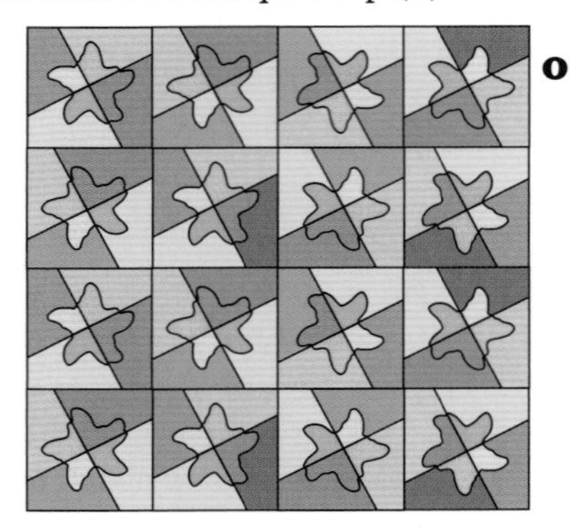

10 Add two of the border strips to the sides of the quilt, and trim them to length; then add the remaining strips to the top and bottom in the same way, and trim them to length (**p**).

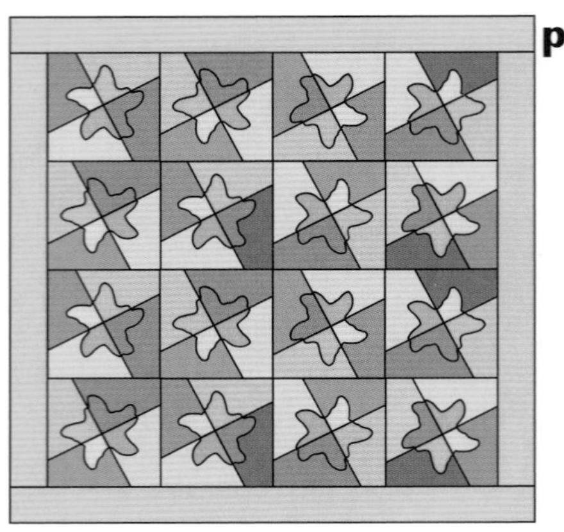

11 Lay the backing fabric right side down on a flat surface and lay the wadding on top, raw edges aligned; cover the wadding with the fused design, right side up, and use your preferred method (see p136) to secure the layers. Now stitch your chosen machine quilting design across the quilt; I free-machined a design of circles in random sizes, outside the starfish motifs, to create the effect of water bubbles (**q**).

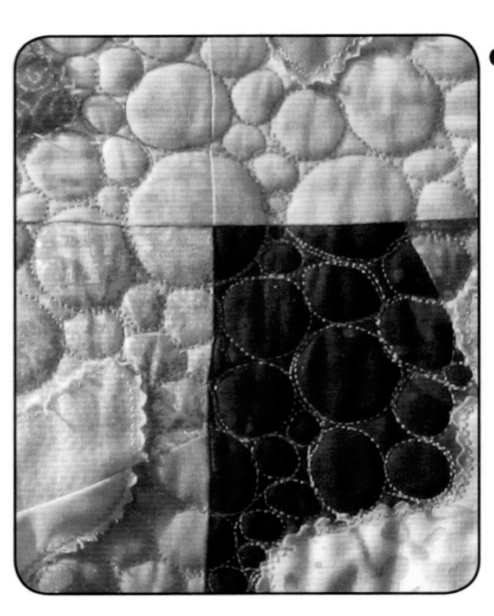

12 Follow the instructions on p136 to bind the edges of the quilt.

VARIATION

For a smaller quilt, suitable for a cushion-cover or bag front (or just a smaller wall-hanging!), just make four starfish blocks. Pick four different background fabrics and four different starfish fabrics, and assemble the blocks as above; when you join them, this will produce a roughly 14in (36cm) square. Add any borders you fancy, then quilt the design by hand or machine.

Starfish template, full-size

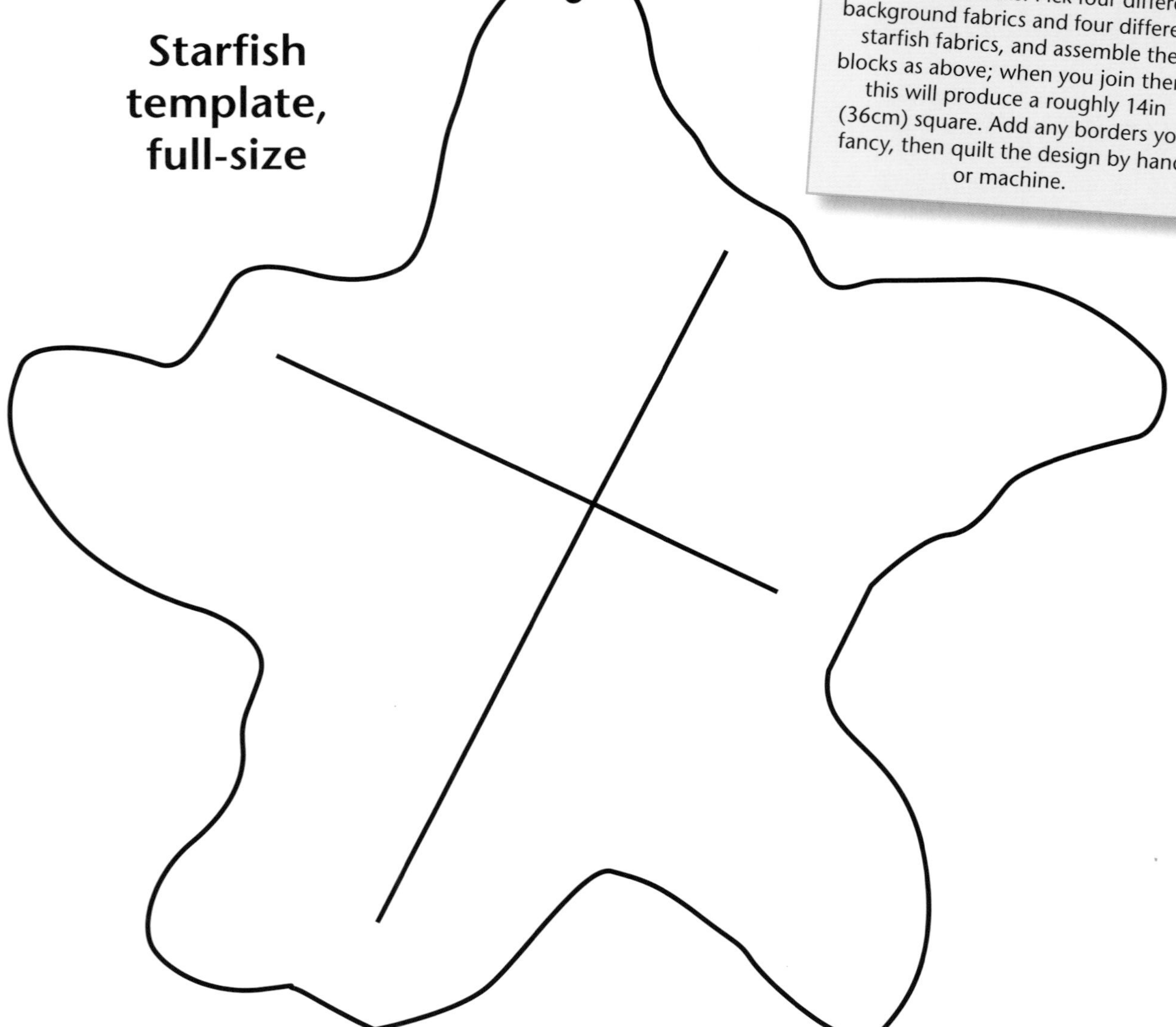

Sunset

In the year 793, Viking raiders arrived on our coasts and a whole way of life came to an end.

When the Scandinavian invaders first arrived on our shores, the north of England had been under Celtic influence for many centuries. The original Celts were a group of tribes that slowly colonised much of central and western Europe, eventually becoming concentrated in Ireland, Scotland, Wales, northern England and western France. Christianity arrived in Britain during Roman times, but flourished under the great Celtic saints such as Aidan (on the left is a statue of him on the Northumbrian island of Lindisfarne), Hilda, Cuthbert, Columba (and, in the Isle of Man, Maughold). The wonderfully-named Venerable Bede (who died in 735) was a monk both on Lindisfarne and in Jarrow; when he wrote one of the first histories of England, he emphasised these spiritual influences. Ancient and modern Celtic crosses appear all over the Celtic regions of our islands.

The target of the first major Viking attack, on June 16th 793, was Lindisfarne itself; the raiders slaughtered some residents (including monks), took others prisoner, and destroyed the Priory. Until then, monks had lived undisturbed on the island for 500 years. It was a seat of learning and industry, and on this tiny windswept island – linked to the coast twice a day by a causeway – one of the most beautiful books in the world was created: ***The Lindisfarne Gospels***.

This exquisite volume is decorated with sumptuous illuminations, particularly featuring Celtic designs, and has been one of the main sources of inspiration in my creative life. As well as including the classic Celtic knots, the designs used by the scribes also include key and fret motifs, spirals, and depictions of people and angels as well as real and mythological animals and birds. Before the raids the book had already been safely removed, but the Norse invasion marked the sunset of Celtic influence in the region (and beyond), and the dawn of the Viking age.

The Viking raids continued for 200 years. They left us their genes (the sandy colouring of many northern Brits, in particular), and their surnames; English names that end in 'son' or 'sen' are all of Norse origin. The Vikings also left us some important treasures: the Lewis (or Uig) Chessmen form the most famous chess set in the world. These characterful figures were found in 1831, in a sandbank on the island of Lewis in the Outer Hebrides; they are carved from walrus ivory, and were probably made in Trondheim, Norway. For many years lots of the Scottish islands were ruled by Norway, and the carvings were possibly part of a shipment being imported by a Norse trader.

And it's impossible to get away from ships when we think about the Vikings. Their habit of burning their boats gave us an important figure of speech; some were incinerated so that the invaders couldn't return to their homeland, and were committed to stay, and boat-burning also played a part in funeral ceremonies. *Up Helly Aa* is a series of Shetland festivals that began as midwinter celebrations; from 1889 onwards *Up Helly Aa* ceremonies have included burning a replica galley (right).

In 1939, at Sutton Hoo in Suffolk, one of the most important archaeological sites in Britain was excavated. It had been known for many centuries that there was a group of ancient burial-mounds in the area, created during the 7th–9th centuries, but no-one know for sure what they held – although there were rumours of 'untold gold.' The excavation was arranged by the then owner of the land, first of all using a local archaeologist plus her gardener and gamekeeper. What they found in the most significant mound was a ship burial; these were particularly associated with Norsemen, and have been found in various places on the British Isles including the Isle of Man and Orkney. ***Beowulf***, one of our oldest epic poems (written some time during the 8th–11th century), is set in Scandinavia; near the beginning the author describes the Danish king Scyld Scefing being laid to rest in a ship burial.

The ship burial had lain undisturbed since it was first covered over, and the treasure recovered from it was breathtaking. The items include a massive circular shield, a helmet, a bronze bowl, an Anglo-Saxon lyre, silver bowls and spoons, a sword and spears – everything the Anglo-Saxon king-about-town needs to help him on his journey to the afterlife. The most famous items, though, because of their exquisite beauty, are a gold buckle, a purse, and a set of gold and precious-stone shoulder-clasps – used to clip the tops of a *cuirass* (a piece of chest armour made from thick leather).

The theme of my quilt is the sun setting behind the island of Lindisfarne, with its distinctive silhouette; although the current castle wasn't built at the time of the Viking invasion, there was an earlier castle on the same site. In the foreground the raiders have decided to burn their longboat, watched over by a baleful Lewis Chessman. The lettering at the top, CELTS, uses an uncial letterform; uncials were used as the capitals in Celtic illuminated manuscripts. The decorative border at the top is taken from the shoulder-clasps found at Sutton Hoo. At the bottom, the word VIKINGS appears in a more chiselled Celtic letterform, bordered by Celtic knots.

Inside information

The Sutton Hoo Society runs a website (www.suttonhoo.org/) with details of ongoing excavations and related issues. At the British Museum (www.britishmuseum.org/) you can see the Sutton Hoo treasure, and 67 of the Lewis Chessmen (the other 11 pieces are in the Museum of Scotland in Edinburgh, www.nms.ac.uk/).

*The **Lindisfarne Gospels** can be seen in the British Library; if you'd like to admire just the most ornate pages, you can see them online at www.bl.uk/onlinegallery/ttp/lindisfarne/accessible/introduction.html. Lindisfarne, also known as Holy Island, has its own website (www.lindisfarne.org.uk/).*

Materials

Much of the quilt is created in cotton fabrics, with metallics used for the lettering, and the decorative borders. I've used sheers and metallics to create the flames, and also to make the waves gleam. The Celtic knot in the sun is painted, and I've embellished the flames with beads (not particularly Venerable ones …)

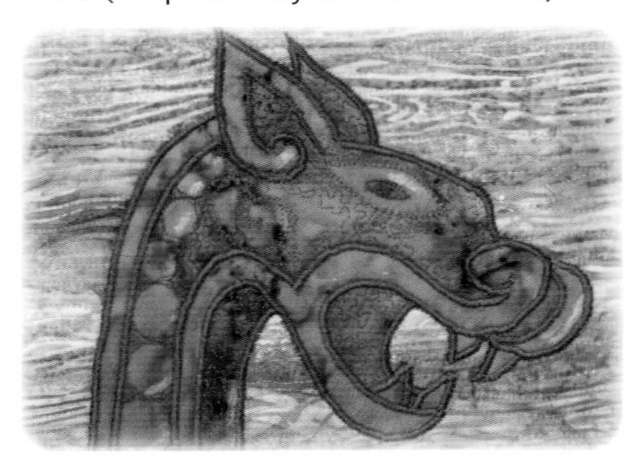

Techniques

After I'd painted the Celtic knot I edged and quilted it with machine satin stitch, then added extra sparkly gold paint to create highlights in the sky and at the top of the sea. The landscape was fused to the background then edged with machine zigzag. Because the Celtic symbol of the Holy Spirit is the wild goose, I've machine-quilted the sky with skeins of Flying Geese patterns. The flames are beaded so that they catch the light. I fabric-painted and machine-quilted the boat and the chessman on wadding, then cut them out and appliquéd them by machine; the lettering panels were done in a similar way.

Backing and binding

To echo the wood of the longship, I've used a wood-print cotton fabric for the backing and the binding.

PROJECT

Celtic Knot Cot Quilt

A new baby is a great opportunity to stitch an exquisite quilt – and this is one that will be treasured for years to come. The quilt top is decorated with beautiful flowing Celtic knots in pastel colours, but you'll be astonished at how quickly and easily the design comes together. I've used some of the decorative stitches on my machine to stitch the knots, but if your machine doesn't have a range of decorative stitches, or if you prefer hand stitching, you could quilt the knots by hand instead. Big-stitch quilting in variegated threads looks very attractive, and is almost as quick as machine-stitching!

finished size: 24 x 36in (60 x 90cm)

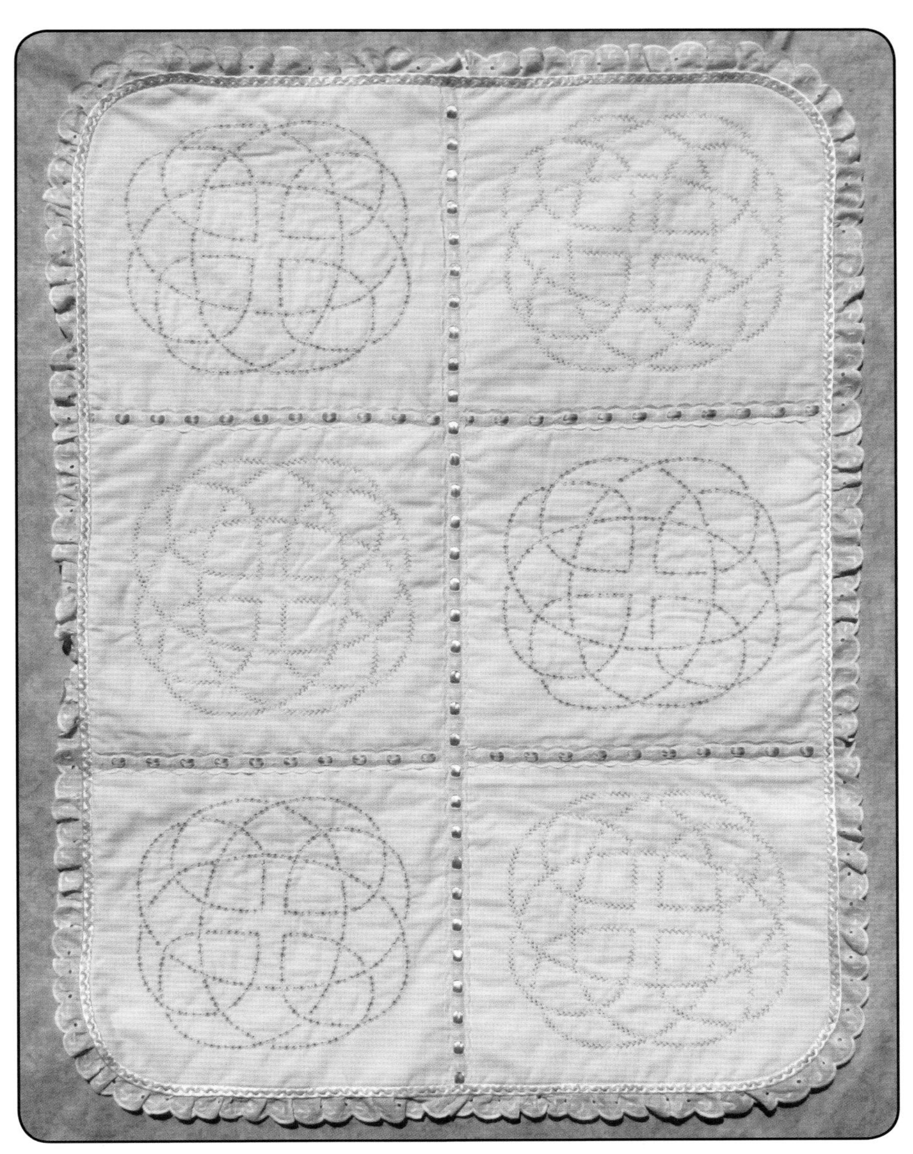

You will need:

- six 12in (30cm) squares of white or cream cotton fabric
- six 12in (30cm) squares of flat white wadding
- white or cream cotton fabric for the backing, 24 x 36in (60 x 90cm)
- white or cream sewing thread
- large reel of machine-sewing thread (or your choice of hand-quilting threads) in pastel colours
- 2½yd (2.5m) white or cream broderie anglaise with eyelets for ribbon
- 2½yd (2.5m) ribbon in a pastel colour that tones with your quilting thread, the correct width for threading through the broderie anglaise
- 4yd (4m) white or cream bias binding, 1½in (4cm) wide (¾in/2cm when the edges are folded under)
- 4yd (4m) ruffled white or cream broderie anglaise with a finished edge
- sewing thread to match the bias binding
- coloured pencils in colour(s) to match your quilting thread(s)
- bodkin or large tapestry needle
- rotary cutter, board and long ruler
- pencil and paper (or photocopies of the template)

Instructions

1 Trace two copies of the knot template on p129 (or use photocopies), then cut them along the dotted centre line (**a**); stick the two copies together, matching the centre lines (**b**).

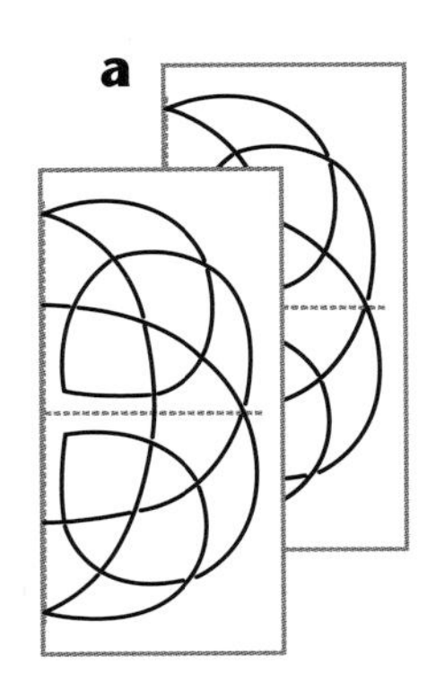

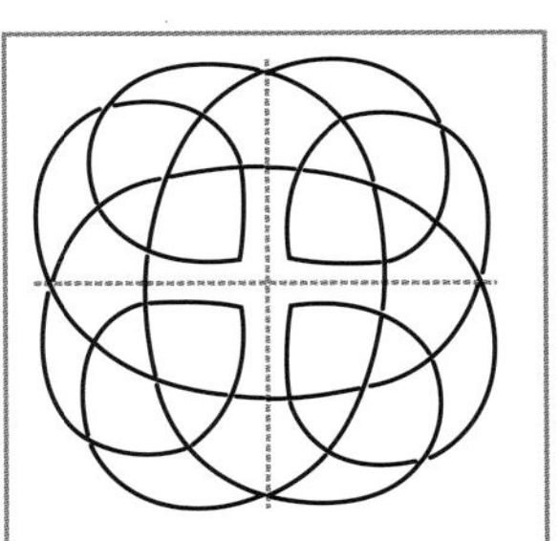

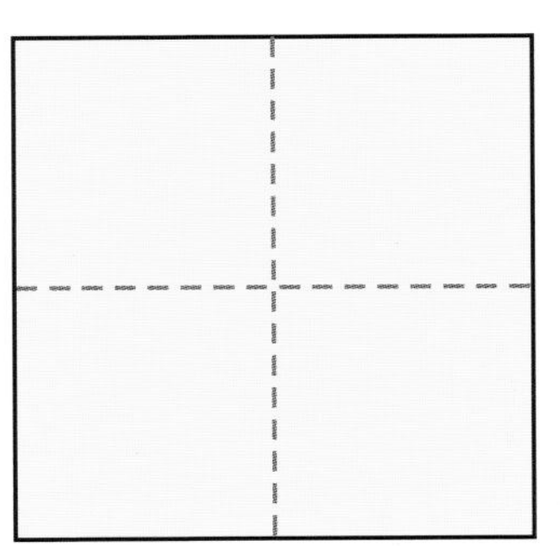

2 Fold one square of white or cream fabric in half, and then into quarters; finger-press the folds lightly to mark the centre lines, then open up the square (**c**). Position the square,

right side up, over the knot template, matching the centre lines; pin in place. Use an appropriately-coloured pencil to trace all the lines of the knot (not the straight centre lines), and unpin (**d**). Do the same with all the fabric squares. Using coloured pencil, and matching the colour to the thread for the embroidery, saves you having to remove the marks after the knots have been stitched.

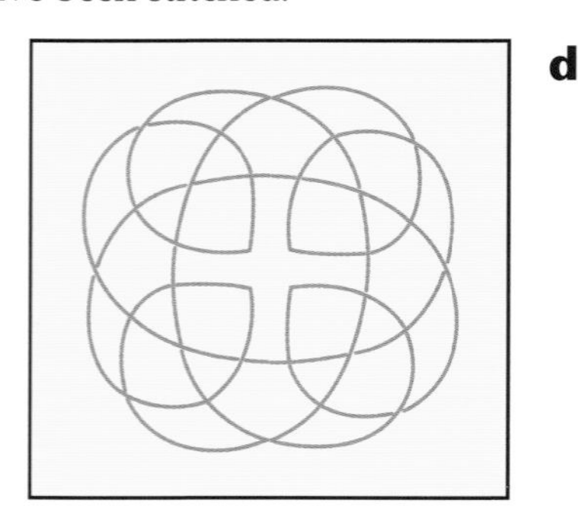

3 Press the squares to remove the folds; do this on the back, just in case you smudge the crayon. Lay each fabric square right side up on top of a square of wadding, and pin around the edge of the square. Use your chosen stitching method (hand or machine) to stitch around all the lines of the knot design on each square (**e**).

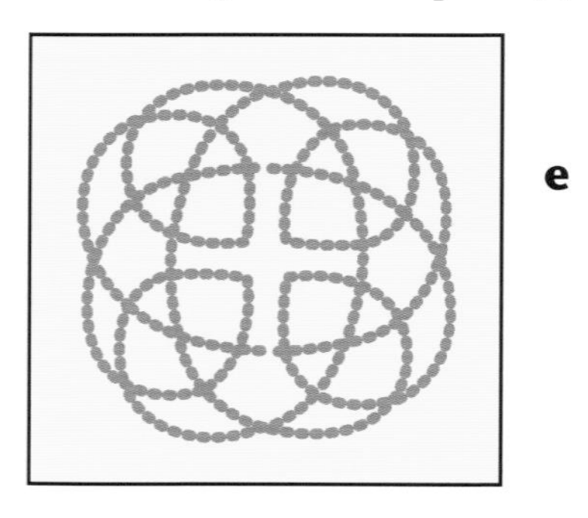

I used the same variegated thread and two different machine stitches, but you could make the stitch the same on all the squares if there's one you particularly like. If you have a walking foot for your machine, you'll find it useful when you're stitching the knots.

TIP

As the decorative stitches use quite a bit of thread, wind two bobbins before you start stitching. This way, if your first bobbin runs out half-way through a decorative line, you don't need to finish off and re-start your top thread – just slip in the new bobbin.

4 Once all the knots are stitched, lay the squares out in a 2 x 3 design (**f**).

Thread the machine with white or cream and use a large zigzag to join the quilted squares in rows, just catching the raw edges of the fabric and wadding together. Don't worry if a couple of bits don't catch; this is, in effect, just tacking, and all the raw edges will be sealed under the broderie anglaise. Once the rows are complete, use the same method to join them together to create the complete quilt top (**g**).

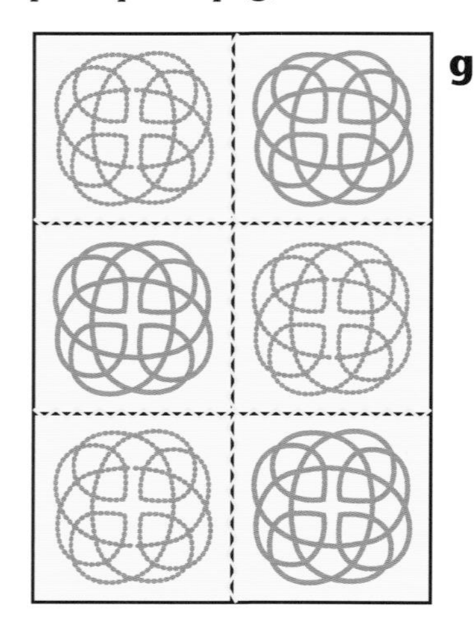

5 Lay the piece of backing fabric on a flat surface and position the quilt top, right side up, on top. Put a couple of pins in each square just to hold the layers together. Cut one 36in (90cm) length of the eyelet broderie anglaise, and two 24in (60cm) lengths. Thread these strips with ribbon – this is where the bodkin comes in handy.

6 Lay the shorter threaded strips of broderie anglaise across the quilt, over the joins between the rows. Pin them firmly in place, through all the layers, and use a small zigzag in white or cream thread to stitch down the edges of each strip of broderie anglaise (**h**). Add the longer strip down the centre of the quilt in the

Below: St Cuthbert's face carved on a rugged cross on Lindisfarne; Right: Bamburgh church, where St Aidan died, and its castle

h

same way. If the broderie anglaise has a scalloped edge, work a straight stitch or a wavy stitch just inside it; this allows the scalloped edge to stand slightly proud of the fabric, which looks rather pretty.

7 Use a rotary cutter, board and quilt rule to square up the edges of the quilt so that you have a nice neat, even rectangle; then round the corners of the quilt into smooth curves. I found it useful at this stage to go round the very edge of the quilt with a large zigzag, just to hold all the layers together. Bind the edges of the quilt with the bias binding, beginning and ending the line of bias down one of the long sides of the quilt so that it's not noticeable.

8 Add the ruffled broderie anglaise round the edge; I used a decorative stitch (in the same variegated thread I'd used for the knots) to attach it, which produced a pretty embroidered edge on the front of the bias binding (**i**). Your beautiful pram quilt is now ready to wrap up its new arrival.

i

VARIATION

As you're building the quilt up from separate blocks, you could use various different pastel colours for the background squares. The design also looks lovely if you stitch each knot in a different colour of thread – try one each in pink, peach, yellow, pale green, pale blue and mauve.

Celtic Knot template, full-size

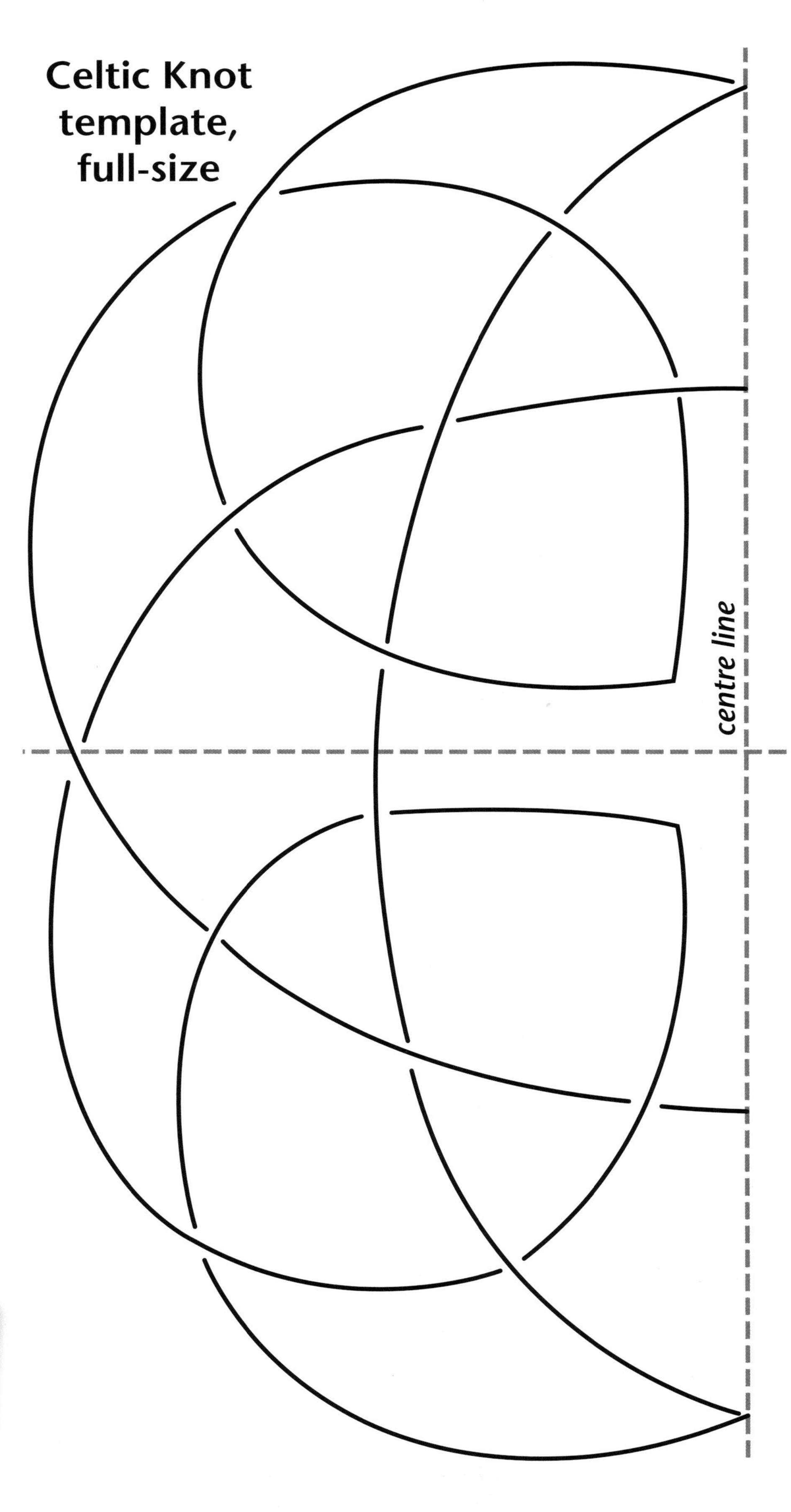

Best of British

To round off my British quilt collection, a celebration of everything that I've left out!

I expect by this stage in the book you're thinking: OK, so you've included Stonehenge/tea/London/Dickens/half-timbered houses/ Johnson's Dictionary/The Battle of Hastings etc etc, but what about all the things you've left out? All those other people, places, foods, traditions, artworks, authors, history? And you know what – I'm thinking pretty much the same! As I was working my way through the quilts, and the research for them, it was great to find so many topics that I could include or refer to; but it was also quite frustrating in a way to think of so many others that there wouldn't be room to include.

For instance: what about Steve Redgrave and Matthew Pinsent, ***Three Men in a Boat*** and ***Messing About on the River***? How can I leave out Dave Allen, Griff Rhys Jones, Billy Connolly and Tommy Cooper? What about bumble bees and Sting? Mulberries and silkworms? Raymond Briggs, Thelwell, Gerard Hoffnung, Posy Simmonds? Hornby trains and the Flying Scotsman? Tadpoles and water-boatmen? Shepherd's pie, star-gazy pie and the pie-eaters of Wigan? Red kites, Red Priest, red squirrels, Red Rum, the red cliffs of Dorset, and red setters? The Dartford warbler and the Beast of Bodmin? The Sitwells, the Brontës, the Corrs, the Krankies (?!), the Rossettis, the Fiennes, the Opies, the Freuds, the Dubliners, the Foxes, the Gallaghers, the Forsytes, the Nolans, the Gambols, the Tradescants?

What could I do about all these orphans, with no home on my other quilts? The answer was to give them a quilt of their own. On the background I've printed some of the many extra good things about Britain, and some of these are featured on the squares that run down the quilt in two rivers. A few years ago there was a craze for stitching tiny one-inch square pieces of textile art, which were called 'inchies':

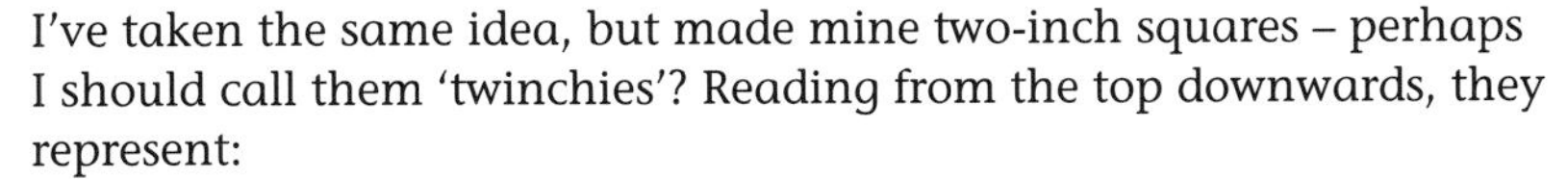

Below left: fireworks night; Above: Jodrell Bank; Right, from the top: shell grotto, classic Mini, a canal scene in Brecon, beech nuts in autumn

I've taken the same idea, but made mine two-inch squares – perhaps I should call them 'twinchies'? Reading from the top downwards, they represent:

- autumn; the season of mists and mellow fruitfulness
- spices for our favourite national dish: curry
- toast – what Wallace (as in Wallace and Gromit) has for breakfast
- Victorian shell grotto
- Valentine's cards; the first ones were created in Britain
- summer
- during the top-secret development of radar, the rumour was started that British pilots could 'see in the dark' because they were eating more carrots
- Bonfire Night and Guy Fawkes; the anarchic side of Britain – celebrating someone who tried to blow up our parliament!
- cider and scrumpy
- Wimbledon
- primroses
- Wedgwood
- Miss Marple's knitting
- Jamie and Delia are always trying to get us to eat more veg …
- lawn bowls
- Ordnance Survey maps
- the corkscrew, first patented by an Englishman (I hope they gave him a knighthood)
- winter
- Eric Morecambe's glasses
- a celebration of our composers
- Lowry
- a reference to our great physicists (and before you e-mail me, I know it's Einstein's theory, but he did lecture in Britain!)
- penicillin mould and Alexander Fleming
- the one and only Thelwell
- the British and their love of cats
- James Farley perfected the penny-farthing bicycle
- William Morris' work included textile design, embroidery, furniture design and printing.
- In 1714 Henry Mill patented a writing machine that was the forerunner of the typewriter
- Florence Nightingale
- Pontefract cakes (actually a form of liquorice)
- hopscotch
- the name's Bond … James Bond …

Part of the LS Lowry trail in Berwick-upon-Tweed

- liquorice allsorts
- the plumage of our brightest bird (I'm talking aesthetics, not intelligence ...), the kingfisher
- arctic and antarctic explorers, both ancient and modern
- bluebells (not to be confused with the Bluebells of Scotland, which are harebells)
- Patrick Moore and star-gazy pie (so-called because all the little pilchards in it have their heads poking out through the pastry)
- the world's best chocolate, Cadbury's Dairy Milk
- pulsars, a British discovery
- mulberries; the lunch of choice for silkworms
- the quintessential English rose
- the printer's device of William Caxton, who introduced the printing press to England.
- Ironbridge, the first cast iron bridge in the world
- the black swans of Dawlish
- zebra-hide, celebrating all our wildlife conservation initiatives.
- sound-waves representing Jodrell Bank and Goonhilly.
- the Penny Black, the world's first adhesive postage stamp.
- Charlie Chaplin
- Roy Castle's trombone
- black velvet: Mole's coat in ***The Wind in the Willows***; the Irish drinking-song ***The Black Velvet Band***, and the drink made from dark stout and champagne.

And if there's anything you particularly feel that I've left out, do feel free to create your own ***Glimpses of Britain*** quilt!

Inside information

There's a museum dedicated to silk and its production in Macclesfield: www.silkmacclesfield.org.uk/. In London, the Museum of Brands (www.museumofbrands.com/) houses much of the material collected by Robert Opie.

At Ironbridge (near Telford in Shropshire), you'll find no fewer than ten museums dedicated to different aspects of this World Heritage Site (www.ironbridge.org.uk/); these include a tile museum, a Victorian town, a tar tunnel, and a china museum.

*If shells (or grottoes) are your thing, visit the ornate shell passageway in Margate (www.shellgrotto.co.uk/), or Groto Cregyn in Torfaen in Wales. You can also read about them in a book called **Shell Houses and Grottoes** by Hazelle Jackson.*

Materials

Most of the fabrics are cottons, including the black velvet square; the background printing is done on a white cotton sateen. I was determined to use a different-coloured thread to edge each of the squares in the rainbow sequence. The black-and-white squares are edged with a gradation of black, grey and white threads; I put the lighter squares nearer the top, and edged them with the darker threads, then worked my way down towards darker squares and lighter threads.

Techniques

To create the background, I typed a series of words from my list of overlooked British items, then put these in many different typefaces to emphasise the variety of the subjects covered. Once I was happy, I printed the images onto fabric, then joined the patches into one large piece. The background is quilted with random lines of straight machine stitching. Most of the small squares were also made by printing onto fabric; I then cut these into squares, fused them onto firm interfacing, rounded the edges, and sealed the edges with machine satin-stitch.

Backing and binding

For the backing I picked a black-and-white print that complemented the front of the quilt without fighting with it. I cut the outside of the quilt around the words, then machine satin-stitched the edges.

PROJECT

Rainbow Wall-Hanging

I've echoed the rainbow colours and monochrome background of the Best of British quilt in this striking wall-hanging; the fused design is quick and easy to make, but looks very effective.

finished size: 15 x 42in (38 x 107cm)

You will need:

- 15 x 42in (38 x 107cm) background fabric; I used a black and white print
- 15 x 42in (38 x 107cm) flat wadding
- 15 x 42in (38 x 107cm) backing fabric
- 8 x 24in (20 x 60cm) rainbow-print fabric
- 8 x 24in (20 x 60cm) bonding web
- 3½yd (3.5m) fabric strip for binding
- rotary cutter, long quilt rule, cutting mat
- machine-quilting thread

Instructions

1 Fuse the rough side of the bonding web onto the wrong side of the rainbow fabric (**a**). Position the fused fabric on the cutting mat and use the rotary cutter and quilt rule to cut the whole piece into 2½in squares, working diagonally across the fabric first in one direction (**b**) and then in the other (**c**). Creating squares 'on point' like this gives each square more colour variation. You will have a few offcuts that aren't large enough to give you 2½in squares; cut these scraps into 1¼in squares.

a

2 Press the background fabric and lay it on a flat surface. Peel the paper off the back of each coloured square, then arrange the squares in a pleasing design across the front of the fabric (**c**) – don't put them too close to the edge of the fabric, as you need to allow room for trimming and binding. When you're happy with the arrangement, fuse the patches onto the background.

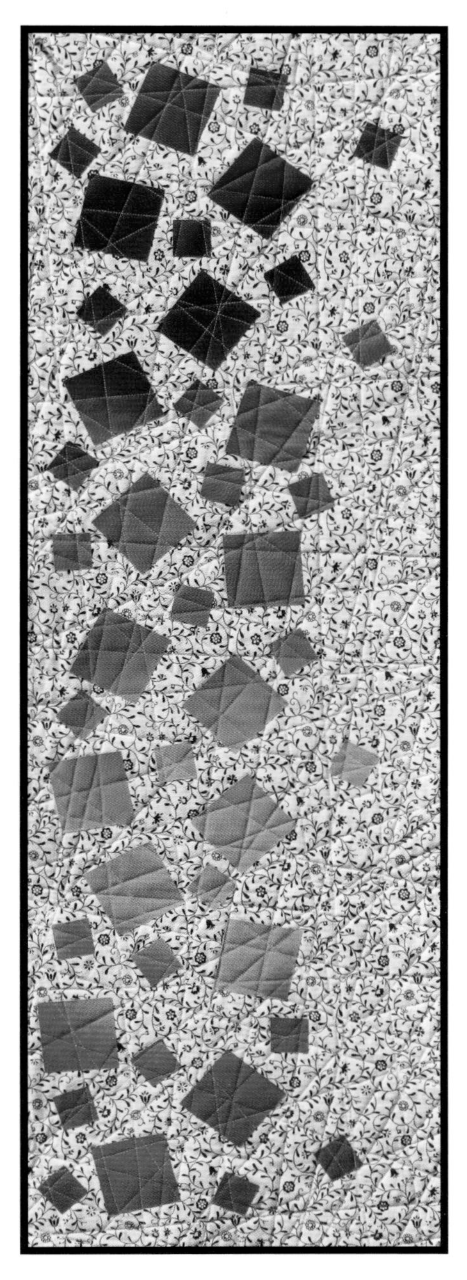

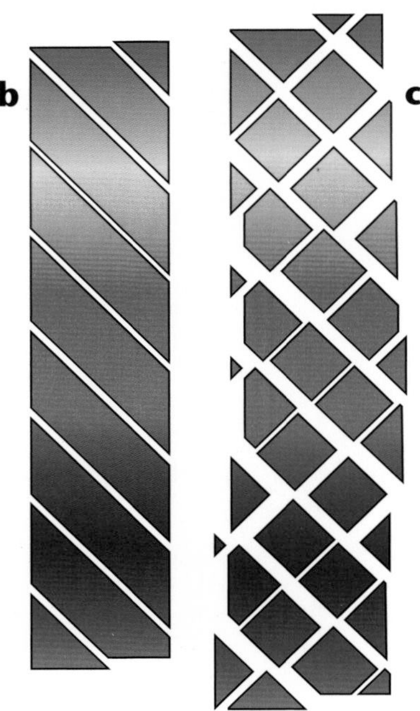

b

c

d

3 Use your favourite method (see p136) to layer the backing fabric, wadding and fused design, right side up, then quilt the design by machine. There are many different quilting patterns you can use to do this; I stitched straight lines at random angles across the quilt. Just ensure that each coloured patch has at least two or three lines of quilting crossing it, to guarantee that it stays in place.

TIP

To mark the lines on the front of the quilt, I used a quilt rule and an unpicker. Lay the quilt rule randomly across the quilt and impress a line with the blunt back of the unpicker; beginning at one end of this line, mark another line across the quilt at a different angle, and so on. I 'draw' about half a dozen lines like this at one go, then stitch them, then continue in the same way – it saves having to think about removing the marking lines once the quilting is complete.

4 Trim the quilt to a neat rectangle, ensuring that all the corners are square, and bind the edges with the binding strip (see p136). I used a 1¼in binding strip; if you'd like to do the same, you will need three strips across the width of standard-width fabric. Add a hidden casing for hanging your design.

VARIATION

Circles, hearts, triangles or star shapes would work just as well as squares on this wall-hanging; cut templates for your chosen shape in several different sizes, then trace them onto the paper side of the bonding web before you fuse it onto the rainbow fabric.

Below: winter, and bluebell woods in spring; Right: typical British allotments, and Hay-on-Wye – famous for its second-hand bookshops and annual literary festival

Techniques

If you're new to quilting, or if you fancy a few reminders, these tips will help you get the most out of the projects in this book.

Enlarging designs

Almost all of the templates in this book are full-size, so you don't need to enlarge them at all. The Tudor Cottage main template and the Nautical Herb Cushion templates need to be enlarged from A4 to A3; do this on a photocopier, enlarging by 141%. The Cornucopia Quilt needs to be enlarged more than is practical on a photocopier, and the best way to do this is by using the grid method. (This is also a very useful method to know for other patterns.)

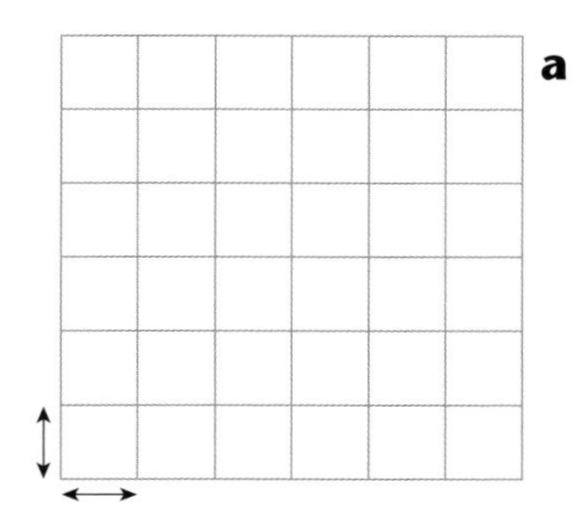
a

1 On a large piece of paper, draw a grid of squares to match the dimensions given on the pattern (**a**). (In the case of the Cornucopia Quilt, that will mean a grid of six by six 6in/15cm squares.)

b

2 Roughly draw the main shapes of the design into the squares of your drawn grid, enlarging as you go (**b**). Don't try to be too accurate at this stage; just rough out the most important areas. Once you're happy with the rough lines, fill in the details (**c**); go over the finished lines of the design with a black felt pen to make them stronger, then you can rub out any unneeded pencil marks.

c

Reverse appliqué

This technique cuts your fabric patch to shape and attaches it to the background in one go, so that you don't need separate templates. You'll find curved-tipped appliqué scissors very useful for this technique; use the scissors horizontally, so that the blades slide between the layers of fabric.

1 Using pencil, trace the full-size design onto the front of a piece of foundation fabric (**a**). (If the design is appropriate, you can use this foundation fabric as part of the design by leaving some parts of it clear of appliqué patches.)

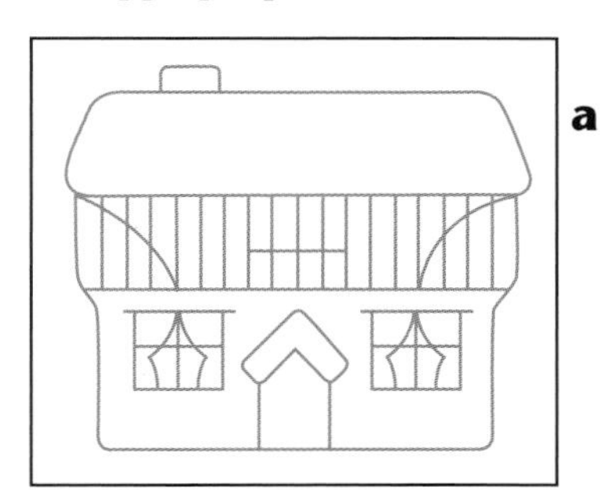
a

Press the fabric you're using for the patch, and lay it right side up on a flat surface; cover it with the drawn design, right side up, so that the patch comfortably covers the shape it will be appliquéd to.

2 Set your machine to a small zigzag (about 1.5 length and width), and stitch along the lines edging the relevant shape or shapes (**b**). On the front of the work, use the small scissors to trim the background fabric away from inside the line of zigzag (**c**), taking care not to cut the underneath fabric. Trim away any excess on the back if necessary.

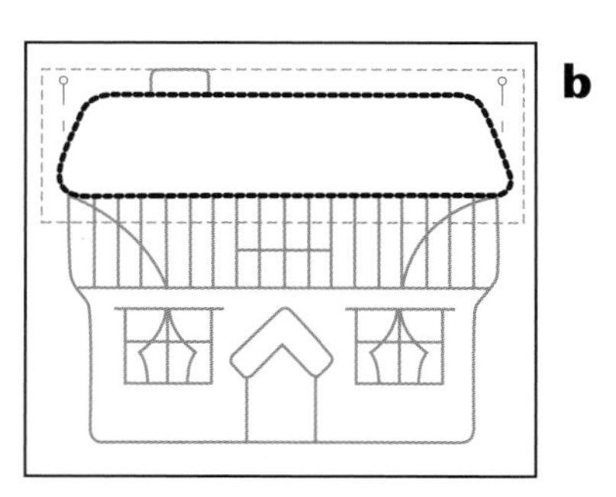
b

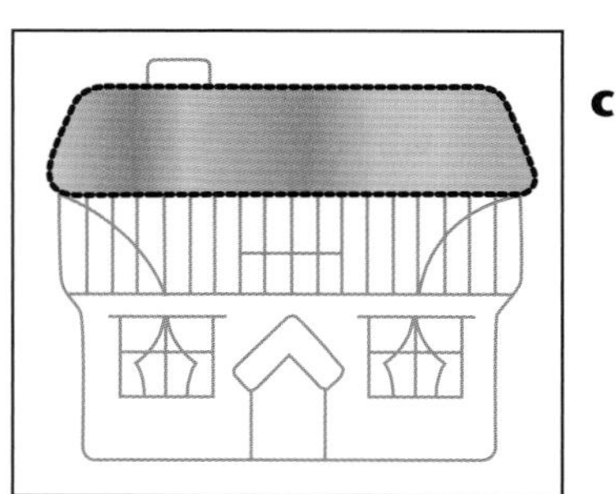
c

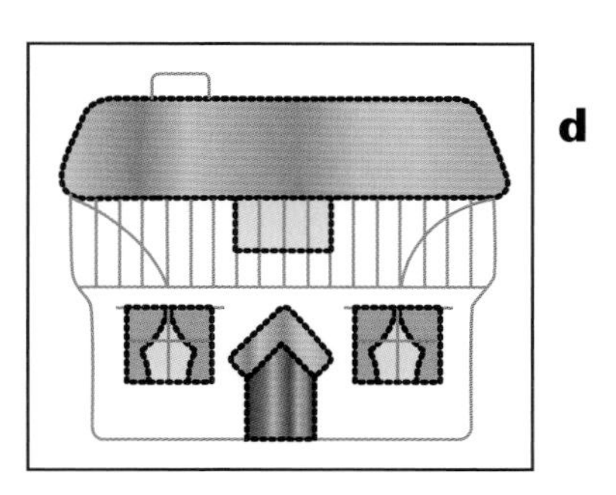
d

3 Continue building up the design until all the patches are in place (**d**).

Applying fusible bias binding

You can stitch fusible binding on by hand or machine, using various methods – simply choose the one you like doing best. I often put a flat wadding under the quilt top before I stitch on the fusible binding; this way, you're quilting it as you add the binding, and can then hide the wrong side of the work with your backing.

- If you're stitching by machine, use a tiny zigzag down each long edge of the binding strips.
- If you're confident with a twin needle, you can stitch both sides at the same time; you'll need a 4mm twin needle and a second reel of cotton to match the bias binding colour.

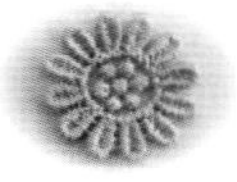

• If you're using gold or silver fusible binding, you can stitch it on using invisible machine appliqué. Use a fine monofilament nylon thread in the top of the machine, and a pale cotton thread underneath; stitch down each side with a very small blind hemming stitch.

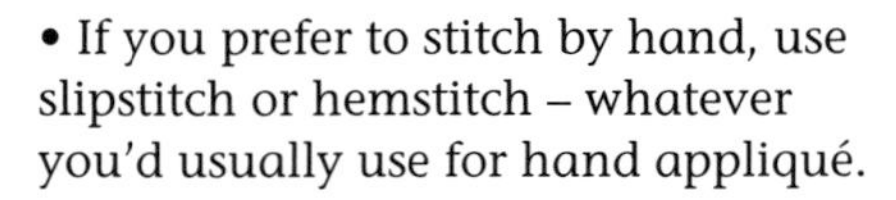

• If you prefer to stitch by hand, use slipstitch or hemstitch – whatever you'd usually use for hand appliqué.

Layering quilts

Traditionally a quilt comprises three layers: the backing, the wadding, and the quilt top. These layers need to be held together in a 'sandwich' before you quilt them (either by hand or machine); securing the three layers stops them from moving out of position while you stitch. There are various methods you can use for layering your quilt: pick the one that works best for you, and suits the project you're working on.

• Tack the layers together with vertical and horizontal lines of large tacking/basting stitches; if it's a very large quilt, work the lines of tacking from the centre of the quilt outwards.

• Use a quilt tack gun to shoot little plastic tags through the layers; once the project is quilted, snip the tags with scissors to remove them.

• If the project you're working on is small, you can hold the layers together with a few pins while you quilt; this is particularly true with the modern compressed waddings.

• If you want to pin a larger project, use safety pins; it's possible to buy slightly curved safety pins, which are easier to insert through the layers.

• Use a special quilt spray glue to hold the layers together.

Binding quilts

I find it most satisfactory to bind my quilts with a continuous strip, rather than binding each edge individually. If the quilt has straight edges and square corners, you can use a binding strip cut on the straight of the grain or on the bias, as you prefer; if the quilt has curved edge or rounded corners, you will need to use a binding strip that has been cut on the bias so that it will ease around the curves. This is the method for binding a straight-edged quilt with square corners:

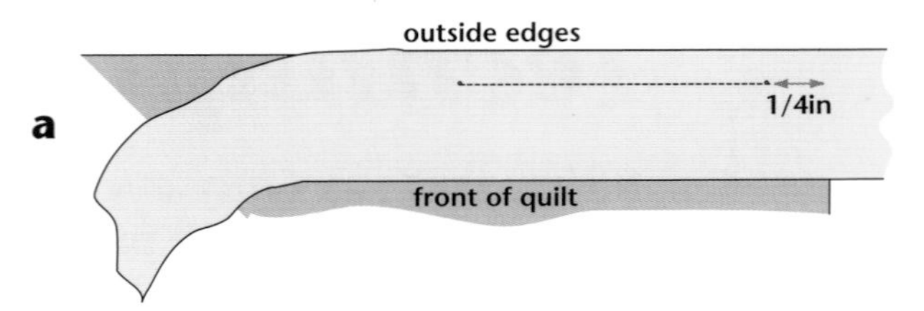

1 Beginning roughly half-way down one long edge of the quilt, lay the binding strip right side down so that the raw edges of the binding and quilt align (**a**). Leaving a reasonable length of binding free (about 12in/30cm on a large quilt), stitch a seam down to the first corner. If you're using a ¼in (6mm) seam, stitch to within ¼in (6mm) of the next corner (whatever width seam you're stitching, stop that same distance from the raw edge).

2 Fold the binding strip at 45° as shown (**b**), then fold it down again square so that the raw edge aligns with the next edge of the quilt (**c**).

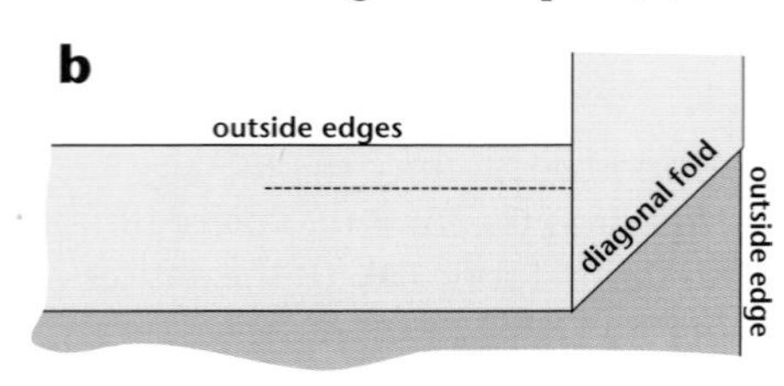

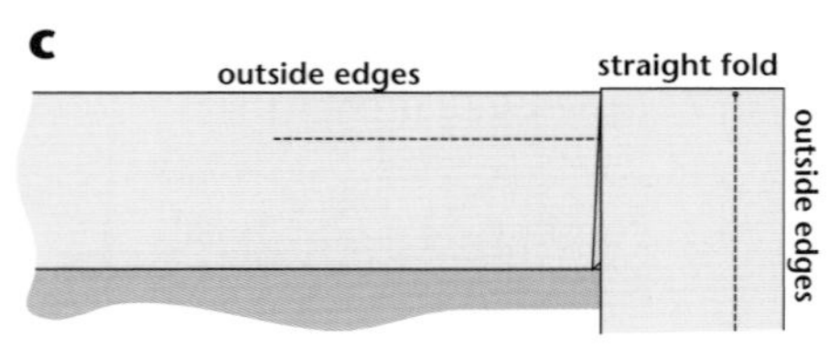

Begin the next seam right at the edge of the quilt, and work round the whole quilt in the same way.

3 When you come to the final edge, stop stitching so that you still have a reasonable length of binding unstitched. Fold one loose end of the binding at 45° as shown (**d**), then fold the other loose end at 45° so that the folds butt up (**e**).

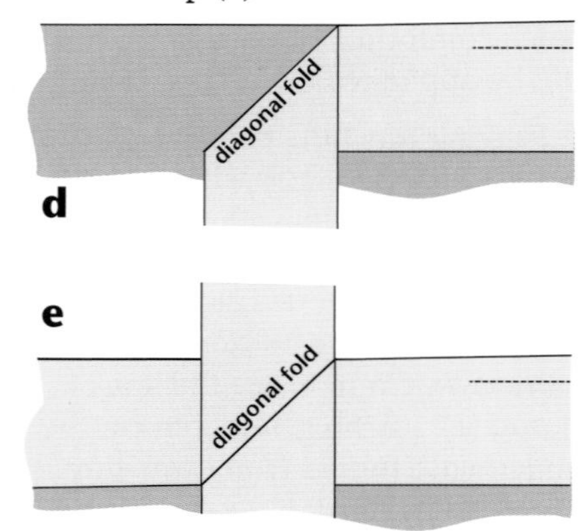

Press these folds lightly, then pin the ends of binding right sides together so that these folds align; stitch along the folds.

4 Check that the binding lies flat on the front of the quilt; when you're happy, trim the seam allowances to ¼in (6mm) and press the seam open (**f**). Complete the stitching line to attach the binding.

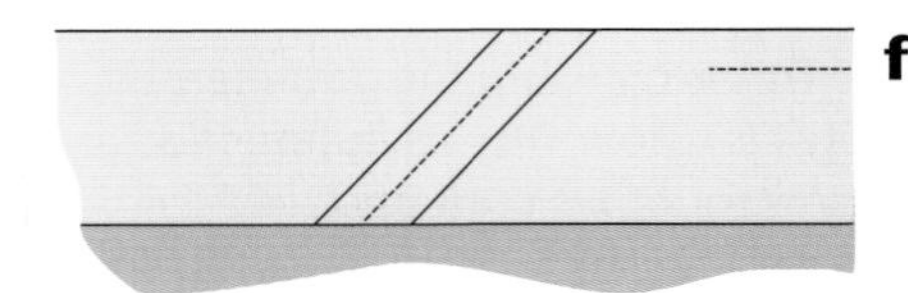

5 Turn the binding to the back, fold under the raw edge (if you're using a single layer of fabric for the binding strip), and slipstitch the folded edge down (**g**).

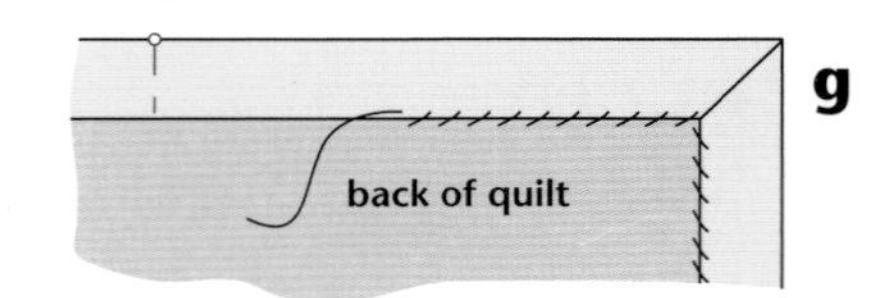

Hanging your quilts

Once again, there are various methods you can use to hang quilts. The method you choose will depend on the size of the project, whether you want the hanging method to be visible or not, and your own personal preference.

• For small projects, you can stitch a curtain ring to each side of the top back of the quilt, then put two hooks in the wall to hang the work.

• You can add a hidden casing on the back of the quilt, just under the top binding; thread through a plain or fancy curtain pole, and rest this on two brackets on the wall (or more, if your quilt is large).

• Stitch hanging loops of ribbon or tape at regular intervals along the top edge of the quilt, then slip these over a pole and attach the pole to the wall as above.